The Complete Idiot's Guide to DOS Reference Card
(Use this card to avoid reading any more than you have to)

tear here

Anatomy of a DOS Command

DOS command   Switch
|
DIR A: /P
|
Parameter

DOS command Tells DOS to perform some specific task.

Parameter Specifies the files, the directory, or the drive with which to work.

Switch Options you can use with a command.

alpha books

Idiot-Proof Tips for Entering DOS Commands

- First, have someone place these commands in your AUTOEXEC.BAT: **PATH=C:\DOS** and **PROMPT PG**.
- Press **Enter** to activate a DOS command after typing it.
- At *most*, there are only two spaces in any DOS command:
  1) After the command itself, and
  2) Either to separate the *from* and *to* parts of a command, as in the COPY command, or to separate a DOS parameter from a DOS switch, as in DIR A: /P
- To stop a command, press **Ctrl+C** at the same time.
- When you enter a DOS command, it acts on the files *in the current drive or directory* unless you specify otherwise.
- To see which drive or directory is current, look at your prompt:
  C:\WORD>
  Here, drive C is the current drive, and \WORD is the current directory.

Idiot-Proof DOS Command Guide

You need at least DOS 4   *You need at least DOS 5*   *You need at least DOS 6*

If you want to do this…	Then type this…	If you want to do this…	Then type this…
Clear your screen	CLS	Make a duplicate of a file.	COPY OLD.docnew.doc
Find out what DOS version you're using	VER	Move a file	C:\newdir\new.doc COPY old.doc DEL old.doc
Get help with the DIR command	HELP DIR	Move a file	MOVE old.doc c:\newdir
List files one screen at a time	DIR /P	Rename a file	REN old.docnew.doc
List files on drive A	DIR A: /P	Delete a file	DEL old.doc
List files across the screen	DIR /W /P	Restore an accidentally deleted file	UNDELETE old.doc
Change to the \WORD directory	CD \WORD	Format a disk	FORMAT A: /V
Create a new directory	MD C:\newdir	Format a double-density 5 1/4-inch diskette	FORMAT A: /F:360
Remove a directory without files	RD \olddir	Format a double-density 3 1/2-inch diskette	FORMAT A: /F:720
Remove a directory with files	DELTREE \olddir	Format a previously formatted diskette	FORMAT A:/Q

Anatomy of a DOS 6.x Shell

Drive list   Menu bar   Menu   File list

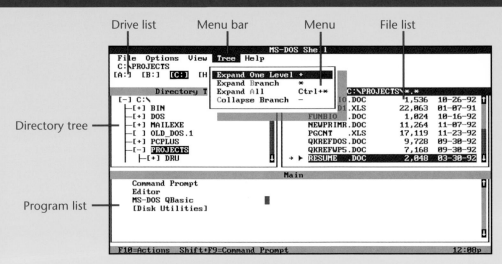

Directory tree

Program list

Drive list Use to change from drive to drive. The current drive is highlighted.

Menu bar Open a menu and select commands by clicking on them.

Menu Displays a list of commands.

File list These are the files in the current directory.

Directory tree These are all the directories on the current drive. The current directory is highlighted.

Program list You can start a program or utility from this list.

Help-O-Rama

Here's a hodgepodge of helpful hints for common situations:

I'm done with my work, now what do I do? Save your file, and then quit or exit the program before you turn off your PC.

I'm done with this diskette, now what do I do? Wait until diskette drive light goes out. Then remove the diskette and place it in its paper sleeve (if the diskette has one).

My program won't start! Are you in the correct directory? Type **CD** followed by the name of the directory you want to change to, and then try starting the program again.

I can't find my file! Don't panic; your file is probably in another directory. If you have at least DOS 5, type something like this:

> **DIR C:*filename*** /S (substitute a real file name)

If you don't have at least DOS 5, perform a directory-by-directory search by typing these two commands:

> **CD*directoryname*** (substitute a real directory name)
> **DIR /W**

Look for your file. Do you see it? If not, change to another directory by using the CD command.

Somebody help me, I deleted the wrong file! If you have at least DOS 5, change to the directory where the file was and type something like this:

> **UNDELETE GOODFILE.DOC**

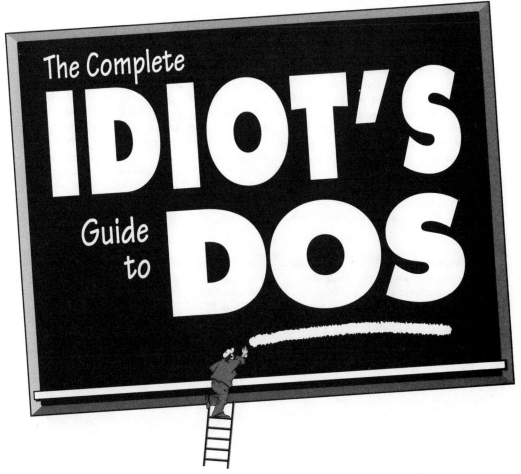

The Complete

IDIOT'S

Guide
to

DOS

by Jennifer Fulton

alpha
books

A Division of Macmillan Computer Publishing
201 West 103rd Street, Indianapolis, Indiana 46290 USA

For Scott, who makes me laugh when DOS doesn't.

©1994 by Alpha Books

International Standard Book Number: 1-56761-496-5
Library of Congress Catalog Card Number: 94-71082

96 95   8 7 6 5 4

Interpretation of the printing code: the right most number of the first series is the year of the book's printing; the rightmost number of the second series of numbers is the number of the book's printing. For example, a printing code of 94-1 shows that the first printing of the book occurred in 1994.

Printed in the United States of America

Screen reproductions in this book were created by means of the program Collage Plus from Inner Media, Inc., Hollis, NH.

Publisher
Marie Butler-Knight

Managing Editor
Elizabeth Keaffaber

Product Development Manager
Faithe Wempen

Acquisitions Manager
Barry Pruett

Manuscript Editor
Barry Childs-Helton

Imprint Manager
Kelly Dobbs

Designer
Barbara Webster

Illustrations
Steve Vanderbosch

Indexer
Johnna VanHoose

Production Team
*Gary Adair, Dan Caparo, Brad Chinn, Kim Cofer, Lisa Daugherty,
Jennifer Eberhardt, Beth Rago, Bobbi Satterfield, Kris Simmons, Carol Stamile,
Robert Wolf*

*Special thanks to Herbert Feltner for ensuring
the technical accuracy of this book.*

Contents at a Glance

This page unintentionally left blank.

Contents

23 Managing (Not Mangling) Files in Windows   **287**

24 Using DOS from Within Other Programs   **299**

25 It's a Portable PC World!   **305**

Part V: Problems That All of Us Have, and How to Fix Them   **313**

26 Help! What Does This Message Mean?   **315**

Introduction

You are an intelligent, mature adult. You know how to balance a budget, book a one-day meeting in Chicago, and get the copier to collate (and staple!). You don't need a computer book that treats you like a child.

On the other hand, you don't need a book that assumes you are (or want to become) a PC wizard. You're a busy person with a real life beyond your computer (which you'll be glad to get back to as soon as you can get your PC to do what you need).

Why Do You Need This Book?

With so many computer books on the market, why do you need this one? Well, first off, this book doesn't assume that you know anything at all about how to use a computer. Every term, every instruction, is fully explained—and *in English!* (Imagine that!) Anyway, I think it's easier to climb a ladder when the first rung isn't over your head, so I've made this guide to the confusing world of DOS as easy to understand as possible.

This book will help you feel comfortable using DOS and your computer, while cleverly avoiding anything that could make you a PC expert. (Believe me, you do not want to become THE expert on anything, especially computers.) Simply open the book when you have a question or problem, read what you need to, and get back to your life.

How Do I Use This Book?

For starters, don't actually *read* this book! (At least not the whole thing.) When you need a quick answer, use the Table of Contents or the Index to find the right section. Each section is self-contained, with exactly what you need to know to solve your problem or to answer your question.

When you need to type something, it appears like this:

TYPE THIS STUFF IN

Just type what you see and press the **Enter** key. It's as simple as that. (By the way, if you're supposed to press a particular key, that key appears in bold, as the **Enter** key does here.)

There are some special boxed notes that I've used in this book to help you learn just what you need:

Bold word   Easy-to-understand definitions for every computer term let you "speak like a geek."

Special hints and amusing anecdotes from me.

Notes and tips showing the easiest way to perform some task.

There's help when things go wrong!

Skip this background fodder (technical twaddle) unless you're truly interested.

Acknowledgments

Thanks to all the great people at Alpha Books for allowing me to write a computer book for regular people, and for realizing learning can be fun!

Special thanks to my friend Rhonda Kuntz, who helped me improve some of my explanations by letting me test them out on her. Thanks, Rhonda.

Thanks also to my brother Mike, who hated DOS for a long time because there was never any book that told him what he wanted to know in a way that made sense. That is, until his sister wrote one.

Trademarks

All terms mentioned in this book that are known to be trademarks or service marks are listed below. In addition, terms suspected of being trademarks or service marks have been appropriately capitalized. Alpha Books cannot attest to the accuracy of this information. Use of a term in this book should not be regarded as affecting the validity of any trademark or service mark.

MS-DOS is a trademark of Microsoft Corporation.

Recycling tip:
tear out this page and photocopy it.

Part One

Dad Does DOS—The Basics of Using a Computer

My dad is a great guy—and smart, too. He can change a tire, sharpen the blades on a lawn mower without getting nicked, and figure a sales discount in his head. He once fixed the toilet with a paper clip, yet he's stumped by this thing called a computer.

The computer age crept up on some of us adults without our even knowing it. One day, we were marveling at pocket calculators the size of toasters; the next day, we were desperately trying to coax OUR OWN MONEY from automatic teller machines. Soon PCs were so fast and so cheap that everyone felt obligated to buy them (including your boss).

So maybe you're sitting there, just like my dad, with a brand-new computer that one of your kids gave you for Christmas. Relax. It's much easier to make a computer do what you want than to paper-train a puppy or coax a two-year-old to eat peas. In this section, you'll start to learn how.

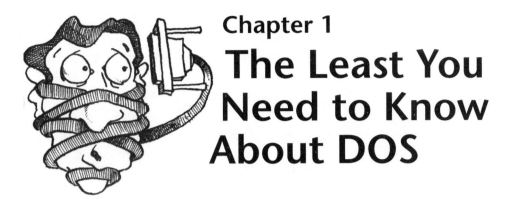

Chapter 1
The Least You Need to Know About DOS

In This Chapter

☛ Stuff you need to know to get started

☛ Things you should do often if you want to avoid trouble

☛ Common beginner's faux pas, and how to avoid them

☛ When to call 911

☛ What's new in the newest DOS versions

OK, so you bought this book. Good start. Maybe you're ready to dive right in. That's OK, but this chapter may not be for you, because this chapter is for those of us who dip our toes in *before* we take a dive into murky waters (and believe me, you can't get any murkier than DOS). In this chapter, you'll learn enough about DOS to get your feet wet, but not enough to feel you got soaked.

The Minimum to Get You Started

We all do it. While a stewardess is busy explaining complex safety procedures which might just save our undeserving souls when or if the plane decides to take a siesta, we're popping peanuts and browsing through the latest issue of "In-Flight Shopper." Let's face it—some things you just don't want to know unless you absolutely have to. Here's a list of the absolutely-have-to-knows for DOS, which you should learn about now, before you do something silly and your computer goes down in fiery ruin. Okay, so your computer *won't* catch on fire, no matter what buttons you press—but now that I've got your attention, here's what you need to know about DOS:

The DOS Prompt Awaits Your Command

The *DOS prompt* is a message from DOS telling you that it's waiting for a command. Think of the prompt as a kid pulling on your leg saying, "Let me do it!" DOS is like that kid who just can't wait to do something.

When you type a command, it appears next to the prompt on-screen. Typical DOS prompts include **C>** or **C:\DOS>**. Next to the prompt you'll find the *cursor*—a horizontal blinking line that acts like the tip of your pencil; when you type commands, they appear on-screen wherever the cursor is located.

Your DOS Version Number

Some commands are only included with the latest DOS versions—DOS 6, 6.2, DOS 6.21, and DOS 6.22. (By the way, DOS *versions* are numbered consecutively; DOS 4 was followed by DOS 5, which was followed by DOS 6, etc.) To see what DOS version you have, type **VER** and press **Enter**. To learn more about the latest DOS versions, see Chapter 9.

Make Things Happen by Pressing Enter

You can type anything you want at the DOS prompt, but until you press Enter, nothing happens. If you want to know more about how to enter DOS commands, see Chapter 4.

Files and Directories

DOS stores information in *files*. Anything can be placed in a file: a memo, a budget report, or even a graphics image (like a picture of a boat or a computer). You use *directories* to organize your files. Think of a directory as a drawer in a large file cabinet: you can keep your files in whatever drawers (directories) you want. To learn more about files and directories, read Chapter 7.

Getting Help

If you are using *at least* DOS version 5 (see "Your DOS Version Number" on how to figure out what DOS version you have), you can get instant help on any command by typing **HELP**. For example, to get help on the COPY command, type **HELP COPY** or **COPY /?** and press **Enter**. To learn more about the DOS Help system (including how to exit it), see Chapter 9.

Those Darn Slashes

You should get to know the difference between the forward slash (/) and the backslash (\). The forward slash is used to designate a *switch*, a part of a DOS command that overrides what that command normally does. For example, if you type just **DIR** you'll get a listing of files in the current directory, running down the screen. But if you type **DIR /W** the files are displayed across the screen instead of downward. *The forward slash indicates the use of a switch*—in this case, /**W**.

The backslash is used in *path names*, to designate a directory, as in **C:\DOS**. In this case, the backslash separates the disk drive name **C:** from the directory name **DOS**. A backslash is also used within a path name to separate a directory name from a filename, as in

C:\WORD\CH10.DOC.

In this case, the backslash separates the disk drive name **C:** from the directory name **WORD**, which is separated from the *filename*, **CH10.DOC**. To learn more about entering DOS commands, see Chapter 4.

Path   The route that DOS travels from the root directory to any subdirectories when locating a file. Think of telling a friend how to find your house. A complete path name looks like this: **C:\WORD\DOCS\CH01.DOC**.

Diskette Disk-cussion

You should learn to buy the type of diskettes that match the kind of diskette drive that your PC has. *Diskettes* (small plastic things that you save your work on) come in many sizes and capacities. If you don't buy the right kind, they may not work, or they may be too much trouble to use. If you want to know more about diskettes, see Chapter 6.

Things You Should Do Often

Now that you have this new PC, what should you do with it? What happens if you get mad and shout at it? (Actually, nothing. I shout at mine quite often, and because it has yet to answer me back, I get a great feeling of superiority out of the exchange.) Does it need watering, or regular feedings? Well, not exactly, but your PC *will* live a lot longer if you treat it properly.

Protect Your PC Against Things That Go Bump in the Night

Okay, so this is something you don't have to do *often*, only once. But it's important. A *surge protector* protects your valuable electrical equipment from spikes in electricity which happen all the time, even when you're not home to enjoy them. Some surge protectors are shaped more like cubes, with four to six electrical outlets. However, a lot of surge protectors look like a power strip—a bunch of electrical sockets all lined up in a row. "Looks like" is the key phrase here—some power strips offer no surge protection at all.

If you're given a choice, pick a surge *protector* over a surge *surpressor*. Also, don't buy the cheapest one you can find, because if it doesn't do its job, you're out a lot more than ten bucks.

Back Up Your Work

You should do this one as often as possible—for instance, at the end of the day. A *backup* is a process where the PC copies files from its permanent storage area (the hard disk) onto diskettes. When you have a backup and something happens to your PC (e.g., it won't start), you're sitting pretty because you've got a copy of everything on your backup diskettes. Think of a backup as a "traveler's cheque" for your work. You can use your backup if the original gets lost or stolen. For more on how to do a backup, see Chapter 14.

Delete Files You Don't Need Anymore

After you're done with a piece of paper, you throw it away, and yet people think nothing about leaving dead files on their PCs for years and years.

When you first buy your PC, you may think you've got loads of room to store everything—but believe me, it's really easy to get that thing full of junk. So pick up as you go, and delete files when you know you don't need them any more. See Chapter 12 for help.

Don't Let Your Emergency Diskette Go Out of Style

An *emergency diskette* contains important system files that help your PC get going again after it dies. After you create one, you should update it from time to time to keep it current. Jump over to Chapter 6 for instructions on how to create some insurance against dead PCs.

Mouse Cleaning

Although you don't need a mouse to use a PC (at least, if you just use a PC with DOS and not Windows), you probably have one. It's that small white thing with a roller underneath, that's attached to your PC through its "tail," a long thin cord. Anyway, when the mouse is rolled around, it tends to pick up lots of dirt; eventually it starts to resent the neglect, and sends weird signals to your PC. To clean the mouse, flip it over on its back and remove the roller ball. Look for dirt on the rollers, and remove with your fingernail or a clean toothpick (Q-tips leave little fuzzies). Don't spray anything in there, because you might ruin the electronics. While you're cleaning house, wipe off your monitor (that TV thing); it's probably dusty too.

Label Your Diskettes

I'm guilty of this too: I just slap a diskette in the drive, copy the stuff I need, and away I go. The next day, I'm looking at the diskette, trying to remember what's on it. And I waste a lot of time trying to find that diskette I used last week—you know, the one with the only copy of the super-important-gotta-get-it-on-my-desk-by-five-*or-else* report my boss is waiting for. So when you reach for a diskette, make sure you reach for a label, too—and save yourself oodles of hassle later on.

On or Off?

You'll hear the great debate later on, the one about whether you should turn off your PC at the end of the day, or whether it's better to leave it running all the time. Whatever you decide, make sure you occasionally turn off the PC to "clean out all the goop." See Chapter 3 for the complete story. Film at eleven.

Be on the Lookout For Escaped Viruses

Computer *viruses* are nasty programs that make things go baha. Believe me, you don't want to get one. Chances are slim that you will, but why take that chance? It's super easy to protect your valuable data from these nasties. See Chapter 18.

Make Hard Disk Go Zoom

The day-to-day stuff you do on your PC sometimes leaves it a wreck. You see, the *file system* (which controls where files are placed on the hard disk) sometimes gets a bit sloppy. It suddenly starts breaking files into pieces, and placing them in different spots on the hard disk. Then when your poor PC has to read the file, it has to run all around the disk. Bottom line: after you use your PC for awhile, it starts to slow down a bit. You can fix this problem by getting the files back into some kind of decent order. See Chapter 5 for details.

What Most Often Goes Wrong and How to Avoid It

Murphy was right—if something can go wrong, it probably will. Here's a list of things you can expect to go wrong sometime:

You Leave a Program Dangling

When you're done with a program such as Lotus 1-2-3 or Microsoft Word for Windows, you've got to exit that program *properly*. By properly, I don't mean simply shutting off (or even resetting) the computer and calling it a day. There's a simple shutdown procedure you go through each time you leave a program; it protects all the stuff you just worked on, and keeps your computer from going crazy. See Chapters 3 and 20 for the gory details.

You Forget to Save Your Stuff

Big-time OOPS. If there's anything I want to impress upon you to do and to do often, this is it. You see, when you work on something like a letter or whatever, it's saved in a temporary area called *memory*. Well, that's a stupid name for it, because as soon as you shut off the PC (or it loses power temporarily), it forgets everything—which includes all the stuff you were currently working on.

But if you've saved your work to the hard disk from time to time throughout the work session, you can retrieve a copy of your letter (or whatever) and start back up as if nothing has happened. True, that copy is missing the latest changes not yet saved to the hard disk, but that's nothing compared to losing the whole thing. So save your pennies, save the whales, save your ticket stub if you want, but *be sure to save your stuff!* See Chapters 3 and 21 for the lowdown.

It Starts Raining Coffee

If you've just spilled the beans (as it were) or some such all over your keyboard, just turn the PC off and let it dry out. Then try starting it again. Learn to keep drinks at a safe distance, so they don't gum up the works. Above all, never give your PC a bath, no matter what gets on it (think of it as a big electrical cat). For more timely tips, see Chapter 3.

You Pull A Diskette Out While It's Spinning

Never, ever, *ever* remove a diskette while the drive light is on. You could damage the diskette or the drive (which costs a whole lot more). Also, while Grandma's giving out advice: never plug anything into your computer while the computer is on. Turn your computer off before you add that new Master Blaster sound system.

You Delete a File Accidentally

Big oops. Well, first thing, DO NOTHING, at least don't do anything else until you've undeleted your file. You see, if you have at least DOS version 5, you can *undelete* files, *but you must try not to do anything on your computer until you've rescued the deleted file.* See Chapter 12 for more help.

There are also some rather boring—but important—things you can do to save your work from accidental destruction. If I just got your attention, good: see Chapters 14, 15, and 18—all others go to the back of the class.

How to Know When It's Time to Call In the Cavalry

Everyone needs help sometime, but when it comes to PCs, it's tough to know *when* to panic (actually panicking isn't so tough). Before you call in the cavalry and get embarrassed because you didn't know you were supposed to point the PC to the East every other Wednesday, here's a quick list of things to check:

Check the cables. Are they all connected? If something's loose, push it back in. Also, be sure to check both ends of the cable. Unlike most home appliances, a PC uses cables that detach at both ends—so make sure one end is plugged into the PC, and the other end is plugged into an electrical outlet.

Is the monitor on? Believe it or not, the monitor has a separate power switch from the PC. That means that you've got to turn it on too. If you're sure it's on, make sure that it hasn't been adjusted so the brightness is so low it looks like it's off. You'll find little control knobs for the brightness and the vertical hold somewhere along the front, back, or sides. Modems and printers also have separate power switches, so check them too.

Turn the PC off, then back on after a minute. Sometimes that simple thing does the trick.

Narrow the problem down. Is it a particular part that isn't working, such as a diskette drive, or the keyboard? When did the problem start? Does it happen every time you try it, or only under certain conditions? If you can determine this much information, you'll do well when you do have to call the calvary, because these are the first questions they'll ask. For a more detailed list of suggestions, see Chapters 26, 27, and 28.

I Just Upgraded to DOS 6-Point-Something. What's New?

You may have just recently upgraded to DOS 6 from an older version such as DOS 5 or DOS 4. There are many different critters in the DOS 6 family now, including DOS 6.0, DOS 6.2, DOS 6.21 and the newest star, DOS 6.22. Here's a brief overview of some of the new stars; you'll find the complete cast list in Chapter 9.

Improved Help system   The new Help system provides descriptions and examples of each DOS command. No more looking in the manual. You'll get more help on Help in Chapter 9.

Improved capability to undelete files   With the DOS 6 somethings (DOS 6, 6.2, DOS 6.21 or 6.22), you stand a better chance of being able to recover files that you have deleted accidentally. How does this magic work? Refer to Chapter 12 for the rabbit trick.

System backup and restore   Since computer data is stored electronically, there's no sense in taking chances. Backing up is a process which protects your data by copying it onto diskettes. The DOS 6 somethings come with an easy-to-use *backup* program that makes backing up your system a breeze. You'll learn more about backing up and restoring in Chapters 14 and 15.

Virus protection   A *virus* is a computer program whose sole purpose is to wreak havoc on your computer system. "Howdy neighbor! I'm Mr. Virus, and I'm here to ruin your day. Where should I start?" Actually, rare as they are, a computer virus is no laughing matter, and protecting your system against a virus is an important job. The DOS 6 somethings come with built-in virus protection. You'll learn more about virus protection in Chapter 18.

Improved memory management   *Memory* (RAM) is the working area of your PC. RAM is your computer's version of your desktop; every program and every file must be placed on the desktop (loaded into memory) before the computer can use it. Effective management of this precious resource improves the speed and efficiency of your PC. The DOS 6 somethings come with a built-in memory manager that makes it easy to customize memory to meet your specific PC needs. You'll learn more about memory management in Chapter 20.

Disk compression   Files can be *compressed* (shrunk) so that they take up less room on your hard drive. With disk compression, you can almost double the amount of data you can store on your hard disk. The DOS 6-somethings come with a disk-compression program, which you'll learn more about in Chapter 19.

The Least You Need to Know

So much for your first dive into DOSland. Here's a recap:

- ☞ The DOS prompt typically looks like **C>** or **C:\DOS>**.

- ☞ Type **VER** and press **Enter** to see what DOS version your PC uses.

- ☞ Press **Enter** after each DOS command.

- ☞ The forward slash (/) is used in DOS commands, while the backslash (\) is used in path names.

- ☞ Perform backups often, delete files you don't need, keep your emergency diskette updated, clean your mouse, label your diskettes after you use them, turn your PC off every once in a while, and defragment your disk every once in a while.

- ☞ Avoid problems by learning how to exit programs properly and how to save your work.

Chapter 2
So You Got a Computer, Whadaya Do with It Now?

In This Chapter

- ☞ What is a computer?
- ☞ Great things you can do with a computer
- ☞ Understanding the parts of a computer
- ☞ How does DOS fit into the picture?
- ☞ How the Shell makes DOS easier to use

This chapter explains all those "little things" about PCs that nobody's ever bothered to tell you. And if you're wondering what all those keys are for, you're about to find out!

Hey, Somebody Replaced My Typewriter with a TV!

One day, my mom walked into her office and found her typewriter missing. In its place was this gray box, with something like a TV sitting on top of it. Did she panic? Not my mom—we're talking about a woman who raised ten kids. She'd watched *Star Trek*, so she knew what a computer was. She turned to the computer and said in her best Spock voice, "Computer on." Mom had entered the computer age.

Learning how to type with the computer keyboard was something of a challenge, but after she got used to it, Mom grudgingly admitted that she *liked* using the computer. With the computer, she could make last-minute changes (the kind her boss was fond of) to memos and reports, without using a single drop of white-out! Printing a copy of last month's budget meeting was as simple as pressing a key.

Making Do with Your New PC

With a computer (which is also called a *personal computer*, or the more "politically correct" term *PC*) you can do more than just type. A PC takes information you type in, allows you to change it as many times as you like, stores that information in something called a *file*, and even prints it out.

If you're doing something with a calculator, or with mere paper and pencil, chances are you could be doing that same task more efficiently and accurately with a computer. (Notable exceptions include various bits of origami, and making those little twirly umbrellas you spin with your hands.) Just imagine it—in a mere 198 weeks (with the proper training, of course), you too could create a five-page report *using your PC*. Thankfully, with the help of this book and its vast storehouse of knowledge, you can cut that time in *half*. Wow.

Great Things You Can Do with a Computer

Find that missing two cents in your checkbook.

Balance your department's budget for this year.

Maintain an address book of sales contacts, account reps, friends, or family.

SPEAK LIKE A GEEK

Personal computer A personal computer (or PC, for short) is small enough to fit on a desktop and is intended for use by an individual to perform daily tasks, such as typing, calculating, organizing, and filing.

File DOS stores information in files. Think of placing papers in a file folder, and you'll get the idea. Anything (or, at least, anything not alive) can be placed in a file: a memo, budget report, or even a graphics image (such as a picture of a boat or a computer). Files you create are called *data files*. Applications (e.g., a word processing program you can use to type letters and reports) are made up of several files called *program files*.

Figure your taxes.

Play games.

Write notes, reports, and the great American novel.

Play music. Write music. Put on a show!

Discover the artist in you, or use predrawn pictures to punch up your reports and impress your boss.

Organize your appointments, to-do lists, and those "gotta-get-'em-dones."

Great Things You Can't Do with a Computer

Keep your checkbook balance from going negative.

Eliminate the federal deficit. (Sorry, Bill.)

Discover just why it is that when interest rates go up, it's a bad thing, but when interest rates go up *again*, it's a *good* thing.

Win the Publisher's Clearing House Sweepstakes.

Undo *Beverly Hills Cop III*.

Figure out why a 12-ounce soft drink costs 3 bucks at the movie theater, and only 50 cents out of a machine.

Taking a Look at a Computer, Inside and Out

A person has many parts—including a heart that pumps blood, a brain that processes information (but not before 10:00 a.m.), and a stomach that changes food into energy. Like a human body, a computer also has many parts. Here's what all those parts do:

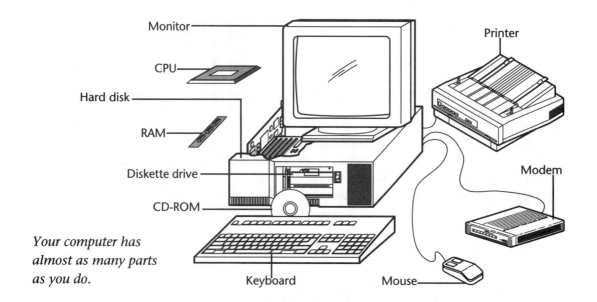

Monitor

CPU

Hard disk

RAM

Diskette drive

CD-ROM

Your computer has almost as many parts as you do.

Keyboard

Printer

Modem

Mouse

TECHNO NERD TEACHES...

Wait a minute! Why should you care about all this stuff? You came here to learn about DOS, so where does DOS fit in? Well, DOS is in charge of everything you see listed here. If DOS was in control of your body, it would be the thing that keeps the heart pumping, the lungs breathing, and the brain braining. DOS links the parts of your computer that store data (diskette drives, hard drives, and the like) with those parts that interpret the data as files (the central processor or CPU, for instance). So DOS is really like this big spinal column . . . but you'll learn more about DOS later. For now, let's find out what these things are for, so we can turn the PC on.

CPU

CPU stands for Central Processing Unit. The CPU is the brain of your computer. Like your brain, this is the part of the computer that "thinks" or processes information. All the logical processes that go on in a computer either take place within the CPU, or are closely monitored by the CPU. The CPU, in other words, is what the CIA always hoped it could be.

RAM

RAM stands for Random-Access Memory. RAM is the place where the computer works on stuff. I think of RAM as a kind of "desktop" or work area. Information is placed on the desktop where the computer processes it, and then it is put away. When you run a program, the program moves into RAM, and stays there until you quit that program. When you type in your information, it is held in RAM as *data*.

For example, if you type a memo, that memo is stored in RAM so the computer can process it and allow you to make changes. The computer erases everything in RAM when you shut off the power, so you need to *save your work onto disks first*. For example, you would need to save your memo onto disk before exiting your program or turning off the computer, or (to paraphrase the theme from *Gilligan's Island*) the memo would be lost—that is, erased from RAM.

Disks and Disk Drives

A disk is a round magnetic wafer on which information is stored magnetically. A *floppy disk* can be removed from the computer, whereas a *hard disk* is usually permanent.

Floppy disks (also known as *diskettes*) are small, portable, plastic storage squares. You can call 'em *disks* for short, but I don't, because then I'd get them mixed up with hard disks. (But you can do what you want—in America, it's your right to be confusing.) Data is stored on diskettes magnetically, using a special film.

Data The way computers see information. You enter facts and figures (information) into a computer, which then processes it, making it into data. The computer then displays this data in an organized manner, so it becomes information again. Just say to yourself, "It's *information* to me, it's *data* to the computer." That's how you tell the difference.

Diskette drives are the slots in the front of the computer where you insert floppy d—(ahem) *diskettes* so you can copy information onto them, or from them. Your computer may have one or two of these diskette drives.

Hidden inside your computer, a hard disk is like a really big diskette. A hard disk stores much more information than a diskette, and accesses that information much faster. Unlike a diskette, a hard disk is typically nonremovable. (Of course, just to make life difficult, some hard disks *can* be removed, but let's not get too confusing here.)

Keyboard

The keyboard is the main device you use to give the computer *input*. It has the standard keys you find on a typewriter (many include a keypad for numbers), plus some additional keys you use to issue special commands.

Input Input is data that you "put in" the computer. When you press a key or click a mouse button, you're giving your computer input. Data that your computer gives back to you is called *output* (because the computer "puts it out").

Monitor

This is the part of the computer that looks like a TV, and gives you eye strain just as conveniently. The computer displays its output on the monitor.

Mouse

The mouse is a device that provides another way to communicate with your computer besides using the keyboard (or, if you don't expect a response, shouting very loudly). The mouse controls an arrow (a pointer) on-screen. When you move the mouse, the pointer moves around the screen. You press the mouse's buttons to select items on-screen; since you can't just tap the screen with your ballpoint and say, "I want *that*," you tap the mouse button instead. A mouse gets its name because it connects to your computer through a long "tail," or cord.

Printer

The "typical" PC user has a printer connected to the computer for printing copies of data. Since the printed data comes out of the computer, it's called (you guessed it) *output*. The *dot-matrix* printer is the most common type—it's designed to work much like a typewriter, but can be used to print graphics (albeit slowly). The most *desired* type is the *laser* printer, which uses the mechanism from a photocopy machine to produce razor-sharp typeset printing.

Modem

A modem is used to transmit or receive information through a telephone line to another computer. A *fax modem* is a special kind of modem which (in addition to a modem's normal abilities) can send and receive facsimiles of documents through a telephone line.

CD-ROM drive

A popular add-on for computers. With a CD-ROM drive, your computer can play ordinary CDs (music) and special computer CDs that store complex programs or large amounts of data. For example, instead of buying a set of encyclopedias for your kids, you could buy an encyclopedia CD, and not have to dust it all the time (or bend your knees when you lift it).

Taking Care of Your Computer

You've invested a lot of money in your computer, so exercise some care. Here are some tips that should extend your computer's life.

SPEAK LIKE A GEEK

Surge-protector power strip A device which protects your PC against sudden power surges. A surge protector is made up of several electrical outlets grouped together in a single unit, and specifically designed to protect your computer against sudden changes in electrical power.

Buy a good *surge-protector power strip* to prevent damage caused by power surges. Since this little gadget needs to protect your already-too-expensive investment, make sure you get one that works. Various models are available, ranging in price and the amount of protection they offer—but beware: not all power strips are surge protectors. Ask your computer dealer to recommend a good one.

Allow proper ventilation so the computer doesn't get hot. This means don't cram the PC into a dusty corner, and don't pile magazines (or anything else) on top of the monitor.

Don't get caught by the Pepsi generation; keep liquids away from the work area. If something does spill on your keyboard, don't attempt to clean it. Just let it dry out, then take it to a PC doctor if it doesn't work.

Don't smoke around your computer. I know, the places where you can smoke without getting arrested are getting fewer and fewer. But that's another story. The politics of smoking aside, any kind of smoke is made up of tiny particles that damage the computer's sensitive parts—so don't put it near the barbecue, either.

Even if you hate housework, dust that computer off every once in a while. Computers collect more dust than a rag full of Pledge! Use a clean, dry cloth—no chemicals, and negatory on the moist towlettes.

Playing with a Full Keyboard

If you've ever used a typewriter, you'll notice that the computer keyboard (at least much of it) is similar. Don't let all those keys intimidate you—the keyboard is easy to use when you learn the functions of the special keys. Understanding the keyboard will be worth your while, since some of the keys let you work faster in DOS.

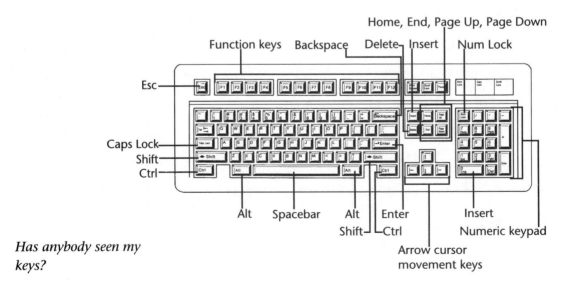

Has anybody seen my keys?

Okay, you're right—the computer keyboard is similar, but *not* identical to that of a typewriter. Here are the functions of some of the keys that are not so obvious:

Enter   THIS IS THE MOST IMPORTANT KEY ON YOUR KEYBOARD! DOS can't carry out a command until you execute it by pressing this key. So what you do is type in a command, then press Enter.

BY THE WAY

The Enter key is something that computer manufacturers like to hide. The Enter key is often marked by a bent arrow pointing to the left, and sometimes by the word *Return*.

Esc   Called the *Escape* key, this key allows you to cancel DOS commands or to back out of an operation.

Function keys   Some programs assign a special purpose to these keys (called the F keys because they all begin with an F). There can be ten or twelve of these keys, generally rowed along the top of your keyboard, though older models place them along the left side. DOS has a purpose for some of them, which you'll learn about later.

Shift   Used just like a typewriter to type capital letters and special characters and comic-book profanity, such as #$%?>. Sometimes used with other keys to issue commands in certain programs. You won't use this key in DOS very often, because you don't have to type your commands in capital letters. You'll only use it when you want to type one of the special characters like *.

Alt and Ctrl   The Alt (Alternate) and Ctrl (Control) keys are used like the Shift key; press one of them along with another key to issue commands in certain programs. See, in some programs you type your regular words, but you also type commands as well. Alt and Ctrl tell these programs you're not typing regular words at the moment, but commands. You'll use the Alt key in the DOS Help system, but you won't really use the Ctrl key when using DOS itself.

Caps Lock   This locks on capital letters. But unlike a typewriter, you will not get ! when you press the **1** key (even with the Caps Lock on). To get !, you must press the **Shift** key and **1** at the same time—likewise with @, #, and other special characters like *.

Spacebar   Just like a typewriter, this inserts spaces. You insert spaces between the parts of a DOS command.

Backspace   Press this key to erase the letter or number to the left of the *cursor* (the point on the screen where new letters appear). Use the Backspace key to erase all or part of a DOS command.

Arrow or cursor movement keys   These keys make the cursor move in the direction of the arrow.

Insert or Ins   This key is used to toggle (that is, to switch back and forth) between *Insert mode* (where text to the right of the cursor scoots over to make room for new text) and *Overstrike* or *Overtype mode* (where new characters replace existing ones). In DOS, you can tell when Insert mode is turned on when the cursor (normally a blinking underline) is now a blinking square block.

Cursor   The blinking box or underline that marks the place where characters will be inserted.

Delete or Del   Deletes the character where the cursor currently appears. Text to the right of the cursor scoots to the left to close the gap caused by the deleted characters.

Home, End, Page Up, Page Down   These keys have limited use in DOS, but in most programs, Home moves the cursor to the beginning of a line; End moves the cursor to the end of a line; Page Down displays the next page of the text on-screen; and Page Up displays the previous page.

Inserting and Removing Diskettes

Well, so far in this chapter, you've learned a little about your computer: how to take care of it, and how to tinker around with the keys. The next item on our agenda is learning about diskettes.

A diskette (as I'm sure you remember from earlier in this chapter, since you wouldn't randomly skip over sections of this great text) is a small, square storage device which contains a flat piece of magnetic film. It's on this film that the diskette stores computer data, in the same general way a cassette tape stores priceless musical treasures such as "Feelings" and "Disco Duck." Before you buy any diskettes, make sure you purchase the right kind for your computer. See Chapter 6 for more help in that department.

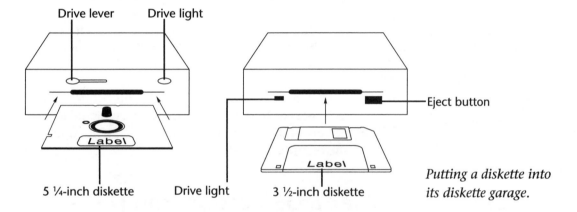

Putting a diskette into its diskette garage.

Diskette drives contain a slot into which you insert a diskette. To insert a diskette properly, hold it at the label end. The label should face up. The exposed area (the hole where the magnetic film shows through) or the metal sliding gate (which covers this exposed area on smaller diskettes) should be pointed away from you. Slide the diskette into the drive until you hear a faint "click." If the drive is a 5 ¼-inch drive, you may need to close the diskette door by rotating the little lever down. (Diskettes come in two sizes, one large, one small. The large size is 5 ¼ inches on a side, while the smaller size is 3 ½ inches square.)

To *eject* (remove) a diskette from its drive, push the drive lever up (on 5 ¼-inch drives) or push the eject button (on 3 ½-inch drives). You'll learn more about the lifestyles of rich and famous diskettes in Chapter 6.

What Is DOS?

DOS (pronounced "DAHS," not "DOSE") is your **Disk Operating System**. DOS is the captain, the head honcho, the big kahuna. DOS controls what your computer is doing at all times.

DOS interprets the commands you give your computer (like a United Nations translator) so your computer can understand them and carry them out. DOS also controls the flow of information to each computer component; like a traffic cop, DOS sends information to the monitor, the printer, the disk drives, etc. when it's each one's turn to receive data.

Don't worry too much. If you do get an error message when entering a DOS command, you can turn to the back of the book and get immediate help.

DOS is *very particular*, and requires you to type commands in a precise way, or else! It's not that DOS is stubborn; it just has a limited vocabulary. You have to use words it knows, and arrange them in the expected way, or DOS won't work for you. (Maybe DOS should stand for Deliberate Obvious Stupidity!)

DOS doesn't care whether you enter commands in upper- or lowercase letters, so use whichever you prefer. In this book, I use uppercase letters to make the commands easier to see.

How to Tell What DOS Version You Have

Some DOS features are available only with the latest versions of DOS. Microsoft DOS versions (as you know if you read Chapter 1) are numbered consecutively. So DOS version 6 is newer than DOS version 5, and so on. DOS version 6.22 is the newest DOS version. To find out your DOS version, try your first DOS command. Just type **VER** and press **Enter**. (If you need help turning on your PC, see Chapter 3. After you get the PC up and running, return here and try out your first DOS command. I'll wait.) You should see something like this:

MS-DOS Version 6.22

If it says **MS-DOS**, that means you're running Microsoft's original DOS and not some revamped version of it. If it says something like

HP DOS Version 6

then you're running a slightly altered version of pure DOS, customized to get the most power out of your computer.

The version number tells you how recent your version of DOS is. (To find out about the latest updates to DOS—and all the goodies they contain—see Chapter 9.)

An Easier DOS: The DOS Shell

If you have DOS version 4 or higher, you have another option for entering DOS commands—through the *DOS Shell*. The DOS Shell is a program that enables you to perform most of the same wonderful things you can with DOS, but without the headache of remembering exactly what to type. You simply point to the names of files with the arrow keys or the mouse, select a command, and *voilà*! If you'd like to use the DOS Shell to enter commands, see Chapter 8.

DOS versions 6.2-something don't include the DOS Shell with the regular disks, so you have to call Microsoft to get it. Don't let that put you off; it's really quite easy to get a copy of the Shell, and the folks at Microsoft are really nice.

If your PC came with Windows installed, you may not want to use the Shell after all, since Windows provides a similar program called File Manager. Read all about it in Chapter 22.

The Least You Need to Know

Now that you've learned a little about computers, you can impress all your friends with these computer tidbits:

- ☞ A computer can imitate many things, such as a calculator, a typewriter, an address book, a notepad, a calendar, a piano, a sketch pad, and a game board.

- ☞ DOS runs the computer and interprets all commands.

- ☞ A PC forgets what is in memory (RAM) when you turn it off, so you must save your information on disk first.

continues

continued

☞ DOS doesn't know that you want it to do something until you type a command and press **Enter**.

☞ The **Esc** key is a good way to cancel a DOS command.

☞ DOS doesn't care whether you use upper- or lowercase letters when entering commands.

☞ To insert a diskette, insert it label-side-up, with the exposed end (or the end with the metal sliding gate) away from you.

☞ You can tell what DOS version you are using by using the DOS command **VER**.

☞ If you have DOS version 4 or higher, you can use the DOS Shell and save yourself the normal headaches of working with DOS.

Chapter 3
Gentlemen (and Ladies), Start Your PCs!

In This Chapter

- ☞ Starting your computer safely
- ☞ Restarting your computer (after the power is on)
- ☞ What is a CONFIG.SYS?
- ☞ What is an AUTOEXEC.BAT?
- ☞ Telling your computer what day it is
- ☞ Turning your computer off safely
- ☞ How to know when something is wrong

The information in this chapter will help you get your PC up and running safely. Even if you've already started your computer, this chapter will answer some questions you might still have about the whole process, such as "What were those funny numbers and other messages for?" You'll learn how to tell when something goes wrong and some quick tricks to use when it does.

Starting Your PC

You don't *exit* an airplane, you "debark," and in the same way, you don't start a computer, you "boot" it (probably the word stands for what the many users before you *did*—or wanted to do—to a PC that wouldn't start). Anyway, to start (*boot*) your PC, you turn the power on. Sounds easy, but it may not be that simple. For openers, it seems a number of computer manufacturers got together and decided on the most obscure places to hide the ON switch.

Booting The process of starting a computer. The word *booting* comes from the phrase "pulling yourself up by the bootstraps," which describes what happens when a computer starts: first it gets power, then it checks itself out, then it loads DOS and awaits your command.

When you're trying to locate that carefully-concealed power switch, don your deerstalker cap, grab your magnifying glass, and follow these clues:

Clue #1: Look for something orange, or white, or some color really different from the rest of the PC.

Clue #2: Look on each side of the *system unit* (the box-thing that the monitor sits on), starting with the front, and moving around to the back. That critter's around here somewhere! And don't feel foolish—each PC is different, and so *everyone* (including Haw-vard graduates) have to spend a minute locating the ON switch. But don't expect to find the familiar words ON and OFF—instead you'll probably find the secret codes I and 0.

Clue #3: I means ON and 0 means OFF!

Clue #4: You probably have to repeat this whole process with the monitor, which usually has its own ON/OFF switch.

What Happens When You Turn Your Computer On?

How can you tell if the PC is working okay? Well, computers go through a self-check (called POST, or power-on self-test) when they start. During POST, each system component is checked to verify that it is connected properly to the main system. For example, the keyboard is checked, the monitor is checked, and so on. You'll see numbers flash on-screen as the

PC's memory (RAM) is counted and checked. Some other messages may appear; they come from the computer system itself, or from two special files: the CONFIG.SYS and the AUTOEXEC.BAT. You'll learn about these files later in this chapter.

What If Nothing Happens?

If you find the power switch and turn it on but nothing happens, check these things:

☛ Is the system unit plugged in? The system unit is that big box that the monitor usually sits on. Make sure that it's plugged in at both ends.

☛ Is the monitor plugged in and connected to the system unit?

☛ Is the monitor on? Most monitors have their own ON/OFF switch, so you have to turn it on too.

☛ Are any of the connections loose, or have any of the plugs fallen out?

☛ If the cords are plugged into a surge-protector power strip, is it turned on? (Power strips usually have their own on/off switches.)

☛ Does the outlet have power? (Pretty obvious, but as a quick check, plug a lamp into the same outlet. It should be illuminating.)

To avoid all this nonsense in the future, try this: insert all of the electrical cords for your system into a surge protector. Leave everything turned ON. When you're done for the day, turn everything OFF by flicking the power switch on your surge protector. (This does not turn off the surge protection, so it's OK.). This eliminates wear and tear on your PC's switches, and wear and tear on your back, as you stretch to reach them.

If you get the error message **Non-system disk or disk error. Replace and press any key when ready**, don't panic. You may simply have left a diskette in drive A. (This is usually the left or top diskette drive.) Remove it and reboot (press **Ctrl**, **Alt**, and **Delete** at the same time) to continue. If that doesn't work, there may be a problem with your hard drive. Refer to the back of the book for more help.

TECHNO NERD TEACHES...

Why *wouldn't* you just "strike any key to continue," as DOS tells you to do? Well, you could, and it would probably be fine. But if that diskette in your drive A had a computer virus on it, that virus could be passed to your system if you continued by pressing a key. For maximum safety, use **Ctrl+Alt+Delete** instead. You'll learn more about viruses in Chapter 18.

Tailor Your PC to a Custom Fit with CONFIG.SYS

CONFIG.SYS is a special file used by DOS at startup—a "DOS tailor" that changes the original settings (*CONFIGuration*) of your computer to work more efficiently with the programs you own. You use a tailor so your clothes fit more comfortably, so why not custom-fit your CONFIG.SYS so the PC runs your programs more efficiently?

CONFIG.SYS is created when you first install DOS (specifically, DOS versions 5 or 6-something). CONFIG.SYS can be modified easily whenever you like, or whenever a new application requires it. You see, even if you don't want to bother trying to change the CONFIG.SYS (and I can't blame you), some programs (especially games) require that you place certain commands into the CONFIG.SYS before they will work. Unfortunately, these commands can't get into the CONFIG.SYS by themselves. To edit the CONFIG.SYS, use the DOS Editor described in Chapter 16.

If you're a beginner, and you find yourself without a CONFIG.SYS (or if you're faced with the task of trying to change the CONFIG.SYS) for one reason or another, buy a box of Ho-Ho's and bribe a PC guru to create the missing CONFIG.SYS for you. If you have one of the DOS 6-somethings (DOS 6, 6.2, 6.21, or 6.22), your guru can even create different sections in your CONFIG.SYS that are customized for the kind of work you do.

What Kind of Commands Go Into CONFIG.SYS?

In your CONFIG.SYS file, you might want commands that:

- ☞ Change the number of files a program can open at one time.
- ☞ Change the number of recently-opened files in memory.
- ☞ Enable your computer to use memory more efficiently.
- ☞ Run special programs called *device drivers*.

If you want to know more about the interesting world of the CONFIG.SYS file, see Chapter 17.

What Is an AUTOEXEC.BAT?

Normally, when you turn on your PC, the default startup procedure begins, which:

- ☞ Displays the current date and asks for confirmation.
- ☞ Displays the current time and asks for confirmation.
- ☞ Displays a *prompt* that looks like C>, and then waits for you to tell it to do something.

If anything else happens when you start your PC—for example, a menu may appear, a program may run—your computer's not possessed; it's being controlled by a file called *AUTOEXEC.BAT*.

Device drivers Special programs (with names that usually end with .DRV or .SYS) that tell your computer how to communicate with certain devices, such as a mouse.

AUTOEXEC.BAT A special file that contains commands which are executed automatically when you boot your computer.

Prompt The prompt is a message from DOS, letting you know that it is waiting for a command. When you type a command, it will appear next to the prompt on-screen. Typical DOS prompts include **C>** or **C:\DOS>**.

AUTOEXEC.BAT is a file which, like the CONFIG.SYS, is created when you first install DOS (that is, with DOS versions 5 and above). In the AUTOEXEC.BAT file is a series of commands that are *AUTO*matically *EXEC*uted (carried out) when the computer is started. If you need to, grab two boxes of Ho-Ho's, and while that PC guru is creating your

CONFIG.SYS, request the creation of an AUTOEXEC.BAT, too. Your friendly guru can even create a customized AUTOEXEC.BAT for different situations, if you have DOS 6.2, 6.21 or 6.22. (It won't hurt to take notes and ask a few questions while this is going on.)

The .BAT in AUTOEXEC.BAT tells you it's a *batch file*—a special file that contains a number of commands. (The commands are batched together in one file, hence the name.) Batch files are handy for all sorts of things. For example, the steps involved in moving several files from one place to another can be quite involved. You can put these commands in a batch file and run that batch file whenever you need to move files.

Anyway, the AUTOEXEC batch file is run automatically when you start the computer, and the commands which are in that file (whatever they may be) are carried out. You can place any command you learn in this book into your AUTOEXEC.BAT and have that command carried out for you, without you doing a thing. For example, if you always use Lotus 1-2-3 every day, why not have the AUTOEXEC.BAT start that program for you when your computer is turned on? Then you can go get some coffee.

TECHNO NERD TEACHES...

What's the difference between CONFIG.SYS and AUTOEXEC.BAT (and why can't I remember the difference)? It seems stupid that DOS has two files that seem to do the same thing—customize what happens when you start your computer.

Actually, DOS is not being redundant. Each file serves a specific purpose; these complement, but don't repeat, each other. CONFIG.SYS contains commands that cannot be run at the DOS prompt—they can only work within CONFIG.SYS. These commands change the way DOS works, so the commands that go into the CONFIG.SYS must be run at a certain point during startup. AUTOEXEC.BAT commands can be executed at any time, not just at startup.

What Kind of Commands
Will You Want in Your AUTOEXEC.BAT?

Commands that tell the computer to:

- ☛ Search for files when it can't find them. (See Chapter 4 for more information on the marvelous PATH command.)

- ☛ Change the default prompt from C> to something different. (See Chapter 7 for more on the fascinating PROMPT command.)

- ☛ Start a favorite menu program or the DOS Shell.

- ☛ Start some other program that you use first thing every day.

If you want to know more about the various commands wandering about your AUTOEXEC.BAT, see Chapter 17.

Does Your Computer
Really Know What Time It Is?

Not all computers have been set up to run DOS in exactly the same way. Some computers display a plain prompt upon starting up, or a colorful menu. Some systems may, during the process of starting, ask you to enter the current date and time.

If at sometime during startup, your PC stops to display the message

Current date is Tue 01-01-1980

Enter new date (mm-dd-yy):

take a careful look at the date (it may already be correct). If it is not correct (if it's only 14 years off, like our example), then enter the correct date in the format *mm-dd-yy* (*month-day-year*, entering a *two-digit* number for each). For example, if the date is October 3, 1994, type **10-03-94** and press **Enter**.

If you are also prompted for the current time, as in

Current time is 14:21:03.10

Enter new time:

then enter the correct time. Use *military time*, which means that 3:00 p.m. is really 15:00. I never bother to enter the seconds, or tenths of a second. For example, if the time is 2:30 in the afternoon, type **14:30** (**14**, colon, **30**) and press **Enter**. If the date and time shown are already correct, just press **Enter**.

On some computers made for non-military minds like mine, you can also type 2:30p for 2:30 p.m. Try yours and see if it takes it, 'cause it's a lot easier to figure out than 14:30.

TECHNO NERD TEACHES...

Where do most computers get the default date of January 1, 1980? Well, that's pretty much when the first version of DOS was invented, so to a personal computer, nothing exists before that date. As a matter of fact, you can't enter a date prior to January 1, 1980, because to the computer, that wouldn't make sense. You also can't enter any illogical date (such as February 31st).

Should You Really Care (About the Date)?

Should you care if your computer thinks it's January 1st, 1980? Yes! Because when you save your work or make changes, the computer remembers the date and time when that was done. By keeping your computer up-to-date, you can figure out when John last updated the department budget report. Or if you have copies of the same document on several diskettes, you can figure out which is the most recent one.

If Your Computer Doesn't Ask You for a Date

If you aren't prompted for the date and time, or if the date and time shown by the computer are correct, it means that the computer already knows what day it is. How? Most recent computers come with a built-in clock that keeps the current date and time updated.

This internal clock runs all the time, even when the power is off, just like the clock in your car. Once in a while, the battery that runs that clock will go dead, and it will need to be replaced. It won't happen for years, but when it does, bully someone into changing it for you. (You can even tell when the critter's getting pooped out when you see that your computer keeps losing track of time.)

Some people put the DATE and TIME commands in their AUTOEXEC.BAT just to verify that the system clock is correct.

You should check the computer's date and time occasionally, because computer clocks sometimes get off track (especially when the battery's running low). To verify the current date (or to enter a new one), type **DATE** and press **Enter**. Your PC displays the current date and asks if you want to change it. If you want to change it, enter the new date in the format *mm-dd-yy*, as described previously. If you don't want to change it, just press **Enter** again.

The TIME command works the same way. Type **TIME** and press **Enter**. Enter the new time in the format *hh:mm* (using military time) as described earlier. If the time is correct, simply press **Enter**.

Turning Off Your Computer—Safely

When it's time to go home, you reach for the old power switch to turn the PC off—*NOT!*

Before you turn off your PC, make sure you've saved your work and exited the program you were using. (See Chapter 21 for help.) When you've exited your program properly and you see the bright lights of the DOS prompt (C> or C:\DOS>), *then* it's OK to throw the ol' power switch.

Shutting Down for the Night (Should You or Shouldn't You?)

Should you turn off your computer at night or leave it on all the time? Even Judge Wapner can't decide:

The prosecution argues that by leaving your PC on all the time, you avoid stressing your computer by supplying it with a constant flow of energy (and not surges). The temperature of the computer parts also remains constant.

The defense argues that leaving a computer on all the time wastes energy and increases the chances of damage by an unexpected power surge. Also, a computer needs to be restarted (booted) from time to time.

The decision? Split down the middle. Roughly 50% of all computer users turn their computers off at the end of the day, and the other 50% leave them on. I turn my computer off every day (probably because of my childhood—"Do you think we own stock in the electric company?"), and I'm happy to report, no damages. What should you do? Do whatever feels best for your situation.

Crash Landings—Shutting Down When You Have a Problem

You may find you need to reset your computer during the working day. You'll be in a program, and the computer may suddenly "pack its bags and fly south." (When I get really frustrated, I buy a ticket and *join* it in Florida.) By "flying south," I mean that maybe your mouse won't respond, or you see a bunch of weird characters on your screen, or your computer simply stops doing anything whatsoever.

The reasons why your PC takes a trip to warmer climes will vary—a sudden power surge can do it, or a glitch in the hard drive. Maybe some poorly-written program has confused DOS, or maybe two of your programs don't get along with each other. At any rate, it's not your fault.

How often does this happen? Maybe never. But if it does, you must restart the computer to get it to respond. Restarting the computer is called *rebooting*. To reboot, press and hold the **Ctrl** and **Alt** keys while you press the **Delete** key. (This sequence is typically shown as **Ctrl+Alt+Delete**.)

Don't reboot a computer unless you have to, because you'll lose any unsaved work (Sorry, but there's no way around this part. That's why you should save your work often). If the computer starts acting funny, try pressing **Esc**. (If you don't know how to tell, see my "Sure Signs That Something's Wrong" in the next section.) If that doesn't work, press and hold the **Ctrl** key while pressing the key with **Break** written on the front edge (this is usually the Pause key). Pressing **Ctrl+Break** tells DOS to stop what it's doing, and can sometimes bring a computer out of its funk. If all else fails, you may need to reboot.

Rebooting The process of restarting a computer that is already on. Press **Ctrl**, **Alt**, and **Delete** at the same time to reboot. Also known as *warm booting*.

Warm booting Same as rebooting (not a treatment for cold feet).

Cold booting Same thing as booting; the process of starting a computer by turning the power on.

Rebooting causes your PC to clear out any electronic "goop" in memory and start over. If your system is really locked up, you may have to perform a *cold boot*, which means you simply turn the computer off, wait a few seconds, and then turn it back on again (but only when all else fails!).

You Should Reboot When . . .
(Jennifer's Sure Signs That Something's Wrong)

Before you decide to reboot and possibly lose some of your work, check out this list of sure signs that something's up:

Pick a key, any key. You press one key (such as G) and you get something else (such as &F%^&*90/?).

Lights on, but nobody's home. You press a key and you get no response. (Kinda like asking your boss for a $100,000 raise—no response.)

Cursor, cursor, who's got the cursor? You press an arrow key and the cursor goes zipping in the opposite direction.

Mouse mania. You move the mouse and the mouse pointer on-screen just sits there munching popcorn.

Did you hear anything? The computer starts making more noises than a two-year-old in church. Be sure to listen for odd beeps and grinding noises—anything that seems out of the ordinary.

The Least You Need to Know

Well, congratulations graduate! Others may quake in fear, but not you—because now you know:

- ☞ How to start your PC safely and without fear. (Remember to look for the power switch on the right side, on the front, or on the back.)

- ☞ If you get the message **Non-system disk or disk error**, you should look for a diskette in drive A (the left or topmost diskette drive). Remove it and press **Ctrl+Alt+Del** to restart.

- ☞ AUTOEXEC.BAT and CONFIG.SYS are special files that issue commands at startup. You can use them to customize your PC's operations.

- ☞ How to keep your PC up-to-date and on time by using the DOS commands DATE and TIME.

- ☞ How to turn your computer off safely. If you are using a program, use the command to save your information before you power down.

- ☞ What to do if your computer acts up, and how to tell if you have trouble. Try pressing **Esc** or **Ctrl+Break**. If that doesn't work, try rebooting by pressing **Ctrl+Alt+Delete**.

What do you want me to do master?

Chapter 4
May DOS Take Your Order, Please?

In This Chapter

- Understanding the DOS prompt
- How to change the active drive
- How to enter a DOS command
- What to do when error messages appear
- Setting up a path so you can use all the DOS commands
- How to repeat commands without retyping them
- Internal versus external commands: the awful truth!

In this chapter, you'll learn the trick of entering DOS commands correctly. If you've ever been frustrated with DOS, or if you're wondering why the computer doesn't do what you want it to do, this chapter is for you.

That DOS Prompt "Drives" Me Crazy!

You enter commands by typing them at the DOS prompt. The DOS prompt is usually some letter, followed by a greater-than sign, as in

C>

Sometimes you may see other letters, such as A, B, or D. The letter you see represents the disk drive you're working on. The letter C refers to the hard drive, and the letters A and B refer to diskette drives. A is usually the left or topmost diskette drive, B is the right or bottommost drive—however, on some newfangled machines, the opposite is true. (PC manufacturers did that just to confuse poor little authors like me.) One way to discover which is your A drive and which is your B drive is to look when you type a command involving that drive, to see which drive light goes on.

If you are working from a diskette drive, you may see this prompt:

A>

Additional letters such as D, E, and so on refer to additional hard drives, a CD-ROM drive, or a tape drive (if any).

Sometimes, you may see a longer DOS prompt, such as

C:\DOS>

This type of prompt tells you not only what drive you're working with, but what *directory*. This prompt is telling you that you are working with drive C and the directory DOS.

Directory   Because hard disks can store thousands of files, you need a way to place related files together on the drive. If you picture your disk as a filing cabinet, then directories are like file drawers. Keeping files in separate directories (drawers) makes it easier to locate and work with related files. You'll learn more about them in Chapter 7.

Putting DOS into Drive

As you just found out, the DOS prompt tells you which drive is active. To work with a disk drive, you must activate it (change to it). For example, if you want to work with files that are stored on a diskette you've inserted into drive A, you must change to drive A. For example, you may have a game on a diskette that you want to play. You have to insert the diskette, then change to that diskette drive by following these instructions.

To change to a drive, enter the drive letter, followed by a colon (:). To change to drive A, type **A:** (that's A, followed by a colon) and press **Enter**. Your prompt will look something like this:

A>

To change back to drive C (the hard disk drive), type **C:** (that's C, followed by a colon) and press **Enter**. Your prompt will change to something like

If you have DOS version 4 or higher, you may have another option for entering DOS commands—the DOS Shell. With the DOS Shell, you can do all the same wonderful things you can do with DOS, but without using the DOS prompt. If you are looking for the easiest way to work with DOS, use the DOS Shell (see Chapter 8 for more details).

> C>

It's that easy! Remember, to use the files on any drive, a hard disk drive, a diskette drive, a tape drive, or a CD-ROM drive, *you've got to change to that drive first*. To change to a drive, just type the drive letter followed by a colon, then press Enter.

Colons and Semicolons, Oh My!

Make sure to include a colon (:) not a semicolon (;). (Doesn't this remind you of your high school English class? We got extra points for semicolons; it was fun thinking up ways to insert them; hey, it got me an A!) Well, no extra points here: to change drives, type the drive letter, followed by a *colon*.

When changing to a diskette drive, make sure there is a diskette in the drive before pressing Enter. If there is no diskette in the drive, you will get the annoying error message: **Not ready reading drive** *x*. **Abort, Retry, Fail?** Place the diskette in the drive and press R for Retry.

Forgetting to Format

Make sure that the diskette is *formatted* (that is, ready to receive data). You will get this error message if the diskette is not formatted: **General failure error reading drive** *x*. **Abort, Retry, Fail?** Press F for Fail, and then format the disk using the instructions in Chapter 6.

Formatting A process that prepares a diskette for use. Formatting creates invisible *tracks* (circles) and *sectors* (pie-shaped wedges) on the surface of the diskette, so data can be stored in known locations. A diskette is usually formatted only once. Some diskettes can be purchased preformatted.

Premature Diskette Withdrawal

Do not remove a diskette until you have changed to a different drive. Don't get fancy and remove the diskette too soon, or you may see the message **Current drive is no longer valid>**. Type the drive letter you want to change to, and press **Enter**.

Unreal Drive Letters

Don't enter a drive letter that does not exist. If you do not have a drive Q, but you type Q:, you will get the error **Invalid drive specification**. Simply type the command again, this time with a valid drive letter.

How to Enter a DOS Command

Entering a DOS command is easy if you know exactly what to type (well, pretty easy, as long as you don't try to type with more than one finger). Simply type the DOS command you want, and press **Enter**.

For example, to find out what day your PC thinks it is, type **DATE** and press **Enter**. In this book, the command will look like this:

DATE

That means, type **DATE** and press **Enter**. You don't have to use capital letters; I do so I can see what I'm doing. DOS thinks lowercase letters are OK too, so use whatever you want.

Make sure you press **Enter** after each command. "Enter" is the (pardon my pun) *key* word here. Nothing happens until you press that magic key.

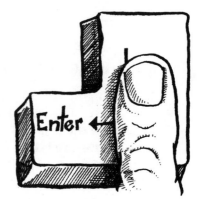

Capitalization is not something to worry about—just forget what Mrs. Haperston taught you—with DOS, it doesn't matter. Use caps or don't; DOS gives all characters equal rights. Most computer books (including this one) show DOS commands in capital letters, as in **TIME**. But if you want to type **time** instead, don't let 'em change your mind.

Much Ado About Spaces

Spaces are the Number One mistake people make when entering DOS commands. How can you tell when to enter a space? Before I can answer that question, you have to understand a little bit more about DOS commands and their structure. Our guest star for this explanation is the DIR command, which is used to list the files in a directory.

A DOS command is made up of three parts:

The command itself   For example, the word DIR.

Applicable parameters   *Parameters* tell the command the files, the directories, or the drives to work with. For example, you can type **DIR HARD2FND.DOC** to get the command to search for and list a specific file. You can type **DIR A:** to get the command to list only the files on drive A. The parameters tell a command such as DIR which drives, directories, or files you want the command to use (if any).

Applicable switches   *Switches* are options you can use with a command. Switches are always preceded by a forward slash (/). For example, the DIR command has a switch (/P for pause) that lists enough files to fill a screen, and then pauses until you're ready to see more files.

Each part of a DOS command is separated by a single space. Don't get spacey and add spaces anywhere else. That means that at most, there can only be TWO spaces in a DOS command.

Let's practice what we know about DOS spaces. The DIR command has a /W switch (for *wide*), which tells it to list files in several columns going across the screen, instead of one column going down. Using what you just learned about spaces, here's the six-million-dollar question: How should you type this command?

DIR /W

DIR   /W

LIST THOSE DARN FILES

The six-million-dollar answer is:

DIR /W

Remember, you type the command (in this case, **DIR**) followed by a *space*, followed by parameters (if any), followed by another *space*, followed by switches (in this case, **/W**). So the command becomes **DIR** *space* **/W**, or

DIR /W

To Err Is Common: What to Do if You Type a Mistake

If you type a mistake *before you press Enter*, try one of these:

Press the Backspace key. Back up and erase the incorrect characters, and retype them.

Insert or delete characters. Using the arrow keys, move the blinking cursor to the place where you want to insert a character. Once you have the cursor positioned, press any character, and it's inserted at that spot. To delete an extra character, press **Delete** or **Del**.

Press the Esc key. This will erase the entire line, and let you start over. On most computers, when you press Esc, you will see a backslash (\), and the cursor will move down one line. Type your command there. (If you feel nervous about typing a command without the DOS prompt, press **Enter** after pressing **Esc**, and Dorothy, you're back in Kansas.)

TECHNO NERD TEACHES...

Pressing the **Ctrl** key produces the character, ^. So if you press **Ctrl+C**, you will see ^C on your monitor. Likewise, if you were to press **Ctrl+D**, you would see ^D, and so on.

Press Ctrl+Break. Hold down the **Ctrl** key while you press the **Break** key. It's the DOS equivalent of "Stop this nonsense or go to your room!" It works like Esc, but will return you to a nice friendly DOS prompt. You can also cancel some commands with **Ctrl+Break** *after you press Enter* (after they've started running). If you can't find the Break key, use **Ctrl+C** instead.

Repeat the command and correct it so that this time, it works. If you pressed Enter but got an error message because you mistyped the command, repeat the command by pressing **F3**. Then use the arrow keys to position the cursor where you'd like to insert or delete characters, and retype the command so it's correct. Once the command is correctly typed, press **Enter** again.

The Most Common Error Messages After Pressing Enter

If you get any errors after typing a DOS command, it's probably one of these (if not, refer to the "HELP! What Does This Error Message Mean, and What Can I Do About It?" section at the end of this book for a more complete listing of error messages):

Bad command or filename

If you get this error, it could be caused by one of three gremlins:

Mistyped command   Check to make sure that you didn't misspell the command or insert extra spaces. Remember, leave one space between one part of a DOS command and the next: the command itself, any parameters, and any switches. That means that the most spaces any command can have is only *two*—don't insert extra spaces where they don't belong.

External command   Some DOS commands are available at every prompt, while others aren't. See "Setting Up a PATH for DOS to Follow" in this chapter.

Missing program   If you get the "Bad command" error message after entering a command to start a program, that program either doesn't exist anymore, or is not in this directory. (Remember that a directory is like a file drawer.) See Chapter 21 for help locating your program.

File not found

If you get this error, it could be one of two foul-ups:

Mistyped filename   Check to make sure that any filenames you typed are valid.

File does not exist   There's a possibility that the file you're looking for is not in the current directory, or the file does not exist. Try a different directory. See Chapter 7 for the how-to's on changing directories.

Invalid parameter or invalid switch

This could be the result of several different gaffes:

You used a parameter or switch that is invalid for this command. Check this book and verify what you typed.

You entered a space between the forward slash and the letter. Easy to do if you type fast. If you want to enter a command with a switch, as in **DIR /W**, do not add an extra space between the slash and the W as in DIR / W.

You used a slash that points the wrong direction. Forward slashes (/) are for switches; backward slashes (\) precede the names of directories.

Required parameter missing

You left out some part of the command. Check this book and verify what you typed.

Setting Up a PATH for DOS to Follow

There are two types of DOS commands: *internal* and *external*. Internal DOS commands are always available (if you're dying to know the full story, read the "Techno Nerd Teaches" in this section). This means that when you type an internal command such as DIR, it works. External DOS commands are not available, which means you could type something like FORMAT, and it won't work. Bummer. But hold on, that's not all! External commands *will* work if

☞ You are in the DOS directory. (How do you get there? Read Chapter 7 to find out.)

OR

☞ You set up a DOS path. (How do you set up this path? Continue reading . . .)

TECHNO NERD TEACHES...

Certain DOS commands are called *internal* because they are loaded into memory (RAM) and are available to use as soon as you turn on your PC. Think of internal commands as being "built in." Unlike internal commands, *external* commands are stored as files in the DOS directory. They are not available until you load them into memory (by typing a command's name and pressing **Enter**). Like a program, external commands cannot be loaded into memory if DOS can't locate them. By setting up a path to the \DOS directory on your hard disk, you are helping DOS find the external commands stored there.

The easiest way to make all DOS commands available (both internal and external) is to set up a DOS path. A DOS path is a listing of directories that DOS should check before it gives you a **Bad command or filename** message, meaning it can't find the command you just typed. If you set up a DOS path, then DOS can find where the external commands are hiding, and it won't give you that error message when you ask for one of the external commands.

How do you know if you've got a DOS path? Well, type **PATH** and press **Enter**. If you see **No Path**, then you don't have one. Go directly to jail and do not pass Go. If you see a bunch of directories listed, make sure you see **C:\DOS** in the list somewhere. If you do, you're OK and you can skip two places.

The installation program for DOS versions 5 or higher creates an AUTOEXEC.BAT for you, complete with a path to DOS, so you may already have a path. To find out, type **PATH** and press **Enter**. If DOS replies **No Path**, then you don't have one. Otherwise, it'll show you what your path is set up to be.

If you don't have a path, or if your path doesn't include the DOS directory (C:\DOS), you need to set up a path so you can use the external DOS commands. Type **PATH=C:\DOS.** This translates as "Set up a search path to drive C, to a directory called \DOS." That's it. Now your external DOS commands are available, regardless of which directory you are in.

Okay, I lied. When you restart your computer, you're going to have this same problem again. To avoid ever thinking about this (ever, ever, ever), bribe a friend (I know, this book is costing you a fortune in Ho-Ho's, but it's worth it) to add the PATH command to your AUTOEXEC.BAT so that the PATH command is executed automatically when you start up your computer. If you want to try editing the AUTOEXEC.BAT yourself, see Chapters 16 and 17 for instructions.

Repeating Yourself

If you're issuing the same DOS command over and over again, you may find that typing it over and over becomes tedious. For example, if you're examining the contents of one diskette after another, you might be typing the following command repeatedly:

DIR A:

The **A:** tells the DIR command to list the files on the diskette in drive A (more about diskette drives in Chapter 6). Instead of retyping the command every time you insert a different diskette in A, simply press **F3**. You'll see the command **DIR A:** redisplayed as if you had really typed it. Press **Enter** to execute the command, and you're on your way!

The Least You Need to Know

When you say "Jump!," DOS will say "How high?" if you remember these things when entering commands:

☛ A DOS prompt tells you what drive you are using (by displaying the drive letter). Some DOS prompts may also tell you what directory you are using.

☛ Drive C is your hard disk, and drives A and B are diskette drives. Other drive letters are additional hard disks.

☛ You can change from one drive to another by typing the drive letter followed by a colon.

☛ There are three parts to a DOS command: the command itself, available parameters (directories or filenames), and available switches. Switches are identified with a / followed by a letter, as in **/P**.

☛ Entering a DOS command can be tricky unless you remember to type only one space between individual parts of a DOS command—and never to use a period, except in filenames.

☛ Setting up a DOS path by typing **PATH=C:\DOS** will make all DOS commands available.

**No, this is not a printing error.
The page truly is blank.**

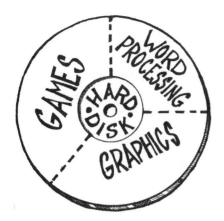

Chapter 5
Becoming a Disk Jockey

In This Chapter

- ☛ Keeping your hard disk in good working order
- ☛ Reorganizing files for efficiency
- ☛ "Defragging" a drive
- ☛ Cleaning up after deleted files
- ☛ Making your hard disk faster with SMARTDrive

Disks and diskettes store your computer data magnetically. This chapter and the next will show you how to "treat them right" so your data is always there when you need it. Your PC uses two different types of disks:

- ☛ A hard disk (hidden inside the computer) that's used to store large amounts of data. This is the type of disk you'll read about in this chapter.

- ☛ Floppy disks (diskettes) that are used to store smaller amounts of data. These munchkins of the computer data world are the stars of Chapter 6.

In this book, I use the word "disk" to refer to the PC's hard disk, and I use the word "diskette" (not "floppy disk") to refer to those portable storage disks. That way, maybe it seems like your PC's had twins.

Jennifer's Soliloquy: Why You Need the Commands in This Chapter

Some of the commands covered in this chapter may make you think, "To use, or not to use . . . That is the question." Before you drive yourself crazy with indecision and start imagining ghosts of old Danes, here's a list to help you sort it all out:

You might also want to increase the amount of space on your hard disk (especially if you're starting to run out of room), but the command you want is discussed in Chapter 19, so you're gonna have to be patient.

DOS path   To use any of the commands in this chapter, you're going to need a path to DOS. (Forget what that is? See Chapter 4 for a quickie review.) Needless to say, such a path is important if you're going to navigate the dark forest of DOS. To see if you have one, type **PATH** and press **Enter**. If you see a list of directories which include C:\DOS, you're fine. Otherwise, type **PATH=C:\DOS** for now.

Defragmenting   Use the DEFRAG command once a month to reorganize the files on your PC, making it *much faster* than it would be if you left the organization task to DOS.

Disk repair   Use SCANDISK or CHKDSK about once a month to clean up any fine messes DOS has gotten itself into. Using these commands frees up hard disk space and allow your programs to run more smoothly.

A speedier disk   Have a guru help you install SMARTDrive into your AUTOEXEC.BAT file, because it makes hard disks go *zoom!*

Whip Your Hard Disk into Shape

A hard disk is one of the most important parts of your computer, because it holds your programs and most of your data. Follow these tips to keep it healthy and strong:

☞ Don't let your hard disk get too hot. Make sure that the system unit is placed in a well-ventilated spot, several inches from any wall. If you add new accessories such as a CD-ROM drive or a tape drive yourself, consult with someone in the know about whether your PC will get too hot.

☛ Putting your system unit (sometimes nicknamed the CPU) on its side is a popular thing to do. But it might lead to problems if the disk has been used in the horizontal position for some time (think of trying to turn a phonograph on its side). If you want a vertical computer, buy one that's built that way (they're called *towers*).

CMOS Pronounced "SEA-moss," CMOS is an electronic device (usually battery-operated) that stores information about your computer. Information stored in CMOS includes the current date and time (if your computer is equipped with a clock), and the number and type of disk drives your computer has.

☛ Always maintain a current backup (copy) of your files (see Chapter 14) in case something happens to your hard disk.

☛ If you're running out of space on your hard disk for new files, a disk compression program, (like DoubleSpace or DriveSpace) will help (see Chapter 19).

☛ Hard disks come in different types. The kind of hard disk your system uses and other important data about your hard disk is stored in something called *CMOS*. Making a copy of this CMOS data is very important; get a guru to help you.

☛ After you use your PC for a while, DOS starts breaking up your larger files and scattering them around your hard disk in various places, instead of in consecutive areas on the disk. This causes the hard disk to huff and puff and take a long time in retrieving files. Solution: a nice defragmenter utility, which you'll learn more about in this chapter. (Talk about timing!)

☛ DOS is also a bit sloppy about file deletions, making it a really lousy housekeeper. Again, you'll learn about how to deal with this sloppiness in this chapter.

Welcome to Defragglerok

DOS will never make Housekeeper of the Year. It's downright sloppy when it comes to keeping files organized on your hard disk. This makes your hard disk really mad, because it takes longer and longer to find a file.

TECHNO NERD TEACHES...

When you tell DOS to save one of your files onto the hard disk, DOS breaks that file into manageable units (which makes sense), and stores them in whatever places it finds convenient. This means that the pieces of the same file are often not together.

Why should you care, since DOS knows how to put those pieces together again? Well, it takes time to put those files together, and that causes your hard disk to slow down every time it has to retrieve a file. This means that as time goes on, and DOS gets sloppier and sloppier with your files, your hard disk gets slower and slower.

So every once in a while, you've got to clean up after DOS. What you need is a utility called a *defragmenter*. If you've got at least DOS 6-something, you're in luck, because it comes with one. If not, you can upgrade your DOS version, or buy a package like The Norton Utilities or PC Tools, each of which comes with a defragmenter.

Upgrading from DOS 6.0 to 6.2, 6.21, or 6.22 might even be worthwhile, because the defragmenter that comes with these later DOS versions is much faster than the one that comes with DOS 6.0.

Is Your Drive Compressed?

Before you follow the directions given here for defragmenting a drive with DOS, you need to know whether that drive is *compressed* or not. How can you tell? Well, you'll see some type of message indicating that the compression program is loading during startup. Restart your PC and look for something like "DriveSpace, DoubleSpace or Stacker drive initialized." If you're feeling adventurous, you can look for the command in

Compressed drive   A disk drive whose storage capacity is increased through a special program which makes more efficient use of space than DOS can by all by its lonesome. (DOS versions 6.0 and 6.2 have a disk-compression program called DoubleSpace; newer DOS versions come with a disk-compression program called DriveSpace.)

your CONFIG.SYS file—see Chapter 16. Otherwise, get a guru to help you figure it out.

By the way, a compressed drive is one which holds about double the amount of files a non-compressed drive can hold (just how is explained later in this chapter). If you know your disk is compressed, defragmenting may not be worth the effort. See the section on compressed drives for more details. If your drive was compressed not with DOS, but with an outside program such as Stacker, you should follow *their* directions, and not the ones given here.

You may have heard of something similar to disk compression, called *file compression*. File compression works by compressing large files into a single compact file which can be easily stored or transmitted via modem to another PC. A popular file compression program is PKZIP.

Disk compression works about the same way, but on a grander scale, compressing all of the files on your hard disk so that they take up less room. However, unlike a file compression program where you must uncompress the file manually before you can use it, a disk compression program handles this task so that the compression itself remains invisible to you. It's really as if your PC's hard disk has suddenly doubled; you don't need to do anything to get the magic to work once the disk compression program is installed.

You'll need at least DOS version 6 to run the DEFRAG command. If you don't know whether you've got DOS 6-something, type **VER** and press **Enter.** As long as it says version 6 and not something lower like 5 or 4, you're OK.

Now, one last warning before we start. This is going to take awhile, especially if you have a large hard disk. So you might want to start the defragmenter late in the day, and not right before an important meeting with say, the IRS. Not that the IRS doesn't have a sense of humor, but they might not like it if you say you don't have access to your accounting records right now because you're *defragging*. They'll think you're de-frizzing your hair, and they'll lock you up for a hundred years with a toothbrush for a comb.

Defragging a Non-Compressed Drive

Now that we've got all of our excuses out of the way, here we go. Actually, there is one more thing. Before you start, exit all programs (including Windows and the DOS Shell). Okay, now you're ready. To defragment your hard disk, type **DEFRAG C:** and press **Enter**. That's **DEFRAG** *space* **C** *colon*. If you got the **Bad command or filename** error message, you need a DOS path (which means, DOS doesn't know where it can find this command at the moment). Chapter 4 can supply you with all the details, but for now, type **PATH=C:\DOS** and press **Enter**. That's **PATH** *equals* **C** *colon backslash* **DOS**. Now try the DEFRAG command again.

May I recommend the red wine with DEFRAG?

DEFRAG analyzes your hard disk and recommends the best procedure for defragging—thank you very much, Uncle DEFRAG. If it says that your hard disk is pretty much "optimized," then just press **Esc** and skip the whole thing.

If you're ready to optimize, press **Enter** to start the whole process. DEFRAG puts on a wonderful sideshow as it reorganizes your disk (for a buck, it'll do your closets too.) DEFRAG is done when a knife inserted into the middle of your hard disk comes out clean (JUST KIDDING!) Actually, it's done when it beeps and displays the helpful message, "Optimization complete—go home now." Press **Esc** and then press **X** to exit DEFRAG.

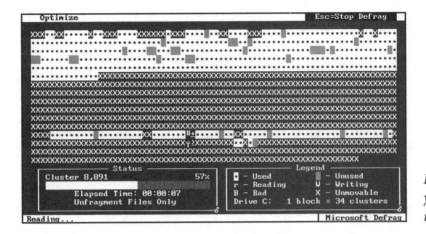

```
┌─Optimize─────────────────────────────────────Esc=Stop Defrag ■┐
│XXX•■XX•••XX•••X•■XXX•XX••■•XXXXXX•XXX•••••X■•••XX■••XXX••••••••X•■■X│
│•••••••••••••••••••••••••••••••••••••••••••••••••••••••••••••••••  │
│•••••••••••••••■•••••••■•••••••••■•••••••••••••••••••••••■•••••••   │
│••■•••••••••■••••••••••••••••••••••••••••••••■•••••••••••••••••••   │
│•••••••••••••••••••••••XXXXXXXXXXXXXXXXXXXXXXXXXXXXXXXXXXXXXXXXXXXXX│
│XXXXXXXXXXXXXXXXXXXXXXXXXXXXXXXXXXXXXXXXXXXXXXXXXXXXXXXXXXXXXXXXXXXX│
│XXXXXXXXXXXXXXXXXXXXXXXXXXXXXXXXXXXXXXXXXXXXXXXXXXXXXXXXXXXXXXXXXXXX│
│XXXXXXXXXXXXXXXXXXXXXXXXXXXXXXXXXXXXXXXXXXXXXXXXXXXXXXXXXXXXXXXXXXXX│
│XXXXXXXXXXXXXXXXXXXXXXXXXXXXXXXXXXXXXXXXXXXXXXXXXXXXXXXXXXXXXXXXXXXX│
│XXXXXXXXXXXXXXXXXXXXXXXXXXXXXXXXXXXXXXXXXXXXXXXXXXXXXXXXXXXXXXXXXXXX│
│XXXX•••••••••■••••••••••xX•••••••■┴+••••••■XX•••••••••••••••••••••□X│
│XXXXXXXXXXXXXXXXXXXXX═≥XXXXXXX■•x□•XXXXXXXXXXXXXXXXXXXXXXXXXXXXXXXXX│
│XXXXXXXXXXXXXXXXXXXXXXXXXXXXXXXXXXXXXXXXXXXXXXXXXXXXXXXXXXXXXXXX     │
│──────Status──────────────────────Legend──────────────           │
│ Cluster 8,891              57%    ■ - Used      ▓ - Unused        │
│ ▓▓▓▓▓▓▓▓▓▓▓▓▓▓▓▓▓▓▓▓▓              r - Reading   W - Writing       │
│ Elapsed Time: 00:00:07            B - Bad       X - Unmovable     │
│ Unfragment Files Only             Drive C:  1 block = 34 clusters │
├───────────────────────────────────────────────────────────────┤
│Reading...                                         Microsoft Defrag│
└───────────────────────────────────────────────────────────────┘
```

DEFRAG optimizes your hard disk by reorganizing its files.

After a good defrag, you should reboot your computer (press the **Ctrl+Alt+Delete** keys at the same time). This ensures that the picture of your hard disk that DOS keeps on its dressing table is the same as say, *reality*. That way, when you go searching for a file, DOS will look in the right spot, and not where the file used to be.

Hey! If this wasn't enough excitement for a Saturday night, why not defragment another drive! Just type **DEFRAG** followed by a space, then another drive letter followed by a colon: **DEFRAG D:** for example. Be sure to press **Enter** and then follow the instructions in this section again for another rip-roaring time.

TECHNO NERD TEACHES...

Ever wonder how DEFRAG does what it does? (Ever wonder how grass grows?) Anyway, if you've ever watched a defrag in-depth (assuming you've already seen the latest reruns on TV), it can be a fascinating thing.

First, DEFRAG cleans off the uppermost unoptimized area, leaving a gap big enough to hold the next file to be *optimized* (organized into consecutive areas). The junk cleaned off that area goes into the most convenient gaps that already exist in the unoptimized zone.

Next, DEFRAG takes all the bytes that belong to the file being optimized, and consecutively writes them into the clean area.

continues

continued

These bytes may come from several sectors, so as they are removed, more gaps emerge. The new gaps may either (1) create more space for DEFRAG's next optimization file, or (2) serve as temporary holding for the former contents of the space that will hold the file being optimized. It's kind of like organizing a bookshelf one book at a time.

DEFRAG Recap

☞ You have to have DOS 6-point-something to use DEFRAG.

☞ You can't be running any programs when you start DEFRAG, so *exit everything*, including Windows and the DOS Shell.

☞ DEFRAG runs on only one drive at a time, so (as it were) rinse and repeat.

☞ Don't use DEFRAG on your diskette drives A and B.

☞ Defragmentation takes a while, but it's worth it.

☞ Run DEFRAG about once a month for best results.

☞ Run DEFRAG on *uncompressed* (not DoubleSpaced) drives. See the next section for help with DoubleSpaced drives.

Defragging a Compressed Drive

If your hard disk was compressed by DoubleSpace (see the last section in this chapter), you can still defragment it if you want. However, defragging a compressed drive really doesn't do much at all, except free up a little space (maybe). That's because a compressed drive is organized differently from a non-compressed drive. If you gotta know the rest of the story, see Chapter 19.

TECHNO NERD TEACHES...

You may still get some advantage out of defragging a compressed drive, and that's extra *room*. A compressed drive is one big file, but that file contains a compressed *image* of the contents of the hard disk drive—dumb file organization, gaps between files, and all. This image is really just a large, salamander-shaped file, containing a compressed image of each section of the hard disk, one right after the other.

Imagine a long line for a popular movie, with each person representing part of a file. On a compressed drive, defragging then reorganizes this large, salamandering file so it can be read consecutively from head to tail. This would be like reorganizing the movie queue so that the tallest people were at the back of the line, just like in grade school. Any gaps in the middle of the drive image (or movie line, if you prefer) would then be moved to the end of the file, making it *smaller*.

If your hard disk was compressed by some other utility such as Stacker, follow their recommendations.

Here's what you do to defrag a compressed drive.

1. Type **DBLSPACE** and press **Enter.**

2. Select a drive to defragment from those listed: use the arrow keys to move the highlight over the drive you want.

3. Open the Tools menu by pressing the two keys **Alt+T** at the same time.

4. Select the Defragment command by pressing **D.**

5. You'll see a message asking you if you really want to do this. Press **Enter** to continue, then go on to step 6. If you've changed your mind, press **Esc** then go on to step 7.

6. When DEFRAG is done, open the Drive menu by pressing the two keys **Alt+D** at the same time.

7. Press **X** to exit and return to the DOS prompt. Whew!

ScanDisk and CHKDSK

Not only does DOS get messy when it comes to storing files, it's downright sloppy when it comes time to delete them. As a result, you probably have little parts of old deleted files sitting around in your DOS junkyard, trading stories and hubcaps. These parts of old files that were never deleted are called *lost clusters* or *lost chains*. There are several commands that come with DOS to help you get rid of these old files and free up otherwise-unused disk space. Which one of these commands you use depends on your DOS version.

TECHNO NERD TEACHES...

When you delete a file, it's not really deleted. Instead, the *reference* to that file is erased, and the spaces it used to occupy are marked "available." The next time you save a file to disk, it may be placed in one of these available spots, overwriting the deleted file.

Sometimes DOS is not as neat as it needs to be, and when it erases the reference to the file, it forgets to mark all the spaces that the file was using as "available." That means that there are parts of old files out there whose space is not being reused because DOS goofed. These dusty parts of old files are called *lost clusters* or *lost chains*.

If You've Got DOS Versions 6.2, 6.21, or 6.22

Before you use ScanDisk, you must exit out of any programs, such a Windows or the DOS Shell. If you're on a network, heed above all, this warning: *don't use ScanDisk on a network drive* such as drive F. If your PC is attached to a network, drive F probably belongs to the network, and not to your computer, or it may be a RAM disk (a simulated disk drive existing in memory) which has little need for ScanDisk anyway.

Now that the preliminaries are over, if you're using DOS 6.2, DOS 6.21, or DOS 6.22, type this **SCANDISK C:** and press **Enter** to scan for lost clusters and chains and fix the problem. If you got the error message, Bad command or filename, you need a DOS path. Chapter 4 can supply you with all the details, but for now, type **PATH=C:\DOS** and press **Enter**. Now try the ScanDisk command again.

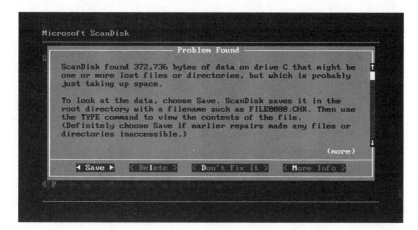

Microsoft ScanDisk

┌───────────────── Problem Found ─────────────────┐

ScanDisk found 372,736 bytes of data on drive C that might be one or more lost files or directories, but which is probably just taking up space.

To look at the data, choose Save. ScanDisk saves it in the root directory with a filename such as FILE0000.CHK. Then use the TYPE command to view the contents of the file. (Definitely choose Save if earlier repairs made any files or directories inaccessible.)

(more)

◄ Save ►   < Delete >   < Don't Fix It >   < More Info >

ScanDisk prompts you if it encounters problems.

ScanDisk entertains you with a magnificent display of checkmarks as it looks for problems. If ScanDisk uncovers a problem, an error message appears. Should ScanDisk uncover lost data, press **Enter** to save the lost data in a file, or press **L** to delete it (which is what I normally do, since it's usually data from some old deleted file I don't even want anymore). If you're asked to create an Undo diskette, you can stick one in drive A and press **Enter**. An Undo diskette allows you to change your mind and undo what ScanDisk does. But take it from me, Undo diskettes are risky, like jumping off the tightrope in hopes there's a net below. You can skip Undo by pressing **S**.

It's worth saying twice: DO NOT use ScanDisk on a network drive. If you do, your network administrator may hang you up by your keyboard, and believe me, it's not a pretty sight.

ScanDisk also checks out your hard disk for physical problems with a surface scan (you should probably do one of these about once a month or so). This is a bit noisy, so if you decide to do it, don't get too worried when it starts crankin'. Just press **Enter** when prompted, or press **N** to bypass this step. Logical problems with your files are rarely the result of a physical defect in your disk; but if the problems you're having don't seem logical (OK, what problem ever does?), a surface scan may be in order.

After the scan is complete, you can view a log of the results by pressing **V**. Press **X** anytime to Exit.

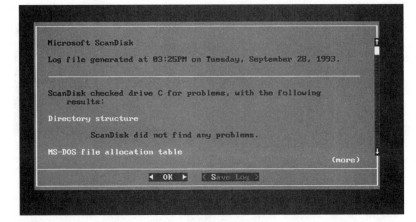

ScanDisk presents the results of your testing. Good news: You'll live.

If You've Got DOS Version 6 or Below

If you have a DOS version earlier than DOS 6.2 (such as DOS 6, DOS 5 or DOS 4), you don't have a SCANDISK command. You have another command which helps to clear away all those lost clusters and lost chains, and it's called the CHKDSK command.

A couple of warnings first: exit all programs before you use CHKDSK, including Windows and the DOS Shell. Also, *don't try to use CHKDSK on a network drive, such as drive F*. OK, now type **CHKDSK C: /F** and press **Enter**. That's **CHKDSK** *space* **C** *colon space* forward *slash* **F**. If you got the **Bad command or filename** error message, you need a DOS path. Chapter 4 can supply you with all the details, but for now, type **PATH=C:\DOS** and press **Enter**. That's **PATH** *equals* **C** *colon backslash* **DOS**. Now try the CHKDSK command again.

If you forget the **/F** switch, CHKDSK will pretend that it's fixing the problem, but when you run CHKDSK again, the problem will still be there. The **/F** switch tells DOS to write the changes to the disk.

If CHKDSK finds an old piece of a deleted file, it displays something like this:

2 lost allocation units found in 1 chains.

8192 bytes disk space would be freed.

Press **Y** to convert them to usable space. DOS creates a file to contain the data that was in each lost cluster. The data is probably unusable because it's part of an old file. To delete the files, type **DEL C:\FILE????.CHK** and press **Enter**. That's **DEL** *space* **C** *colon backslash* **FILE????** *period* **CHK**.

If you're using CHKDSK and get a message like this:

Errors found, F parameter not specified

Corrections will not be written to disk

then you have forgotten to type /F. Retype the command and be sure to include the /F switch.

Making Your PC's Hard Disk Faster with SMARTDrive

If you have one of the latest DOS versions, you can really "cache in" on your investment. A disk *cache* (pronounced "cash") makes your hard disk faster by making it *smarter*. How it works is unimportant (OK, if you have to know, read the "Techno Nerd Teaches" in this section); all you've got to do is install it once, then forget it.

TECHNO NERD TEACHES...

A *disk cache* stores in memory (RAM) a copy of data when it's read from the hard disk. The next time that data is needed, the PC gets it from memory. Getting data from RAM is quicker than getting it from the hard disk because RAM is faster. As the disk cache gets full of recent data, the least requested information is overwritten, ensuring that the cache stays full of often-requested data.

SmartDrive also caches data being written to the hard disk. Instead of stopping every few seconds to write one thing or the other, multiple requests to save data are held until the write cache gets full, then it's all written to the hard disk in one step.

Things You Should Know About SMARTDrive

OK, here's the price you pay for speed:

☞ First, you have to have DOS 5, or one of the DOS 6 somethings. If you've got an earlier version of DOS (like DOS 4), use this opportunity to convince your boss it's worth upgrading.

☞ Second, you have to have some *extended memory*. What's that, you ask? Well, that's a question and a half. Jump on over to Chapter 20 for the payoff.

☞ If you've got Windows, SMARTDrive is already set up for you. So stop sweating it and go get yourself some Ben & Jerry's.

☞ Actually, DOS itself installs SMARTDrive for you when you install DOS, so again, it's Ben & Jerry's time!

☞ One thing: before you turn off your PC, you need to make sure that SMARTDrive has dumped everything it's been storing in RAM, and has saved it to the hard disk. Just to be sure, wait a few seconds before powering down, or just type **SMARTDRV /C** and press **Enter**. This command clears SMARTDrive's stuff out of RAM. If you have DOS 6.2, 6.21, or 6.22, you don't have to worry about this little glitch. When you see a C> prompt, you can safely turn off your PC.

Installing SMARTDrive?

You may not have to install SMARTDrive, because if you have one of the DOS versions which includes SMARTDrive, or if you have Windows (which also comes with it), then it's already installed.

The command to start SMARTDrive may already be included in your AUTOEXEC.BAT. It looks like this:

C:\DOS\SMARTDRV.EXE

or this:

C:\WINDOWS\SMARTDRV.EXE

If you see something like this:

LH /L:0;2,45456 /S C:\DOS\SMARTDRV.EXE

The mystery codes were added by MemMaker as it wedged SMARTDrive into its best memory-fit. *MemMaker* is a utility that gets the most out of your computer's memory, and it's featured in Chapter 20.

If one of your programs encounter a problem with SMARTDrive, you can remove it. To do that, you've got to edit your AUTOEXEC.BAT file. See Chapter 16 or bribe a friend to help you.

The Least You Need to Know

Dealing with DOS is just another day at the races for a "disk" jockey who remembers these basic rules:

- ☛ Always maintain a current backup (copy) of the files on your hard disk, in case something happens.

- ☛ Disk compression utilities like the ones you'll read about in Chapter 19 allow you to put more files on your hard disk.

- ☛ Fragmentation is caused when files are split up all over a hard disk drive.

- ☛ You can defragment a drive (reorganize the files) with DEFRAG.

- ☛ To clean up after deleted files, use ScanDisk (for DOS versions 6.2 and above) or CHKDSK (for DOS version 6 and older).

- ☛ SMARTDrive makes hard disks more efficient, and therefore faster.

"Look, another blank page!"

Chapter 6
Diskette Disco

In This Chapter

- Choosing the right diskette for your PC's decor
- How to insert a diskette into its drive
- How to keep sleet, rain, and gloom of night from damaging your diskettes
- Preparing diskettes for use by ordinary human beings like yourself
- Down and dirty formatting
- Unformatting a diskette
- Creating an emergency diskette
- Copying diskettes

They're small. They're square. They're small and square. They don't slice, they don't dice, but they're great for leveling off lopsided office furniture. Used in a more conventional manner, diskettes are handy for storing copies (backups) of important files. Diskettes also make good taxis for transporting files from one PC to another.

The welter-weights of PC data storage, diskettes contain a thin, round piece of film covered in magnetic coating which allows them to store data in a way that's similar to how the hard disk does it. Floppy disks (let's use *diskettes*—it's more polite) come in a variety of sizes and types, which you'll learn about in this chapter, along with their proper care and feeding.

A Bit About the Commands in This Chapter

If you've just tuned in to our show, here's an update:

☞ **Remember to press Enter to execute a command.** Until you press Enter, nothing will happen.

☞ **If you have an older DOS version, you should be especially careful when using the FORMAT command.** Be sure to include a drive letter to format, or you may accidentally format your hard disk if you are not careful (this would be a really, *really* baaaad thing).

☞ **The most common error message you might get** when using these commands is Bad command or file name. If you get this error message, you need to set up a DOS path so that DOS can find the command. See Chapter 4 for more details.

Why Our Critics Give These Commands Two Thumbs Up

"I laughed, I cried, I formatted diskettes."

"These are the best commands you'll use in this chapter!"

"This chapter changed my life. I can't wait 'til Diskettes, Part II!"

Here's a sneak preview of when you might need this chapter:

Using new diskettes. Sorry, gotta format them first, unless you bought preformatted diskettes, you clever person, you (see page 74 "A Dirty Job, but Somebody's Gotta Do It: Preparing a Diskette for Use").

Formatting a low-density diskette in a high-density drive. Although this is not recommended, sometimes "ya gotta do what ya gotta do"— for example, if you need to transfer files from your PC to a PC with a lower-density drive (see "Formatting a Double-Density Diskette in a High-Density Drive").

Reusing a diskette. One way to erase the files on an existing diskette is to reformat it (see "Performing a Quick Format").

Preparing for the worst. Creating an emergency diskette will prepare you in case you encounter a problem when starting your PC (see "Calling 911: Creating an Emergency Diskette").

Protecting your investment. After you buy a new program, you should copy the program diskettes so you'll have a backup in case something happens to them (see "Copying Diskettes").

A Brief Disk-cussion About Diskettes

Diskettes really aren't that hard to understand, but you need to know some of the factors that go into selecting the right diskettes for your system, such as size and density.

What Size Is Right?

Diskettes come in two sizes: 5 1/4-inch and 3 1/2-inch. You buy the diskette that fits your diskette drive.

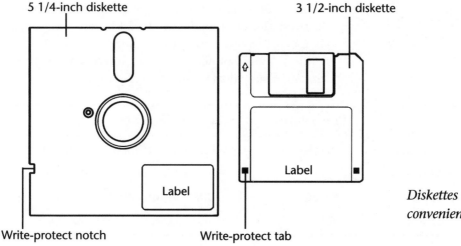

5 1/4-inch diskette

3 1/2-inch diskette

Label

Label

Write-protect notch

Write-protect tab

Diskettes come in two convenient sizes.

Physical size does not have anything to do with the amount of data a diskette can hold. In fact, the 3 1/2-inch diskettes can hold *more* than the 5 1/4-inch diskettes! Size is only a measure of the physical size of the plastic part.

Feeling a Bit Dense About Diskettes?

Each diskette size comes in two densities. The *density* of a diskette refers to how closely data can be packed onto the disk. A diskette that's more dense than another diskette holds more data. Imagine one phonograph record with 100 grooves, and a second record (the same size diameter) with 200 grooves. On the latter, the grooves are closer together, so more music fits on the record.

Density A measure of how closely data is packed onto a diskette. A high-density diskette holds more data than a double density diskette because its data is packed closer together.

Capacity A measure of the storage capabilities of a diskette, which depends not only on its *size*, but its *density*.

The two most common densities are *high-density* and *double-density*. The exact capacity depends on the diskette size, but a high-density diskette holds at least twice as much data as a double-density diskette of the same size.

Diskette Capacity: Fill It Up!

The amount of data a diskette can hold is called its *capacity*. Capacity is determined by a combination of the diskette's size and density. Diskette capacity is measured in *bytes*. A byte is the amount of space it takes for a computer to store one character, such as the letter Q. A *kilobyte* is 1,024 bytes. A *megabyte* is 1,048,576 bytes sometimes shortened to "1 million bytes" or about 1,000 kilobytes. Kilobytes are abbreviated as K, and megabytes as MB.

Size...	Plus Density...	Equals Capacity
5 1/4-inch	Double	360K (about 360,000 bytes)
5 1/4-inch	High	1.2MB (about 1,200,000 bytes)
3 1/2-inch	Double	720K (about 720,000 bytes)
3 1/2-inch	High	1.44MB (about 1,440,000 bytes)

Choosing the Right Diskette for Your System

Obviously, you have to use the right size of diskettes in your drive, or the disk won't fit. But you must also use the right *density*. If your PC has a double-density 5 1/4-inch drive, you must use 5 1/4-inch double-density diskettes. So, when buying diskettes, match the diskette drive's *size* and *density*. Check your owner's manual to find out what kind of diskettes your diskette drive uses.

If you have a high-density drive, you can use either density diskette: high or double. But you can run into big-time problems that way, so I wouldn't use anything other than a *high-density diskette* in a *high-density drive*. And in case you decide to forego my infinite wisdom and buy double-density diskettes because they're cheaper, just don't put anything too important on those diskettes once they're formatted. OK?

Also, so you won't get too confused—even if you buy double-density diskettes and format them in your big ol' high-density drive, they *still won't hold any more information*. In other words, they will only hold the same amount as regular double-density diskettes, so you're not really gaining anything but a bunch of headaches, because they are harder to format with you big ol' high-density drive. So don't buy them if you have a high-density drive—*please*.

DD, HD, What Does It All Mean?

The first time I went to buy diskettes, it seemed that the store was full of them! Different sizes and types (not to mention formatted and unformatted). I had a hard time figuring out which ones to buy. Look for these abbreviations:

DD   Double density.

HD   High-density.

2D   Double-density.

4D   Quad-density, an old term for twice-double-density.

ED   Extended-density. Avoid these unless you have a special extended-density drive (there are only about twelve of these, so if you're not sure you have one, you don't. Besides, geez, they're expensive!).

DS   Double-sided. This is the norm because most diskette drives write data to both sides of a diskette.

SS   Single-sided. Physically, it seems this is about as possible as a single-sided coin or a one-party Congress. Despite the obvious fact that you can flip over a single-sided diskette and find a reverse side, SS diskettes are designed for older PCs that could write data to only one side of a diskette. (They're actually double-sided, but have only been tested on one side.)

Changing Diskettes

You already learned this trick in Chapter 2, but here's a quick review. To place a diskette in a drive, hold the disk so that your thumb covers the label, *with the label pointing up* (or to the left, if your drive is vertically mounted).

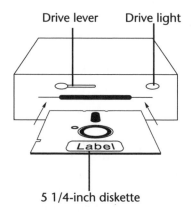

Drive lever   Drive light

5 1/4-inch diskette

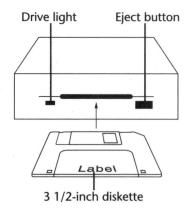

Drive light   Eject button

3 1/2-inch diskette

Inserting a diskette.

3 1/2-inch diskette   Push the diskette into the drive, metal-covered area first, until you hear a soft click.

5 1/4-inch diskette   Push the diskette into the drive, exposed area first (label up or to the left). Then close the drive door by pulling the lever down across the slot or pressing the button.

To eject (remove) a diskette:

5 1/4-inch diskette   Open the drive door by pulling the lever up.

3 1/2-inch diskette   Press the eject button.

Care and Treatment of Diskettes

Here are some easy guidelines:

Wait until the light changes, then ease into the intersection...   Don't remove a diskette from its drive while the drive light is on. It could damage both the drive and the diskette.

Watch your fingers   When handling a diskette, don't touch any exposed area—you'll damage the magnetic film inside the diskette and erase data.

If a 3 1/2-inch diskette gets stuck, I push it back into the drive, and the spring inside usually bounces it back out. On a 5 1/4-inch drive, pulling the lever down and then back up usually works.

Is it hot in here?   Keep diskettes away from heat sources (such as the top of your monitor or the inside of a car on a hot day).

Magnet magic   Since data is stored on diskettes magnetically, keep them away from any magnetic source (like your telephone, your cat (such a shocker), your modem, or even your CPU).

Look for the union label   If you use 5 1/4-inch diskettes, complete your labels *before* placing them on the diskettes. If you have to write on a label that is already on the diskette, use a soft-tipped pen. Since the casing on a 3 1/2-inch diskette is hard, you can write on its label with an ordinary pen or pencil if you want. Acetylene torches, however, are still not advisable.

Put your toys away when you're done playing with them.   If you use 5 1/4-inch diskettes, place them back in their paper sheaths (envelopes) when not in use. Remember: never unholster a diskette unless you *intend to use it.*

Remove the diskette from the drive when you're finished with it, and you know for sure the computer's finished with it, too. If you start the computer with a disk in drive A, you may get an error message: **Non-system disk or disk error. Replace and strike any key when ready.** If that happens, remove the diskette and *press* **Ctrl+Alt+Del** (don't take that "strike" too literally, either).

Prepping a Diskette for Use

Diskettes come in two sizes: 5 1/4-inch and 3 1/2-inch, and two types of *density*. You should buy diskettes of the same size and density as the type of diskette drive your PC comes with (see the "disk-cussion" earlier in this chapter).

Before you can use a purchased diskette to store your own personal data, it has to be *formatted*. Imagine printing lines on a piece of notebook paper so the person who uses it will be able to write legibly, and you'll get an idea of what formatting does. Although you can purchase diskettes that are preformatted, I've found that diskettes that have been formatted in the actual drive they'll be used in are more reliable—it's like knitting a sock around the actual foot that will wear it.

To format a diskette for drive A that is the same density as its drive, type **FORMAT A: /V** and press **Enter**. That's **FORMAT** *space* **A** *colon space slash* **V**. In DOS 5 and below, the /V switch allows you to enter an electronic *volume* label (a fancy-though-optional name for "diskette" that shows up when you display the contents of the diskette). If you have one of the DOS 6-somethings, you can omit the /V and get the same results.

But why bother with a volume label at all, when you have a paper label on the outside of the diskette? Well, when you use the DIR command, as in **DIR A:.** you'll see a listing of files on the diskette in drive A, along with the volume label. If you use good descriptions in your volume labels, you'll be able to quickly identify the diskette and what is stored on it— even if the paper label has fallen off!

When I'm talking about diskettes you'll need to format, I mean the ones you've bought to store your own personal stuff. Don't *under any circumstances* format a diskette that came with some program such as Microsoft Word, Lotus 1-2-3, or WordPerfect. Formatting such a diskette would erase the program from the disk, and make your PC guru very upset (not to mention the person who paid for the program, such as your ex-boss.)

After you type the FORMAT command, you'll see a message telling you to insert the diskette into its drive. You may already have inserted it, and that's OK, DOS'll tell you this anyway. (Feels good to be *one step ahead of DOS*, doesn't it?) After the diskette has been inserted, press **Enter** to continue.

After the diskette has been formatted, you'll be asked to enter a *volume label* (remember, that's what the /V switch is for). You may use up to 11 characters, including spaces, so type something informative such as 94 TAXES or PERSNL STUF. You can also press **Enter** if you don't want to label your disk. After a summary is displayed, you'll be asked if you want to format another diskette of the same density. Press **Y** or **N**, then **Enter**.

At your command . . .

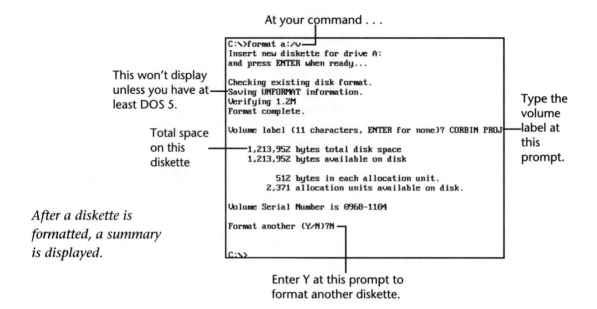

This won't display unless you have at least DOS 5.

Total space on this diskette

Type the volume label at this prompt.

```
C:\>format a:/u
Insert new diskette for drive A:
and press ENTER when ready...

Checking existing disk format.
Saving UNFORMAT information.
Verifying 1.2M
Format complete.

Volume label (11 characters, ENTER for none)? CORBIN PROJ

   1,213,952 bytes total disk space
   1,213,952 bytes available on disk

       512 bytes in each allocation unit.
     2,371 allocation units available on disk.

Volume Serial Number is 0968-1104

Format another (Y/N)?N

C:\>
```

After a diskette is formatted, a summary is displayed.

Enter Y at this prompt to format another diskette.

The diskette summary tells you how much room is on the diskette, and whether there are any *bad sectors* (unusable spots) on the diskette. You can still use a diskette with bad sectors, but I wouldn't copy irreplaceable data onto it.

You can use a diskette with bad sectors because those bad spots have been *marked* as "unusable" by the system. However, bad sectors are like slimy bacteria (I know, I just *had* to give you at least one disgusting mental picture before the end of the chapter). A diskette that has bad sectors typically develops more of them over time, so you may not want to use it. Also, a diskette is fairly cheap and easily replaced, so why take the chance?

As an interesting side note, a diskette with bad sectors may not actually *be* bad, but simply misformatted (formatted for the wrong density). See the next section for instructions on formatting a double-density diskette in a high-density drive.

Formatting a Double-Density Diskette in a High-Density Drive

You should try to use only high-density diskettes in a high-density drive. (It's their density, I mean *destiny!*) However, if you need to use a double-density diskette in your HD drive, don't use it to store data that's irreplaceable.

You may find that you want to format a double-density diskette in your HD drive because your neighbor George has only a DD drive. (Poor George.) That's OK, but in all honesty, George is better off formatting a diskette in his drive and giving it to you to copy data on. A DD diskette formatted in a HD drive is simply not reliable, so I just plain wouldn't do it except when I don't have any real choice, like when it's 10:00 at night and the only things in the house include a day-old bagel, a half-used package of cream cheese, some corn crunchies, my sleeping husband, me, and some double-density diskettes.

To format a *double-density 5 1/4-inch diskette* in a high-density drive, use this command (you must have at least DOS 4):

> **FORMAT A: /F:360 /V**

If you have a DOS version less than DOS 4, use this command instead:

> **FORMAT A: /4 /V**

Formatting   A process that prepares a diskette for use by creating invisible magnetic *tracks* (rings) on the surface of the diskette and dividing them into pie-shaped wedges called *sectors*. The number of tracks and sectors that a diskette is divided into determines its *density*.

Density   Describes the amount of data a diskette can store. There are two kinds of densities: *high* and *double*. High-density diskettes hold at least twice as much as the same size double-density diskette.

Volume label   A brief description or name for a diskette, recorded electronically on the disk itself. A volume label will appear on-screen when you use DIR to list the files on the disk.

To format a *double-density 3 1/2-inch diskette* in a high-density drive, use this command (you must have at least DOS 4):

FORMAT A: /F:720 /V

If you have a DOS version less than DOS 4, use this command instead:

FORMAT A: /N:9 /T:80 /V

Yech! See why it's best to buy the right type of diskette for your drive, and not to use double-density disks in a high-density drive? It's just not worth the trouble (never mind the dents in your digits from typing too much!)

Unformatting a Diskette

If you have at least DOS 5 and you format a diskette, it's formatted *safely* (unless you specify otherwise). This means that file locations are erased, but the files themselves still exist on the diskette. Because the files are not really erased, you can use the UNFORMAT command to "unerase" a formatted disk, in case you suddenly realize you've just formatted an important diskette with meaningful data on it, such as names and picks for this year's football pool.

I should note here that in previous DOS versions—the ones *before* the Paleozoic Era and DOS 4—once a diskette was formatted, the data was irretrievable. You couldn't unformat a diskette with those early DOS versions.

If, however, you're one of the lucky ones (or unlucky ones, if you think about what you just did to a poor, helpless diskette), then you can unformat your accidentally-formatted diskette. To unformat a diskette, *wait for the FORMAT procedure to complete itself first* (UNFORMAT won't work otherwise). Then, once you're back to the DOS prompt, type **UNFORMAT A:** and press **Enter**.

Performing a Quick Format

If you have at least DOS 5, you can perform a quick format on a previously-formatted diskette. That's because a diskette only needs to be formatted *once*. From then on, all you're really trying to do is to erase the data. Use this command when you want to clear old data from a diskette so you can reuse it. A quick format does everything a regular format does, but it does not check the disk for bad sectors—so if that diskette's been sputtering on you lately, don't use quick format. A quick format takes less time than a regular format. To perform a quick format, type **FORMAT A: /Q /V**.

Calling 911: Creating an Emergency Diskette

An emergency diskette is used to boot your system when you have trouble starting your PC. An emergency diskette contains DOS, your AUTOEXEC.BAT, and your CONFIG.SYS. When your PC doesn't start properly (its startup information has been damaged somehow), simply place the emergency diskette in drive A, and restart your PC from it.

Here's why it works: When your PC boots (starts), it usually checks drive A first. If there's a diskette there, the PC boots using the information on the diskette. If not, the PC boots from the information on the hard disk. You use your emergency diskette when the information on the hard disk becomes damaged, and you can't start your PC any other way. Some of the newer PCs think it's fun to check drive C first, then any other hard disks, *before* checking drive A. How rude. Anyway, your emergency diskette will work on them too.

To create an emergency diskette (sometimes called a *boot diskette*), use a special variation of the FORMAT command to format a diskette:

FORMAT A: /S /V

That's **FORMAT** *space* **A** *colon space slash* **S** *space slash* **V**. The /S switch tells DOS to place a copy of the operating system on the diskette after formatting it. (The /V switch is optional, but it lets you place an electronic label on the disk—a good idea if you can't find a pen.) After formatting the diskette, copy your AUTOEXEC.BAT and CONFIG.SYS files with these two commands:

> **COPY C:\AUTOEXEC.BAT A:**
> **COPY C:\CONFIG.SYS A:**

That's **COPY** *space* **C** *colon backslash* **AUTOEXEC** *period* **BAT** *space* **A** *colon*. The second command is similar to the first, except you type CONFIG.SYS instead of AUTOEXEC.BAT. What these commands do is place a copy of these two files onto the diskette in drive A. You'll learn more than you ever cared to know about the COPY command in Chapter 11.

Put your emergency diskette in a safe place, and make sure it's well marked, so you can find it when you need it. *If you (or any close friend you con into it) ever change your AUTOEXEC.BAT or your CONFIG.SYS files,* be sure to copy these crucial files onto this diskette again, to keep your emergency diskette current.

Copying Diskettes

Whenever you purchase a new software program, the first thing you should do is make a copy of the original diskettes, because if Uncle Bill borrows the disks and then returns them to you in pieces, you're out of luck.

When you have DOS make a copy of a diskette, you make an exact duplicate. This is different from using the COPY command to copy all the files from a diskette. The DISKCOPY command copies all the files and the *formatting* of a diskette, all in one big step.

Now, because you're making an exact duplicate, the two diskettes you use must be the same kind. This means they have to be the same *size* and *density*. It also means that you'll be using only one diskette drive during the entire affair, because if your PC has two diskette drives, they are probably different types. Follow? Good. Then we're ready to go.

You cannot use DISKCOPY to copy a hard disk, only diskettes.

To make a copy of a diskette, use one of these commands (choose the command which matches the diskette drive you're going to use, either A or B):

> **DISKCOPY A: A:**
>
> OR
>
> **DISKCOPY B: B:**

After you enter one of these commands, you will be prompted to insert the *source diskette*. That's a computer term for the original diskette. What you do is: place the *disk you want to copy* into the drive, and press **Enter**. Then, when prompted, switch the original diskette for the *target diskette* (fancy-schmancy name for the diskette you're using to make a copy). You may need to do this back-and-forth business a coupla times, depending on your PC. Just watch for the prompts, and do whatever the PC tells you to do.

When the copying process is complete, you'll be asked if you want to copy more diskettes. Because most programs nowadays come on several diskettes, answer Yes by pressing **Y**. When you've copied the last diskette that came with your new program, answer No by pressing **N**.

If you have two diskette drives and they are the same type and density (it's unlikely, but it could happen, especially on older machines), you can save a bit of time by using this command instead:

> **DISKCOPY A: B:**

In this case, y'put ya original diskette in drive A, and ya target diskette in drive B, then press **Enter** and let it do its thing. No switchin' diskettes on this one.

The Least You Need to Know

Performing diskette surgery is easy if you remember these tips:

- ☞ Diskettes come in two sizes (5 1/4-inch and 3 1/2-inch) and two densities (double and high). Density refers to how closely information is placed on the diskette.

- ☞ To protect diskettes, remove them from the drive when not in use. Keep diskettes away from magnets, heat, and your kid's sticky fingers.

- ☞ To format a diskette that is the same density as its drive, type **FORMAT**, a space, the letter of the diskette drive to format, then a colon. You can add the switch **/V** to the command if you want to enter a volume label.

- ☞ If you have at least DOS 5, you can unformat a diskette if it was formatted by accident. Use the UNFORMAT command.

- ☞ If you have at least DOS 5, you can perform a quick format on a previously formatted diskette by including the /Q switch.

- ☞ To make an exact copy of a diskette, use the DISKCOPY command.

Chapter 7

Navigating the DOS Jungle of Files and Directories

In This Chapter

- ☞ What are files?
- ☞ Appropriate monikers for files
- ☞ PBS documentary: "Directories: The Awful Truth"
- ☞ Naming that directory
- ☞ The truth about dinosaurs and how their mere mention can sell another 20,000 copies of any book
- ☞ Setting up a customized prompt

The unthinkable has happened. You turned around for *one second*, and now you're alone, alone in the dark and forbidding jungle of files, directories, and DOS. Don't panic—armed with only a small flashlight, a can of OFF! and this chapter, you'll be out of this mess in no time and back to the civilized world of notepads, manila folders, and file drawers.

What Are Files?

Hard disks and diskettes are used to store your data. You store data in *files*, which you can think of as tiny books scattered on your PC's hard disk. If

File DOS stores information in files. A file can be anything: a memo, a budget report, or even a graphics image (like a picture of a boat or a computer). Files you create are called *data files*. Applications (like a word processing program that you can type letters and reports with) are composed of several files called *program files*.

you write a memo about the copier, you might save it in a file called COPIER. If you create an analysis of shipping costs, you might save it in a file called SHIPPING. Each file you create has its own name (just as books have their own names).

Naming Your Files

Files have a first and a last name, just like people—except really famous people who don't need a last name because they are *way too talented*, such as Cher, Madonna, Fabio, and Lassie. The first name of a file can have up to eight characters (letters, numbers, and special characters such as #). The last name of a file is used to identify what type of file it is. For example, a word processing file might end in DOC, which is short for document. The last name of a file is called its *extension*, and it can have up to three letters. The first and last names of a file are separated by a period, as in REPORT.DOC.

The extension of a file tells you a lot about what type of file it is. Most word processors use a .DOC extension. Lotus 1-2-3 (a spreadsheet program which creates worksheets) uses extensions such as .WKS and .WK4 for its files. Excel (another spreadsheet program) uses .XLS for Excel spreadsheet. Use the DIR command to check the files in each of your program directories to see what extensions they use.

Program files end in .COM or .EXE. If you were looking for the command to start a program, you could use the command **DIR *.EXE** to list files ending in .EXE. One of these .EXE files is probably the one to start the program. To find out more about starting programs, see Chapter 21.

Use care when naming files, so that you can easily identify them. BUDGET.DOC might not be as descriptive as BUDGET93.DOC, and MEMO.DOC might not be as clear as PRODMEMO.DOC or MAYSALES.XLS. If you misname a file it's no crime, just as it's no crime to name your dog Fred when it should be called something more like Trash-Eating-Moron-Who-Never-Comes-When-I-Call-Him. However, misnaming a file might make it take longer to identify the correct file when you need it.

What Are Directories?

You organize files on the PC's hard disk just as books are organized in a library. In a library, books are neatly organized by subject, taken out, then never returned until they're found under the front seat of your car three months later. On a computer, files are usually organized by type: *word processing* files are placed in one directory, while *spreadsheet* files are placed in a different directory. In this analogy, a *directory* is like a shelf where you place your books (files).

Typically, you create a directory for each program that you use, so if you think back to the shelf analogy, you'd end up with a shelf (directory) for every program that you install on your PC. By keeping related files (all the files having to do with a single program) in the same directory, they're easier to locate and use.

Getting to the Root of Things

There is a special directory that your computer only has one of: the *root directory*. The root directory is the main directory; other directories branch off the root directory. Directories are also called *subdirectories*, because they are subordinate to the one and only root directory.

Root directory The main or central directory. All other directories branch off the root.

Subdirectories Means the same thing as directories. The prefix *sub* is used to emphasize the fact that all directories are subordinate to the root directory. Sometimes the word *subdirectories* is used to describe a directory under another directory.

Word processing program A computer program that is used for typing letters, reports, envelopes, and other tasks that you would normally use a typewriter for.

Spreadsheet program A computer program that organizes information in columns and rows and performs calculations. If you want to balance a checkbook or last year's budget, try using a spreadsheet program.

When you turn on your computer, you are placed in the root directory, so I like to think of the root directory as being the lobby of my computer. From the lobby, I can move to other directories (I think of these as rooms off of the lobby). You can even create directories within directories (like little closets in a bigger room). Even though subdirectories and directories are supposed to mean the same thing, I think that's stupid so I reserve the use of the word subdirectory to mean a directory within a directory.

Let's look at an example. Most programs create their own directory for storing their files. For example, if you bought Microsoft Word for DOS, it would create a directory on your hard disk called WORD. If you wanted to, you could create a subdirectory underneath the WORD directory for storing all of the documents you create with Word, such as letters, memos, and stuff. You might even call this subdirectory MYSTUFF. You would then have the root directory, then a branch off of it called WORD, then a branch off of that called MYSTUFF. Using my analogy of rooms, to locate a memo you'd written using Word, you'd start out in the root directory hallway or lobby, enter a room called WORD, then cross over to the closet called MYSTUFF.

When you think of your directories as rooms, its easier to understand what's happening when you start issuing DOS commands to move from one directory to another—which, unfortunately, is something you're gonna have to learn how to do in order to use your PC.

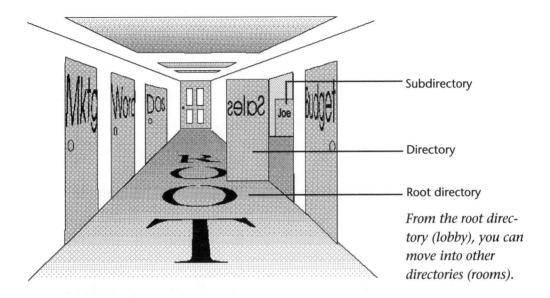

Subdirectory

Directory

Root directory

From the root directory (lobby), you can move into other directories (rooms).

To Get Where You're Going, Change Directories

Because each program you own is placed in its own directory, you change directories as you switch from program to program. For example, if you owned WordPerfect and Lotus 1-2-3, each of these programs would create their own directory on your PC's hard disk. One directory might be called WP (for WordPerfect, aren't they clever?) and the other might be called simply 123. Anyway, to switch from WordPerfect to 1-2-3, you have to switch from the WP directory to the 123 directory. Now that you know *why* should know some of this stuff, let's go on.

To change directories, use the CD command (CD stands for change directory). Type **CD**, then a backslash (\), followed by the name of the directory you want to go to. To change to the DOS directory, use the command **CD\DOS**. That's *CD backslash DOS*. To change to a directory called WORD, use the command **CD\WORD**.

Sometimes, you'll have directories within directories (*subdirectories*). For example, if your word processing directory is called WORD, you might have a directory within the WORD directory called MYSTUFF, to separate the files you create from the rest of the program files (you'll learn to make your own directories in Chapter 13). To change to the MYSTUFF directory, you'd have to go through the WORD directory (just as you'd have to go through a bedroom to get to its closet). Use the command **CD\WORD\MYSTUFF.** That's *CD backslash WORD backslash MYSTUFF.* Notice how an additional backslash (\) separates the directory names.

To change to the root directory, type **CD\.** That's *CD backslash.* The backslash by itself means root directory.

What Goes Wrong When You Change Directories

Basically, only a few things can go wrong when you change directories, and none of them will cause irreparable damage to fish, fowl, or your data:

You type a forward slash instead of a backslash. A backslash looks like this: \ and not /. The backslash is usually located above the Enter key on the right hand side, or on the lower left on the keyboard.

You are trying to change to a directory that doesn't exist. Type DIR *. to see a list of actual, real-life directories.

You forget to place a backslash between a directory and a subdirectory name. Remember to follow the CD\WORD\MYSTUFF example, which changes you to the directory MYSTUFF, which is a subdirectory of WORD. Notice how a backslash separates each directory name.

You insert a space where there shouldn't be one. The CD command runs everything together—no stopping. So don't type CD \WORD \MYSTUFF when you mean CD\WORD\MYSTUFF.

Changing Your DOS Prompt (So You Can Tell Where You Are)

DOS is not very informative at times, especially when you change directories. When you type **CD\WP** to change to the WP directory, you might expect some type of fanfare or something. But instead of doing anything wild, the DOS prompt just sits there with its usual

C>

blinking at you, waiting for you to do something else to entertain it. Because DOS is so uninformative, as you move from program to program changing directories, it's easy to get lost and forget which directory you're in.

TECHNO NERD TEACHES...

If you customize your prompt to display the current directory, the prompt changes as you move from one directory to another. For example, if you are in the root directory, your prompt might look like this:

C:\>

If you type the command **CD\123** to change to the 123 directory, your prompt changes to

C:\123>

If you then type **CD\WORD\MYSTUFF**, your prompt changes to

C:\WORD\MYSTUFF>

Notice how the prompt keeps changing to let you know which directory you are in? Be sure to read the following section, "Creating Some of the Most Popular DOS Prompts" to find out how to change your prompt so it will do this.

If DOS doesn't care enough to tell you what directory you're currently in, why should you care to know? Well, DOS commands *act on files in the current directory*. For example, if you issue the command to delete files, you could accidentally delete files in the *wrong directory* unless you realized by some miracle that you were in the wrong directory and stopped yourself from issuing the delete command.

You don't need a miracle; what you need is a *customized DOS prompt*—a squealer of the upmost degree, who'd sell his mother to tell you what directory you were in. And that's not all; you can customize the DOS prompt so it displays the current directory, the current time (for those of us who don't wear watches), and other neat things. So instead of having a boring and uninformative DOS prompt like **C>**, you can change your DOS prompt into something really exciting, such as these nifty prompts:

C:\DOS>

14:32 C:\DOS>

Enter a command, why don't ya?>

Enter a command, why don't ya?
C:\DOS>

There are lots of weird (or cool, depending on your perspective) things that you can do with the DOS prompt to customize it. (If even these prompts aren't enough to make you sit up and take notice, check out the colorized prompts in Chapter 25.)

Creating Some of the Most Popular DOS Prompts

To get a prompt that displays the drive and directory, type **PROMPT PG**. The PROMPT command is used with special characters that are preceded by a dollar sign. The $P tells the prompt to display the current drive and directory, while the $G causes a greater-than sign to display. The result is a dazzling new prompt which looks something like this:

C:\WORD\PROJECTS>

The current drive and directory followed by the greater than sign, as promised. To get a prompt that displays the time and then the drive and directory (separated by a space), type **PROMPT $T PG**. That's *PROMPT space $T space PG*. By using $T, the current time is displayed. However, keep in mind that the time is only updated when you press **Enter** to redisplay the command prompt. So what you get is a prompt which looks like this:

14:30:02.59 C:\>

To display a silly message, followed by the greater-than sign, type

PROMPT Enter a command, why don't ya?$G

And here's what your prompt would actually look like:

Enter a command, why don't ya?>

Of course, this type of prompt is not anymore informative than the regular C> prompt. So you might want to display your silly message and the current directory with this double-decker two-line prompt. To get a two-line prompt, use a dollar sign and an underscore (be careful; two-line prompts take a bit of getting used to):

PROMPT Enter a command, why don't ya?$_$P$G

That's *PROMPT space Enter a command, why don't ya? $ underscore PG*. This prompt would look something like this:

Enter a command, why don't ya?
C:\>

With this kind of prompt, you enter the commands on the second line, after the greater than sign.

Getting Your Old Prompt Back

If you want to return to a standard DOS prompt (C>), simply reboot the computer (press **Ctrl+Alt+Delete**). If you don't want to reboot, you can type **PROMPT;** and press **Enter**. The semicolon returns you to normal.

Keeping Your New Prompt

If you like your new prompt and want to make it permanent, buy a bag of Snickers (your guru's getting tired of Ho Ho's) and head for the nearest PC wizard. Have him add the PROMPT command to your AUTOEXEC.BAT file, and it will be set up each time you start your computer. (If you don't add the command to your AUTOEXEC.BAT, you will return to the default system prompt when you reboot.) If you want to save yourself some time (not to mention a fortune in Snickers), why not try editing the AUTOEXEC.BAT yourself? See Chapter 16.

The Least You Need to Know

The jungle of DOS's files and directories will soon become familiar tramping ground if you remember these things:

☛ Files are used to store your work. A file name can contain up to eight characters, followed by a period, and up to a three-character extension, as in BUDGET.DOC.

☛ Directories are places for storing files. You usually create one directory on your hard disk for each program you use.

☛ The root directory is the central, or main, directory.

☛ To change directories, type CD, a backslash (\), and the name of the directory you wish to change to, as in **CD\DOS.**

☛ To change your prompt to display the current drive and directory, use the command **PROMPT PG.**

Chapter 8
Worth the Price of Admission— The DOS Shell

In This Chapter

- Cracking the DOS Shell
- Mousing around
- Changing the DOS Shell display
- The Shell Answer Man's tips on working with files and directories
- The best beaches in the Caribbean for collecting shells
- Running programs with the DOS Shell

The DOS Shell is a graphical interface that keeps you safe and warm, miles away from the nasty world of the DOS prompt. Inside the Shell you can perform the same commands that you could outside the Shell, but with greater ease (and understanding). This chapter is devoted to the DOS Shell, so if you feel you must issue commands at a cold, gray prompt, refer to other chapters to perform these same tasks.

One little catch to upgrading: if you upgrade to the latest versions of DOS, you will not get the DOS 6 Shell, since it's no longer included. (The last time it was included was with DOS 6, but not with DOS 6.2 and later versions.) To get a copy of the DOS 6 Shell shown here, call Microsoft Technical Support and ask for the supplemental diskette.

Don't let DOS gurus keep you from using the Shell (gurus prefer the prompt because it's what they cut their teeth on). What you'll learn to do with the Shell in this one chapter will take five chapters to learn to do with the DOS prompt—and the Shell's less frustrating!

Once in the Shell, you can get help at any time. Simply press (that's a function key at the top or left side of your keyboard). Press **Esc** to exit a Help screen.

A Word to DOS 4 Users

If you have DOS 4, make things easy on yourself and upgrade to DOS 6 something. The DOS 6 somethings include many nifty features for the first-time user, and the DOS 6.x Shell (featured in this chapter) is much easier to use than the DOS 4 Shell. (Some of the things you'll learn in this chapter are different for DOS 4 Shell users.) If you're interested in making the switch to the latest versions of DOS, see Chapter 9 for more details.

By the way, if you've got DOS 5, you're okay as far as this chapter is concerned because the DOS Shell shown here is the same as the one you got with DOS 5. (You may still want to upgrade to DOS 6 something for its other features, which are quite nice. See Chapter 9.)

Playing the Shell Game

You can start the DOS Shell by typing (yes, you guessed it) **DOSSHELL**. If you get the error message **Bad command or file name**, DOS can't find the Shell program. Type the command **CD\DOS** and press **Enter**. Then type **DOSSHELL**. To learn how to set up a DOS path so things like this won't happen again, refer to Chapter 4.

Drive icons   Menu bar   Selected command   Menu

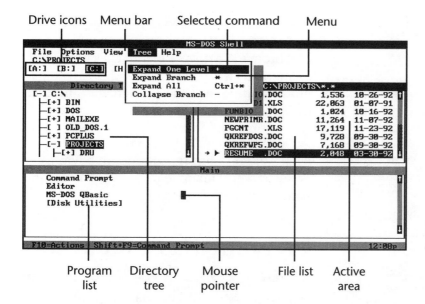

The DOS 6 Shell in all its beauty.

Program list   Directory tree   Mouse pointer   File list   Active area

Making Friends with a Mouse

Using the Shell without a mouse is like trying to pull something out of the oven without oven mitts. It can be done, but why go through the agony? If you plan to use the Shell, get a *mouse!*

To use the mouse, you either *click* or *double-click* with the left mouse button. Some actions require that you *drag* the mouse. (No, not along the floor—along the mouse pad!)

Would You Like to See a Menu?

One of the best things about the DOS Shell is that you don't type commands; instead, you just select something off a menu, and it's done! Look back at the picture of the DOS Shell screen. You'll find a menu bar hanging around the top of the screen loaded with five choices: File, Options, View, Tree, and Help.

SPEAK LIKE A GEEK

Mouse A device attached to your computer that controls a pointer on your screen. To move the pointer to the left, move the mouse to the left. To move the pointer to the right, move the mouse to the right, and so on.

Click To click with the mouse, press the mouse button once.

Double-click To double-click with the mouse, press the mouse button twice in rapid succession.

Drag To drag with the mouse, first move the mouse pointer to the starting position. Now click and hold the mouse button. Drag the mouse pointer to the ending position, and then release the mouse button.

You don't even have to know what you want to do in the Shell; you can just open a menu and browse. To open a menu, click on the menu name with your mouse. (Bring the mouse pointer over the menu name, and click the left mouse button.)

Once the menu is open, you can select whatever you want (go ahead, I'm buyin'). To select a command, click on the command name with your mouse.

Everyone Has a Right to Change His Mode

Here's an exercise that'll help you practice using menus, and—better yet—you get to play around with the video! When you start the DOS Shell, it starts in *text mode* (a display mode that uses lines and such to show screen elements, like in the first figure). If your PC has a monitor that supports graphics, you can change the DOS Shell display to *graphics mode* (a display mode that uses pictures and boxes to show screen elements, as wonderfully displayed in our second figure of the day).

As if changing modes is not enough excitement for one day, you can also select from several screen *resolutions*. The resolution you choose determines the number of text lines that fit on your screen at once. The higher the resolution you select, the smaller (and harder to read!) the text on your screen will appear.

To change the DOS Shell to a different video mode, follow these steps:

1. Open the **Options** menu. (Click on the menu to open it.)
2. Select the **Display** command. (Click on the command.)

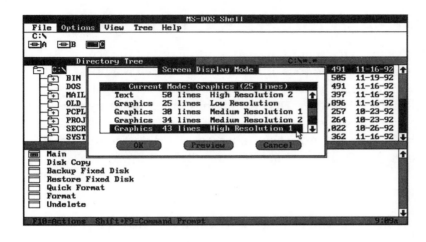

This Screen Display Mode box lets you select a video mode.

3. Choose the mode you want. (This click is getting repetitive.)

4. Click on **OK** or press **Enter**. The screen changes to the resolution you selected.

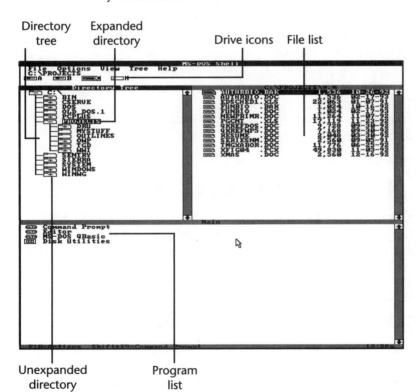

This is what choosing Graphics 60 lines High Resolution 2 looks like. Pretty tiny, huh?

Moving Between the Areas on the Screen

Now that you've mastered menus, let's look at the rest of the screen. As I take you through our guided tour, imagine that the Shell is a house with many rooms. Unfortunately, it's a house furnished by DOS, so it doesn't come with electricity. However, DOS isn't totally cruel; we've got one flashlight, and we can shine it on any room we want to use. To work in an area of the Shell, you must move the cursor (the flashlight) to that area. Moving the cursor to an area *activates* the area (lights it up).

The Shell screen is divided into several areas:

The Drive icons area, where you choose which drive to use.

The Directory tree, which displays the directories on the chosen drive.

The File list, which displays the files in the chosen directory.

The Program list, which lists programs set up to run from the DOS Shell.

The active area shows up highlighted on-screen. Looking back at the first picture in the chapter, you can see that the file list area is active because its title bar (the part that says C:\PROJECTS *.*) is darker than the title bars of the other areas.

To move from room to room in your house of shells, just click anywhere within that area with the mouse.

Displaying Files on a Different Drive

Now that we've got the run of the house, let's see what we can do. The disk drive that you're currently looking at is highlighted at the top of the screen. To display files on a different drive, click on that drive in the drive icons area.

Displaying Files in a Different Directory

Selecting the right drive may get you into the neighborhood, but the directory tree will get you to the right house. The directory you select in the directory tree determines which files are displayed in the file list area.

To choose a different directory from the directory tree area, just click on a directory with your mouse.

If you see a plus sign in front of a directory, that means that there are some subdirectories hiding. You can make them show their faces by clicking on the plus sign with your mouse.

TECHNO NERD TEACHES...

The Tree menu is used to expand and contract subdirectories. For example, in the picture above, the PROJECTS directory is expanded, showing the subdirectory DRU. A minus indicates that a directory is displaying its subdirectories, and a plus indicates that a directory is hiding them. Use the plus and the minus keys to expand and contract a directory.

Selecting Files to Work On

Before you can do something to a file (for instance, copy it or delete it), you need to *select* it. You can select one file or lots of files—whatever you want to work on. To select a single file, just give that file a little click. To select several files, hold down the **Ctrl** key while you click on the files, one by one, with your mouse. Then release the Ctrl key. Now that you've got some files selected, let's see what you can do to them.

Copying Files

When you copy files, the original file is left where it is, and a copy is placed where you indicate. For example, you might want to copy files to a different directory or disk as a backup.

To copy files with the mouse, select them, and then hold down the **Ctrl** key. Drag the copies where you want them.

Don't forget to hold down the **Ctrl** key when copying files with the mouse, or you may end up moving them instead!

(You can drag them to a drive icon in the drive icons area to copy the files to a different drive or to a diskette; drag the files to a directory on the directory tree to copy them to that directory.) When the confirmation box appears, click on the **Yes** button.

Moving Files

When you move files, the files are relocated where you indicate. For example, you might want to move files that you seldom use into a different directory to get them out of your way.

To move files with the mouse, select them, hold the **Alt** key down, and then drag the files to their new home. You can drag them to either a different drive in the drive icons area or a directory on the directory tree. When the confirmation box appears, click on the **Yes** button.

Creating New Directories

In Chapter 7, you learned all about directories and how you use them to organize your files. You can create a directory under the root directory (a room right off the lobby) or a subdirectory under an existing directory (a closet within an existing room). With the Shell, it's easy to remodel. Just follow me:

1. Click on the directory tree area, and highlight the root directory (or the existing directory that the new directory should appear under).

2. Click on the **File** menu to open it.

3. Click on the **Create Directory** command.

4. Type the name of the new directory (up to eight characters), and click **OK**.

Deleting Files and Directories

When a file or a directory is no longer useful, get rid of it. Files are easy to get rid of, but directories are always the last ones to leave a party. To get a directory to go, you need to delete the files in the directory first.

To delete files, select them and press the **Delete** or **Del** key. If you selected more than one file, click on **OK** or press **Enter**. To confirm the deletion of each file, click on the **Yes** button; to skip a file, click on the **No** button.

After all the files are gone and the directory is empty, you can delete it. Highlight it on the directory tree and press **Del**. Click the **Yes** button when you're asked for confirmation.

Renaming Files or Directories

If you don't like the name of a file or a directory, change it! First, select the file or directory. Then open the File menu and select the Rename command by clicking on it. Type the new name in the box that appears, and then press **Enter**.

A file name can contain up to eight characters, followed by a period, and up to a three-character extension (for example, APRBUDGT.WKS). A directory name follows the same rules, but most people do not give a directory name an extension. For example, GAMES and PROJECTS are common directory names.

Running Programs

You can select a program to run using several methods, but the easiest way is to use the program list (located at the bottom of the screen). Within the program list, double-click on the program's name to start the program. For example, if there was an entry called Word Processing in your program list, you could double-click on it and your word processor would start right up.

If you want to run a program that's not listed on the program list and don't have time to wait for someone to set it up for you, here's an alternative method:

☛ Double-click on the program file in the file list (for example, click on **WORD.EXE** to run Microsoft Word).

TECHNO NERD TEACHES...

The DOS 5 and 6.x Shells come with neat task swappers that allow you to run more than one program at a time and to switch between them. For example, you could start a letter in your word processing program, switch to your spreadsheet program to calculate some numbers, and then return to your letter. Task swapping is beyond what you need to know (it's even beyond the scope of this book). If you can talk someone into setting up your program list, have them show you how to use the task swapper.

Exiting the DOS Shell

To exit the DOS Shell and return to the cold gray world of the DOS prompt (**C/:>**), press **F3**. (That's a function key at the top or left side of your keyboard.) Or, open the File menu and select the Exit command.

If you have a mouse (and you really should), simply click open the menu and choose the command.

The Least You Need to Know

You'll be picking up sea shells by the DOS Shell shore when you remember these tips:

☛ If your PC uses DOS 6.2, 6.21, or 6.22, you may not have a DOS Shell. Call Microsoft Technical Support for help.

☛ Start the DOS Shell by typing **DOSSHELL**.

☛ Change directories by clicking on them.

☛ Select multiple files by holding the **Ctrl** key while you click on them.

☛ Holding down the **Alt** key while dragging files moves them; holding down the **Ctrl** key while dragging files copies them.

☛ Create directories with the **File Create** Directory command; delete them with the **Del** key.

☛ Rename files and directories with the **File Rename** command.

☛ Run programs by selecting them from the program list, usually located at the bottom of the Shell screen.

☛ Exit the DOS Shell with the **File Exit** command.

This page requires the Alpha Books secret decoder mood ring.

Chapter 9
What's Your Version?

In This Chapter

- ☞ Checking under the hood to determine your DOS version
- ☞ The newest DOS versions speak out!
- ☞ The DOS 25th Anniversary show
- ☞ Help with DOS Help
- ☞ Losing 10 pounds with the DOS Help diet
- ☞ Navigating the DOS 6.x Help system without a map

In this chapter, you'll learn about DOS versions—what the differences are and how to tell which one you have. After making you read a shameless plug for upgrading to one of the latest versions of DOS, I'll tell you how to access DOS's built-in Help system (versions 5 and above only, void where prohibited).

Version? What's That?

Every year or so, software manufacturers update their products. To distinguish one year's model from another, they assign new version numbers. DOS is no exception to this update madness—new DOS versions come rolling out of Microsoft every few years.

TECHNO NERD TEACHES...

MS-DOS version 1.0 was the first, back in 1980. Since then, there have been lots of major releases: DOS 2.0, DOS 3.0, 3.1, 3.2, and 3.3, DOS 4.01, DOS 5.0, DOS 6.0, DOS 6.2, DOS 6.21 and now DOS 6.22. Each major DOS version improved on its ancestors by adding more features and supporting more kinds of hardware. For example, the earliest versions of DOS didn't support hard disks (they weren't invented yet), and up until version 4.0, DOS did not support large hard disks (bigger than 30 megabytes).

The most recently released version is MS-DOS 6.22, which is *very similar* to DOS 6.21 and DOS 6.2, so don't panic if you don't have DOS 6.22 yet. You'll learn about all the "DOS 6 somethings" later in this chapter.

If you followed the example at the end of Chapter 2, you've already learned what version of DOS you have. If you can't remember what it was because, after all, that was yesterday, type **VER** and press **Enter**. You should see something like this:

MS-DOS Version 6.22

(or whatever version you have, if not 6.22).

The DOS 25th Anniversary Show: A Blast from DOS's Past

Okay, I admit I'm about 11 years early for a 25th anniversary show, but I thought you might like to know something about the DOS version you own (if you're not lucky enough to own one of the DOS 6 somethings).

Hey, I told you this chapter would be a shameless plug for DOS 6, DOS 6.2, DOS 6.21 and DOS 6.22, and it will, but what better selling tool than to point out the pathetic lack of features in earlier versions? Really, unless you have an "*aversion*" to it, I'd save myself a lot of cares and woes and upgrade to one of the DOS 6.2 somethings. Okay, enough. Any more of this, and Microsoft will have to put me on their payroll.

DOS on parade.

DOS Version	Nominations for best new DOS feature	What the critics say
1.0	Single-sided diskette drives	Golly, Gomer, welcome to the computer age.
1.1	Double-sided diskette drives	You mean I can use both sides of a diskette without flipping it? Talk about convenience!
2.0	Hard disk support	A diskette that stays in the computer? It's just a fad—it'll never catch on.
3.0	High-density 5 1/4-inch diskettes	What am I gonna do with all this room?
3.3	3 1/2-inch diskettes	So I can still use my 5 1/4-inch disks if I fold them, right?
4.0	Support for hard drives over 32MB	You've got to be kidding! Heck, we'll never need more than 32MB!
5.0	Upper and expanded memory support	You mean I can use conventional memory to *run programs* and not DOS? Gosh! All this, and a Shell, a help system, and a full-screen editor. I'll never ask for more (until DOS 6 something).

The Best and the Brightest: The DOS 6 Somethings

DOS 6, DOS 6.2, DOS 6.21, and DOS 6.22 are the latest versions of DOS. Actually, there is no real difference between all of the DOS 6.2 somethings, so if you don't mind, I'm going to shorten my list and talk about the DOS 6.2 somethings together.

TECHNO NERD TEACHES...

Okay, you dragged it out of me—the reason that there are several DOS 6.2 somethings is because of a program called DoubleSpace which increases the storage capacity of your hard disk. Microsoft ran into a legal thingie and took it out of DOS 6.21. In the new DOS 6.22, DoubleSpace was replaced by DriveSpace, which basically looks and acts the same to you, the user, so like, who cares?

DOS 6.0 Enhancements

AUTOEXEC.BAT and CONFIG.SYS   You can create several versions of your CONFIG.SYS file and select which one to use when you start your computer. You can bypass the AUTOEXEC.BAT or CONFIG.SYS files, or both. See Chapter 16 for more info.

DELTREE   Use the new DELTREE command to delete a directory and its subdirectories, without having to remove any of its files first. See Chapter 13 for details.

DoubleSpace   Double your pleasure, double your disk drive space with DoubleSpace! It also allows you to compress a disk or diskette so it holds up to two times more data. Once DoubleSpace is installed, it works invisibly. See Chapter 19 for the lowdown.

EMM386   Improvements allow EMM386.EXE to take better advantage of unused areas in upper memory. Programs are able to use either expanded or extended memory as needed, without changing your PC's configuration. Yawn. OK, so you may not know that your new and improved EMM386 is doing anything, but your programs will love you for it! See Chapter 20 for the hoopla on memory.

Help   On-line Help has been expanded to a complete, graphical, on-line reference to all commands which real people can actually use! See the end of this chapter for more help on the new Help.

Interlink   Provides the ability to link two computers (such as a laptop and a desktop computer) together to transfer files, etc. Cool if you own a portable and want to link it to your desktop at work. See Chapter 24 for the whatsis.

MemMaker   MemMaker configures your PC automatically to take the best advantage of the memory you have. (Of course, you have to remember to use it.) MemMaker moves stuff out of conventional memory, providing a bigger playground for all of your programs to run around in. See Chapter 20 for more details.

MEM   MEM provides more details about your system's memory usage. Using the new /P switch causes MEM to display information one screen at a time, instead of displaying it like movie credits, which run off the screen before you can read them. See Chapter 20 for more info.

Microsoft Anti-Virus   DOS now comes with a complete and easy-to-use program for virus detection and removal, based on Central Point's Anti-Virus. There is also an Anti-Virus for Windows. Don't let the bed bugs byte; see Chapter 18 for the whatsis.

Microsoft Defragmenter   It's a new track record! Based on the Norton Utilities, the Defragmenter reorganizes files on your PC for faster disk access. See Chapter 5—*quickly*.

Microsoft Mail   If you're on a network, why not use this nifty utility to send and receive electronic mail (E-mail)? Sorry, DOS version only. If you want the version for Windows, it's available at your local computer store.

MOVE   Move files and rename directories with this versatile command. See Chapters 11 and 13 for the latest.

MSBACKUP   Replacing DOS's antiquated BACKUP program is MSBACKUP, a graphical backup and restore program based on Norton Backup. See Chapter 14 for the nitty-gritty. And that's not all folks! A version of MSBACKUP is also provided for Windows.

POWER   Anybody got triple E batteries? This nifty command won't leave you sitting in the dark because it helps your laptop make better use of its power. See Chapter 24.

SMARTDrive   Improvements in writing and reading information allows SMARTDrive to make best use of system resources. In English: this little guy makes diskette drives go fast. Hurry and look at Chapter 5.

UNDELETE   New and improved, this guy helps you out of stickly situations where you've accidently deleted an important file. Worth its weight in gold. There's also an UNDELETE for Windows. See Chapter 12.

Workgroup Connection   Provides the ability to use shared directories and printers. Kind of like a mini network, minus the usual headaches.

New DOS 6.2 Somethings Enhancements

If you're upgrading from a previous version of DOS to DOS 6.2, DOS 6.21, or DOS 6.22, you may want to review the list of enhancements that were introduced with DOS 6. You'll find that list in the previous section. In this section is a listing of the *additional* enhancements introduced with DOS 6.2 (these enhancements exist in DOS 6.21 and DOS 6.22 as well).

DoubleGuard   Provides extra protection against wetness. OK, just kidding—what it really does is help DoubleSpace protect your data against loss caused by sloppy programs. See Chapter 19 double-quick.

DoubleSpace Enhancements   Besides DoubleGuard, DoubleSpace now performs a surface scan on each disk before double-spacing it. This makes a lot of noise, but it also ensures the integrity of the compressed data, so it's a good thing. You can now uncompress a compressed drive, if you wish. In addition, compressed diskettes are now mounted (made ready for you to use) automatically. In DOS 6.21 and DOS 6.22, DoubleSpace was replaced with DriveSpace which looks and acts basically the same way. See Chapter 19 again.

SMARTDrive Enhancements   SMARTDrive now performs primarily read-caching. Write-caching is turned off by default. In English, this means that SMARTDrive is smarter and faster, doing a better job of making your diskette drives more efficient. Caching of CD-ROMs is now supported. See Chapter 5 if you want to be a SMARTDrive speed demon.

ScanDisk   ScanDisk replaces the old command, CHKDSK, which was getting too old and fat to use. Like CHKDSK, ScanDisk scans disks and performs file repairs, but it does a better job at repairing file damage. ScanDisk works on DoubleSpaced drives, in addition to non-compressed drives. In addition, ScanDisk performs surface testing on a disk. Way cool. See Chapter 5 for the lowdown.

Multiple Configurations in AUTOEXEC.BAT—Two, two, two files in one! Similar to the multiple configuration enhancement for CONFIG.SYS that was released in DOS 6.0, the DOS 6.2 somethings now support the same thing in the AUTOEXEC.BAT. In addition, you can now select individual commands to be executed at startup in both the CONFIG.SYS and AUTOEXEC.BAT. Picky, choosy. See Chapter 17.

Other Enhancements   DOS 6.2x introduces many subtle but nice enhancements, such as:

- **Faster DISKCOPY**   DISKCOPY now uses the hard disk to store data temporarily, which speeds the copy process and reduces disk swapping. Great when you're making a copy of a high-density diskette.

- **Copy protection**   COPY, MOVE, and XCOPY now prompt the user before copying a file over an existing version. This is good news for careless copiers like me.

- **A comment on commas**   Commands which typically display large numbers, such as DIR, FORMAT, and MEM, now display those numbers with commas as in 1,023,476. This means that ordinary people like you and me can now read the numbers displayed everytime we do DIR.

- **Goodbye, Shell!**   The DOS Shell is not included with the DOS 6.2 somethings, but if you're upgrading from a previous version of DOS, it still exists on your hard drive as it did before you upgraded (in other words, the DOS 6.2 somethings don't go out of their way to erase the DOS Shell if it's already there—they just don't provide it if it's not. If you want to learn how to use it, see Chapter 8.

Help, I Need Somebody!

If you have at least DOS version 5, you can access DOS help—oh, goody. Type the command you want help on, followed by the switch /?. For example, if you need help with the DIR command, type **DIR /?** and press **Enter.** You'll see a listing of possible switches and parameters that can be used with the command. If you have one of the DOS 6 somethings instead, you get even more help than just a listing of switches and parameters— read on...

Using the DOS 6 Somethings Help System

With the DOS 6 somethings (DOS 6, 6.2, 6.21, and 6.22) you get the new, improved (now with 50% less fat) DOS 6 help system! You can still type **DIR/?** like you could in DOS 5, and you'll get the same listing of possible switches and such. But to access the new improved DOS help, type HELP followed by the name of the command you need help with. For example, to get new improved help for the DIR command, type this:

HELP DIR

Press **Enter**, and you're whisked away to the DOS 6 something Help System. When you first access the DOS 6 something help system, you see a listing of the syntax and the parameters for your command.

Click on these to see examples or additional notes

The syntax tells you how to type in the command correctly

The new, improved DOS 6 something help system.

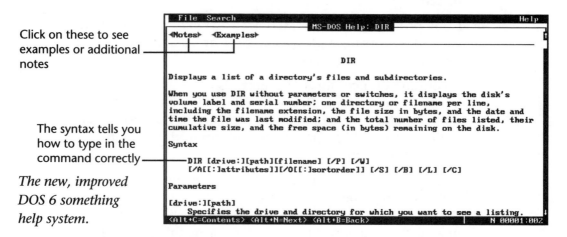

The syntax is fairly difficult to read, and why bother, since you have this book to translate it all for you? But if you're interested, the lower-case stuff represents words for which you substitute real names. For example, you don't type **DIR** *filename*, but **DIR** followed by the name of the real file you want to list. The stuff in [square brakets] is optional; you don't have to type any of that to make the command work. Since everything's in brackets, the only part you have to type with this command is DIR.

If you want to see more, press **Page Down** (press **Page Up** to go back).

If you see a word in angle brackets, such as **<Tree>**, it is a *jump term*. Press **Tab** until the cursor moves to a jump term, then press **Enter** to select it. If you've got a mouse, click on that jump term instead. You will move to another section of the help system that contains information about the jump term.

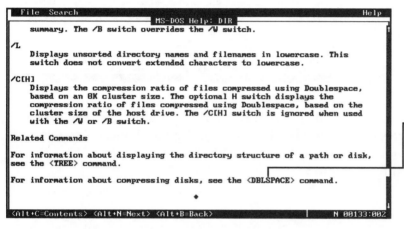

Jump term

Selecting a jump term moves you to another part of Help.

On the first page of every command, you'll see **Notes** and **Examples**. Click on one of these if you want, or use the **Tab** key until the cursor moves to either of these items, and press **Enter** to select it. Notes lists additional tips and cautions about using the command. Examples lists several ways to type the command, which is much easier to understand than trying to decipher the syntax on the first page.

SPEAK LIKE A GEEK

Jump term A highlighted term in the DOS 6.X help system that, when selected, "jumps" to a related section of the help system.

Examples of the
DIR command

*This section of Help
provides easy to
follow examples for
the DIR comamnd.*

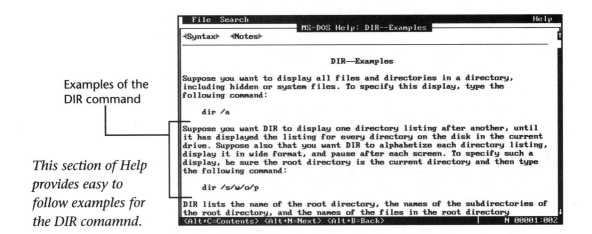

To exit the help system and return to a DOS prompt, press the **Alt** key, and then press the letter **F**. The File menu is displayed. Press **X** to select Exit. (This works just like it did in the DOS Shell in Chapter 8. Nice to have something that looks familiar, isn't it?)

The Least You Need to Know

Glad you could join me! Would you care for a nightcap—I mean a recap? In ths chapter, you learned:

☞ To tell what DOS version your system is using, use the **VER** command.

☞ DOS 6 something includes many enhancements that make it easier to use your PC, especially if you are a first-time user, including an improved help system and an easy-to-use backup system for protecting your files.

☞ DOS 6 something also provides some thoughtful enhancements, such as a virus-protection program, a program that customizes your system's memory usage, and a disk compression program that saves disk space.

☞ Both DOS 5 and the DOS 6 somethings include help for each command. Type the command name followed by /? to get help in DOS 5. For example, type **DIR /?**.

☞ DOS 6.X includes a more extensive help system than DOS 5, which is accessed by typing **HELP** followed by the command. For example, type **HELP DIR**.

Virtual text page: there's virtually no text on it.

Part Two
A Daily Dose of DOS

In this section, you'll find everything you need to know about completing daily tasks with DOS. Since one-third of the job of using a computer is maintaining and organizing your information (PCs should come with a maid), this will be your most-used section of the book. Each chapter is chock-full of exactly what you need to know to maintain your files, your directories, and your sanity.

Although you'll use this section a lot, you probably won't remember how to use every command. (The only thing that's EASY about DOS is forgetting everything you did the last time you used a particular command.) So read, and then forget; everything you need to know will still be here when you need it again.

Chapter 10

Lost Something?
Finding Files
with DIR

In This Chapter

- Understanding the DIR file listing
- Locating your lost files
- Listing files on another drive or directory
- Listing files in Cinemascope, across the screen
- Listing files according to age, weight, and religious preference
- Tricks for listing only the files you want to see
- Printing a file listing

This chapter is all about listing and finding files with the DOS command DIR. Using the DIR command is like reading a table of contents for a book—it's a great way to become familiar with your PC and find out what's on it.

Also, if you've ever had the frustrating experience of misplacing a file that you were working on just moments ago, those times are past. This chapter will show you how to find lost files and lots more stuff. Learn how to print a list of all the files in a directory or on a diskette. You'll even learn how to look inside a file to see what's in it, to find out if it's a file you need, or just to satisfy an itchy curiosity.

Some Things You Should Know About the DIR Command

So you don't have to go scrambling back to previous chapters, here's a quick review of some important concepts about entering DOS commands such as DIR correctly:

Remember to press Enter to execute a command. Until you press Enter, nothing happens.

The DIR command is made up of three parts: The command itself (DIR), parameters (specific file names you want listed), and switches (a forward slash (/) followed by a letter; switches modify the DIR command to make it display files in several ways). Separate each part with a space.

The DIR command lists files in the current directory or drive unless you specify otherwise. If you don't specify a different directory or drive, DOS assumes the DIR command refers to the *current drive and directory*. To switch drives so you can list files on another drive, type the drive letter followed by a colon, as in **A:**

To switch directories, type **CD** *followed by the name of the directory that you want to go to,* as in

   CD\DOS

or

   CD\WORD\PROJECTS

Why and When You'd Want to Use the DIR Command

I thought I'd interrupt this potentially boring stuff to remind you why you might want to use the DIR command in the first place. Here are some reasons:

DIR is an easy way to see an overview of what's on your hard disk. Use the DIR command to list all of the main directories on a disk. Because there is usually a directory for each program, this list helps you figure out what *programs* you have available (see "Locating a Lost Directory").

DIR helps you figure out how to start a new program. Use the DIR command to find the file that starts the program (see "Listing Selected Files").

You can locate files with DIR. Files get lost. How? How can a memo get lost in an In-basket? Who knows? It just does. The fastest way to find a misplaced file is with the DIR command (see "Locating a File Across Several Directories").

DIR helps you identify diskettes. If you forget to label your diskettes (like I do), the only way to tell what they contain is by using the DIR command (see "Listing Files on Another Drive").

Which is the latest copy? DIR knows. If you have several copies of the same file, the DIR command can tell you which copy is the most current (just check out the date).

DIR is easy to use. Only three letters: D-I-R. Gotta love a command like that!

Listing All the Files in a Directory

Listing all of the files within the current directory is the computer equivalent of reading a soup label. Need to find what's on your hard disk? Simply type **DIR /P**.

Other books will tell you to simply type **DIR** and be done with it, but you'll usually end up with files scrolling off your screen (like movie credits) if you do. That's why I automatically add the **/P** switch, which means, "List all the files until they fill the screen, then pause."

If your directory has a lot of files to list, you'll see the message **Press any key to continue . . .** at the bottom of the screen. Press **Enter** when you are ready to see the rest of the files in the directory.

What Does It All Mean? (Understanding the DIR Listing)

Using the DIR command is easy. Understanding what it's trying to tell you is not. Here's what a DOS directory listing typically looks like and what it contains:

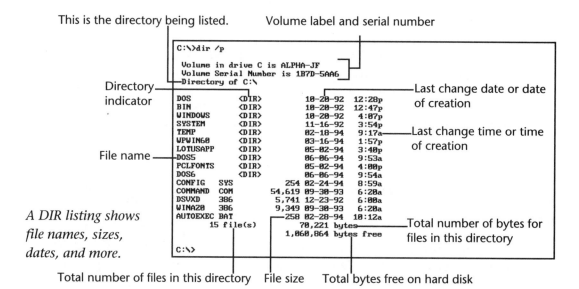

A DIR listing shows file names, sizes, dates, and more.

Volume in drive C is ALPHA-JF   The *volume label* is the name that was given to the disk when it was *formatted* (prepared for use). Your PC may be called something equally as clever, or nothing at all (names are not required). This is followed by the volume's serial number (a number that is generated when the disk is formatted).

Directory of C: *This line is very important*; it tells you what drive and directory are being listed.

File or directory name   The first column lists file and directory names. File names consist of a first and last name, separated by a period, as in CONFIG.SYS. However, in the DIR listing, this same file is displayed as

    CONFIG   SYS

with several spaces separating the first and last names, instead of the usual period.

<DIR> indicator   The <DIR> notation helps you identify subdirectories (directories that are under the current directory).

File size   This column lists each file's size in *bytes*. A total of all the files in this directory is displayed at the bottom of the listing. Subdirectories do not have a file size; their size is determined by the files within them.

Last change date   This date tells you when a subdirectory was created or when a file was created or last changed.

Last change time   This is like the last change date, telling you what time a subdirectory was created or what time a file was last changed.

Total files   At the end of the DIR listing, you'll see the total number of files in the directory, along with the total number of bytes being used by the files. DOS is overzealous and counts subdirectories as files, too, so if a directory has two subdirectories and three files, you'll see a total of five files. However, DOS likes to keep things interesting, so although subdirectories are counted for total files, their contents are not counted in total bytes. Go figure.

> In case you forgot what a byte, kilobyte, and megabyte are, here's a reminder. A byte is equal to a single character, like 4, J, or %. A kilobyte is about 1,000 bytes (it's really 1,024 bytes for you sticklers out there). A megabyte is about 1,000,000 bytes. (Okay, it's really 1,048,576 bytes.)

Total bytes free   This one's self-explanatory; it's the number of bytes of free space left on the disk. By the way, if you have DOS 6.2 something, all the size listings will have little commas in them. Neat, eh? And to think, it only took 14 years or so to come up with that little improvement.

Listing Files on Another Drive

A quicker way to list files on another drive is to include the drive letter to list with the DIR command. So instead of changing to drive A, simply type **DIR A:**. Because you specified drive A, the files on drive A will be listed instead of those on C. This saves you the trouble of switching between drives.

When you're "talking" to DOS through the command prompt, it assumes that the current drive and directory is the "subject" of your conversation. That's why you get a listing of the files in the root directory of your hard disk when you type **DIR** at the C:\> prompt.

To list files on another drive, change to that drive by typing the drive letter followed by a colon (:). For example, if you were in drive C but you wanted to list the files on a diskette in drive A, you would type **A:** and press **Enter**. The prompt changes to A:\> or to some variation of that. Then you could use the DIR command to list the files in drive A, because the drive A is *now the current drive*. Just type **DIR** and press **Enter**. When you are ready to switch back to your original drive, type the drive letter followed by a colon (:), as in **C:** and your prompt will return to C:\> (or something similar).

Listing Files in Another Directory

By default, DIR lists files in the current directory only. To see the contents of a different directory, you must either make the desired directory active by changing to that directory, or you must specify its name as part of the DIR command.

First, let's try it by changing to the desired directory, using the CD command. For example, to change to the 123 directory, type **CD \123** and press **Enter**. Now you're in the 123 directory. To get the directory listing, type **DIR /P.** This command lists the files for the current directory, \123. To get back to your original directory, you use the CD command to change directories again.

You can get dizzy changing directories all the time, so an easier way to see the files in another directory is to include the directory name as part of the DIR command. For example, if you wanted to list the files in the 123 directory *without leaving the directory you're in,* you would type **DIR \123 /P**.

That's *DIR space backslash 123 space forward slash P.* Even though you might be in, say, the WORD directory, the files in the 123 directory would be listed instead. It's like seeing into the next room without actually going into that room. This command comes in handy for lousy typists.

Listing Files Across the Screen

Sometimes, you don't need all the information that the DIR command provides. If you are looking for a specific file, it is simpler to look at only the file names. Try **DIR /W /P**. The /W switch modifies the DIR command so file names display across the screen in wide format. The /P switch is optional, but I use it just in case there's more than one screen full of names. After I use this command, my screen looks like this:

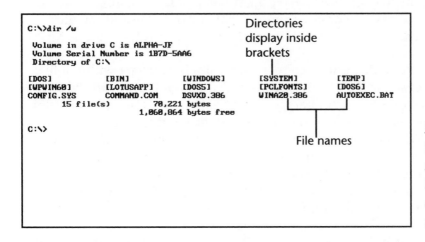

Displaying file names in a wide format shows fewer details, but more files can fit on-screen at the same time.

Listing Files in Alphabetical Order

Files normally display in the order in which they are stored on disk, which is about as useful as a calendar without months. *If you have at least DOS version 5,* you can force DOS to display the files in some kind of reasonable order, such as, dare we say it, *alphabetically.* **Type DIR /O /P.** This command lists subdirectories first, then files, sorted by first name.

Listing Selected Files

If you're looking for a particular file, or a particular file type (extension), you can use *wildcards* to list selected files.

A DOS *wildcard* is just like the wildcards in card games, where each wildcard can be substituted for the Queen of Spades or whatever card you need to win. In a similar fashion, a DOS wildcard represents a character or characters within a file name. Wildcards create a general file name *pattern* so that several files can be used with a single DOS command. There are two DOS wildcards: the asterisk (*) and the question mark (?).

The asterisk * is kind of like having a whole handful of wildcards. The single * represents several characters within a file name. For example, *.DOC means "use files that have any first name, but a last name of DOC." Using K*.DOC means "use files that begin with K, followed by a bunch of miscellaneous characters, and have a last name of DOC. Using *.* means "use files with any first or last name," in other words, "use all the files." *Any characters after an asterisk are ignored,* so M*RCH.* is the same as M*.*.

The question mark ? is used to represent a single character within a file name. For example, JO?N.WKS means "use files that begin with the letters JO, followed by any single character, followed by an N, and the extension .WKS." The files JOHN.WKS and JOAN.WKS match this pattern, but the files JEAN.WKS and JOHNNY.WKS do not. You can use additional question marks to represent other characters, as in JO??.WKS, but the number of characters must also match. The files JOHN.WKS, JOKE.WKS and JOAN.WKS would match this file name pattern, but JOKES.WKS would not because it has five characters in its first name.

To list selected files, simply type **DIR** followed by the wildcard pattern, as in **DIR TAXES??.* /P.** This command lists (one screen full at a time) all the files in the current directory that start with the letters TAXES, followed by two characters, and any extension.

TECHNO NERD TEACHES...

Here's a practical use for all this wildcard business. Let's say you've found a new program on your hard drive but no one is around to tell you how to start it, change to that directory and try **DIR *.EXE /P.** This will list all of the program files; look for one that matches the name of the directory (or comes close), such as WP.EXE, 123.EXE, and so on. Type its name, as in **WP**, and the program will probably start. If you don't find an .EXE file, look for a file that ends in .BAT or .COM.

Locating a File Across Several Directories

My mom created a letter one day, saved it, and went to lunch. When she came back, the letter file was gone! She figured that maybe she hadn't saved it properly, so she retyped it, saved it again, and took a coffee break. When she returned, the letter file was nowhere to be found. Just as she was ready to look for the prankster who was messing with her files, a friend came over and showed her the following command. Her files were there; they were simply in the wrong directory!

If you have at least DOS version 5, you can use this command to locate a file anywhere on your hard disk. For example, to find the file LOST.DOC, you would type **DIR C:\LOST.DOC /S /P.** That's *DIR space C colon backslash LOST period DOC space forward slash S space forward slash P.* Whew! The /S switch tells DIR to look in the current directory, and all subdirectories. By adding C:\ in front of the file name, DIR will start its search in the root directory (neat, eh?).

BY THE WAY

You could probably leave the /P switch off this time (unless there are so many copies of LOST.DOC all over your hard drive, that you expect the listing to scroll off the screen).

You can use wildcards to conduct more extensive searches. For example, if you want to list *all the .DOC files* on your hard disk, type **DIR C:*.DOC /S /P**.

Locating a Lost Directory

Directories (especially subdirectories) can get lost, too. Because most hard disks today are so large, directories have a lot of space to hide in. Use this command to find the directory LOSTDIR (you must have at least DOS 5.0 to use this command):

DIR C:\LOSTDIR. /S /P

That's *DIR space C colon backslash LOSTDIR period space forward slash S space forward slash P.* This command translates to "List all the files that begin LOSTDIR and have no extension, beginning with the root directory, going across all directories, one screenful at a time." Because directories don't usually have extensions (last names), looking for a "file" with no extension gets you a listing of directories instead. (Clever, huh.) To list all the directories *on your C drive*, use this command:

DIR C:*. /S /P

Printing a File Listing

When you use the DIR command (or any other command, for that matter), the result of that command is displayed on the monitor. You can redirect the output to a different device, such as your printer. Why do this? Sometimes it's easier to flip pages than to scan through a directory listing on-screen. Also, a printout of their contents makes a great way to organize diskettes. Besides, you learned all this stuff about DIR, so why not have a nice printout to show for all your hard work? (Custom framing is extra.) To send a listing of all the files on a diskette to the printer, use this command:

DIR A: /W >PRN

The greater-than sign (>) is the *redirection symbol*; PRN is DOS's name for your printer. So this is the DOS equivalent of one of those guys with the funny orange vests pointing his big thumb to the left, making you park in oblivion instead of in that free space right next to the door. The redirection symbol forces DOS to send the output of the command to whatever device you list (in this case, it's the printer.) Because you'll probably want to print only the file names (and not the other DIR information), I included the /W switch.

You can also send the file listing to another file, so you can save it permanently, or print it out later. To save a listing of the current directory in a file, use a command like this:

DIR >FILE.LST

If you have at least DOS 5, you can print a file listing with the name of each file appearing on a separate line, going down—instead of across—the paper. Use this command:

DIR A: /B > PRN

The Least You Need to Know

I gotta admit, the DIR command is one of my favorites (probably 'cause it's so easy to spell). But seriously, look at all the stuff you learned about the DIR command:

- ☞ To list the files in a directory, type **DIR /P.**

- ☞ The DIR command lists the files in the current directory only. To list files on another drive, use a command like this: **DIR A: /P.** To list files in another directory, use a command like this: **DIR \PROJECTS /P.**

- ☞ The file listing includes the name of the file or directory; followed by its size; and then the date and time that file or directory was created or the file was changed. The file listing also displays the total number of files in the directory and the amount of space left on the disk.

continues

continued

☞ To list file names across the screen, type

DIR /W /P.

☞ If you have at least DOS 5, use this command to list files alphabetically: **DIR /O /P.**

☞ The DOS wildcards, * and ?, can be used with the DIR command. The * replaces several characters in a file name, and ? replaces only one. For example, DIR JOE?.* lists files like JOE1.DOC, JOE2.DOC, and JOES.WKS.

☞ You can locate a file anywhere on your hard disk by typing something like this:

DIR C:\LOST.DOC /S /P.

☞ Create a paper listing of your files by adding **>PRN** to the end of the **DIR** command.

Chapter 11
Standing at the Copier, Copying Files

In This Chapter

- Making a twin (duplicate) file
- Copying files from one directory to another
- Copying files to a diskette
- Calling your files something else
- Moving files in less time than it takes to move your sofa

This chapter is all about copying files, one of the most common DOS tasks. You can use the COPY command to copy files from the hard disk to a diskette for safekeeping, or copy files from a diskette to the hard disk so you can access them more quickly. When you copy a file, the original file stays where it is, and a copy is placed in the location you indicate. If you want to move a file instead of copy it, the last section in this chapter gives you easy instructions on how to move files instead.

I once had a friend who was having trouble with one of her document files. I asked her to make a copy and send it to me so I could take a look at it. When I opened the interoffice mail the next day, I found a photocopy of the diskette! (I guess I should have been more specific.)

Because the COPY command is one of the hardest DOS commands to get right, I've included many examples. Just follow the examples and substitute the names of your directories and files (and hopefully, you'll find the process pretty painless).

Things You Should Know About the COPY Command

So you don't have to go scrambling back to previous chapters, here's a quick review of some important concepts to remember when using the COPY command:

Remember to press Enter to execute a command. Until you press Enter, nothing will happen. Ever. Believe me.

The COPY command is made up of three parts: The command itself (COPY), followed by the name of the file(s) to copy, followed by the place to copy the file(s) to. Insert a space between each part of the command.

Unless you have one of the DOS 6.2 somethings, the COPY command overwrites existing files without telling you. Talk about not nice! So if you don't have DOS 6.2 something (DOS 6.2, 6.21, or 6.22), be careful or you'll overwrite existing files with the same names.

Naming your copy. When you copy a file, you're making a duplicate of the original. You can give the duplicate a new name, or let it keep its original name (*but no two files can have the same name, unless they are in different directories or on different disks*).

The COPY command copies files FROM/TO the current directory or drive, unless you specify otherwise. You can include other directories and drives (*path names*) as part of the command, if you want.

The most common error message you get when using the COPY command is File not found. If you get this error message, try using the full path name for the file; maybe the file is not in the current directory. If needed, use the DIR command to list the files in the current directory so you can check the spelling; maybe you misspelled the name of the file. See this section coming up for more about path names.

Path Finders: One Way for DOS to Locate a File

Using a *path* to designate a file is like telling a friend how to find your house. You use a path name in the COPY command to copy files located in other directories or drives. It's a lot more typing to include a path name with the COPY command, but it's a lot less hassle than changing back and forth between directories just so DOS can find the files you want to copy!

A path name to a file consists of three parts:

- ☛ The drive the file is located on followed by a colon, as in C:.

- ☛ A backslash (\) followed by the complete directory path to the file. Start with the parent directory, then add another backslash, and a subdirectory name if applicable. Finish up with a final backslash, as in **\PROJECTS\DOSBOOK**.

- ☛ End the path name with a file name or file specification, as in **CHAPTR11.DOC**.

The completed path would look like this:

C:\PROJECTS\DOSBOOK\CHAPTR11.DOC

Now, use the path name with the COPY command, as in:

COPY C:\PROJECTS\DOSBOOK\CHAPTR11.DOC A:

In English, this command tells DOS to copy the CHAPTR11.DOC file (which it will find in the \PROJECTS\DOSBOOK directory on the C: drive) to the diskette in drive A:. Hold on, there's more about the COPY command coming up. Just remember that in any of the examples, you can include the full path name to any file you want to copy.

The COPY Command—Gotta Love It

Before you wade through all this stuff about copying files, I thought you might like to know why you'd want to use the COPY command in the first place. (This is how I get you to stay and read the whole chapter.)

COPY can create duplicates of important files before they get ruined. Files like your AUTOEXEC.BAT and CONFIG.SYS (which you paid several Ho Ho's to obtain) are important and hard to reconstruct from scratch. Safeguard them against disasters by twinning them with the COPY command (see "Cloning 101: Making a Duplicate of a File"). Better yet, copy them onto a diskette, and store that diskette in a safe place (see "Copying Files from a Directory to a Diskette").

COPY makes room for a new program. If you have more than one disk drive, such as C or D, you may want to move files from one drive to another. The COPY command can help you (see "Copying a File from One Directory to Another"). If you're simply out of room, you can copy files onto diskettes and then delete them from your hard disk (see "Copying Files from a Directory to a Diskette").

With COPY, you can keep your versions straight. Before you make changes to an important document, you might want to put the original in a separate directory on the hard disk, in case you want to refer to it later. Use the COPY command to place a copy of your original file into a separate directory. Then you can make changes with confidence (see "Copying a File from One Directory to Another").

With COPY, you can use your files on a different PC. If your PC doesn't have the program or printer to finish the job, use the COPY command to copy the file onto a diskette, so you can transfer the file to another PC. The COPY command is also great for sharing documents with co-workers or with people you pass on the street (see "Copying Files from a Directory to a Diskette").

Cloning 101: Making a Duplicate of a File

The simplest form of the COPY command is used to make a copy of a file, placed in the same directory *but with a different name*. (Remember, no two files in the same directory can have the same name—it would cause a ripple in the time-space continuum, and then where would we be?) For example, to make a backup copy of your AUTOEXEC.BAT file, you could type this:

COPY AUTOEXEC.BAT AUTOEXEC.BKP

That's *COPY space AUTOEXEC.BAT space AUTOEXEC.BKP.* This tells DOS to "Copy the AUTOEXEC.BAT file and name the copy AUTOEXEC.BKP. Place this copy in the current directory." If the COPY command is successful, you'll see the message **1 file(s) copied**. If not, you may get **File not found**. If you have DOS 6.2 something and there's already a AUTOEXEC.BKP file, you'll be asked whether you want to overlay it. Press **Y**.

File not found? You may be in the wrong directory. The COPY command assumes that you are in the directory *where the file to copy is located*. If you're not, you need to tell DOS where the file is, so include the complete path to the file name, as in

COPY C:\AUTOEXEC.BAT C:\AUTOEXEC.BKP

The two parameters of the COPY command act like the "From" side and the "To" side of a gift tag. ("Yes, dear, I waited until the last minute to get your present, and I'm sorry, but all they had left was the COPY command.") So the command **COPY AUTOEXEC.BAT AUTOEXEC.BKP** translates as "Copy the file AUTOEXEC.BAT *from* the current directory, *to* the current directory, and call the copy AUTOEXEC.BKP." Because you didn't type any explicit directory locations, COPY assumes you mean a "From" file and a "To" file *in the current directory*.

If the file AUTOEXEC.BAT was not in the current directory, what could you do? Well, you could change directories with the CD command (see Chapter 7 for help), or you could include the *path to the AUTOEXEC.BAT file*. Including the path would make the command come out like this:

COPY C:\AUTOEXEC.BAT C:\AUTOEXEC.BKP

This command translates to "Copy the file AUTOEXEC.BAT *from* the root directory, *to* the root directory, and call the copy AUTOEXEC.BKP."

Cloning an Army: Duplicating Several Files at Once

You can use DOS *wildcards* to specify more than one file to copy. Wildcards create a general file name pattern so that several files can be used with a single DOS command. There are two DOS wildcards, the asterisk (*) and the question mark (?). The asterisk * represents several characters within a file name (as in *.WK1), and the question mark ? represents a single character within a file name (as in CHAP??.DOC). For more info on wildcards, see that wild and crazy chapter, Chapter 10.

For example, suppose you want to create a duplicate of all the .WK1 files in the \SPREADST directory. Issue the following commands, pressing **Enter** after each one:

```
CD\SPREADST
COPY *.WK1 *.BKP
```

These commands first change you to the \SPREADST directory, then create a copy of all the files in the current directory with an extension of .WK1, and change the extension on the copy to .BKP. Use wildcards in place of file names in any COPY command to copy multiple files at once.

TECHNO NERD TEACHES...

If you want to copy the files in one step, without changing the directory, include the full path names:

COPY C:\SPREADST*.WK1 C:\SPREADSHT*.BK1

Whew! Even though you save a step, it's a lot more typing. Choose whichever "path" is easier for you.

From Here to Eternity: Variations on a Copy

The basic parts of the COPY command never change:

COPY[space]*what you're copying*[space]*where to place the copy*

Here are some basic rules to keep in mind:

- ☞ If you don't specify a drive, DOS assumes you mean the *current drive*.

- ☞ If you don't specify a directory, DOS assumes you mean the *current directory*.

- ☞ *You have to specify a file name for the "what to copy" part.* If you want to make the name of the copy different from the original's, specify a new name in the "where to copy" part.

Remember, if you have DOS 6.2 something and you try to copy over top of an existing file, you must press Y and Enter when prompted. Ready for some examples? Here we go.

Copying a File from One Directory to Another

Suppose you want to work on an important document and to protect your originals, you always copy them into a directory called (cleverly enough) ORIG. After copying the original to a safe place, you can work on the copy without fear of losing anything to the great DOS abyss. So let's say you need to copy the file BIGBUDGT.WK1 from the \SPREADST directory to a directory called \SPREADST\ORIG. Follow these steps:

First, go to the source directory:

CD\SPREADST

Now, copy the file from the current directory (\SPREADST) to the \SPREADST\ORIG directory:

COPY MAYBUDGT.WK1 \SPREADST\ORIG

That's *COPY space MAYBUDGT.WK1 space backslash SPREADST backslash ORIG.* This command translates as "Copy the MAYBUDGT.WK1 file from the *current directory* (since you didn't specify any directory with the MAYBUDGT file) to the \SPREADST\ORIG directory." The original file is still in the \SPREADST directory, and an exact duplicate is in the ORIG directory, safe and sound. If you want to copy the file in one step (without changing directories or drives), include the full path names:

COPY C:\SPREADST\MAYBUDGT.WK1 C:\SPREADST\ORIG

If you want to copy the file to a different disk drive such as drive D:, tweak the command a little:

COPY C:\SPREADST\MAYBUDGT.WK1 D:\GRAPHICS

Copying Files from a Directory to a Diskette

Suppose you need to print one of your spreadsheets on a printer that is attached to another PC. To do this, you want to copy your spreadsheet file, YEAREND.WK1, from the \SPREADST directory to a diskette. Then copy the file from that diskette to the other PC.

Here are the two commands that accomplish the first part of this task:

CD\SPREADST
COPY YEAREND.WK1 A:

This COPY command translates to "Copy the file YEAREND.WK1 from the *current directory* (since you didn't specify any directory for the YEAREND file) to drive A." If you want to copy the file in one step, include the complete path names, as in

COPY C:\SPREADST\YEAREND.WK1 A:

Copying Files from a Diskette to a Directory

The following COPY command translates as "Copy the file YEAREND.WK1 from the current drive (which in this example, is the A: drive) to the 123 directory on the drive C."

A:
COPY YEAREND.WK1 C:\123

To do this operation in one step, try this:

COPY A:YEAREND.WK1 C:\123

Copying Files from One Diskette to Another

If your PC has two diskette drives, copying files from one diskette to another is easy. Suppose you have a file called SALES.DOC on a 5 1/4-inch diskette and you want to copy that file to a 3 1/2-inch diskette so you can use that file on a different PC. Start by changing to drive A, then copy the file:

    A:
    COPY SALES.DOC B:

To do this operation in one command:

    COPY A:SALES.DOC B:

If you want to copy all the files from one diskette to another diskette that is the exact same size and density, you can use the DISKCOPY command. Refer to Chapter 6 for more details.

A File by Any Other Name

By now, you're probably pretty accustomed to the COPY command. If you want to make a *duplicate* of a file, use the COPY command, as in

    COPY SALES.DOC SALES.DUP

If you want to rename a file rather than make a duplicate of it, you don't create a copy of the file (as you do with the COPY command); you simply change the file name. Let's say that you want to rename a file called SALES.DOC to something more descriptive, such as APRSALES.DOC. Use this command:

    REN SALES.DOC APRSALES.DOC

That's REN space SALES.DOC space APRSALES.DOC. This command translates to "Rename the file SALES.DOC in the current directory to APRSALES.DOC."

The error **Duplicate file name or file not found** will appear if you try to rename a file to the same name as another file. Files with the same names cannot exist in the same directory, so choose another name, or move the file to another directory, as explained later in this chapter.

Get a Move On!

For years, DOS users complained about the fact that they couldn't easily move files. They had to copy the files to the new location and then, in a separate step, delete the files from the old location. Then came DOS 6, with the MOVE command which allows you to move files in one step. By the way, if you have one of the DOS 6.2 somethings, you're protected against moving files on top of existing files. If you want to replace the files, press Y and Enter when prompted.

If you have at least DOS 6, you can use the new MOVE command to move files in fewer steps than with the clumsy COPY command. Suppose you want to move the file INVOICES.WK1 from the \SPREADST directory to the the \ACCTG directory. First, type **CD\SPREADST** to change you to the \SPREADST directory. Now, use the MOVE command:

> **MOVE INVOICES.WK1 C:\ACCTG**

That's *MOVE space INVOICES.WK1 space C colon backslash ACCTG*. This command translates to "Move the INVOICES.WK1 file from the *current directory* (since you didn't specify a directory for INVOICES.WK1) to the \ACCTG directory on drive C." You can include the file path with the MOVE command to perform the move in one step:

> **MOVE C:\SPREADST\INVOICES.WK1 C:\ACCTG**

This command translates to "Move the INVOICES.WK1 file from the \SPREADST directory on drive C to the \ACCTG directory on drive C."

How to Move Files If You Don't Have at Least DOS 6

You can still move files without DOS 6 something; you just have to do it the old-fashioned way: copy, then delete. For example, suppose you have a file called INVOICES.WK1 in a directory called \SPREADST and you want to move the file to your \ACCTG directory instead, so you can locate it easier. Use these two commands:

> **CD\SPREADST**
> **COPY INVOICES.WK1 C:\ACCTG**

These commands change you to the \SPREADST directory, then copy the file INVOICES.WK1 to the \ACCTG directory. The original file is still in the \SPREADST directory, so make sure you delete it, or you'll have two copies of the file on your hard disk:

DEL INVOICES.WK1

The DEL command removes files, as you'll learn in Chapter 12. This command translates to "Delete INVOICES.WK1 from the current directory."

The Least You Need to Know

To avoid standing at the COPY command all day, you should know these things:

- ☛ A path name consists of the drive the file is located on, a colon, a backslash, the directory path, another backslash, and the name of the file: C:\WORD\CHAP11.DOC.

- ☛ Unless you specify, DOS assumes you want to copy within the current directory. If you change to the directory first, you'll have to type less later.

- ☛ The copy command has three parts: the command COPY, what you're copying, and its destination. For example, COPY CONFIG.SYS CONFIG.BKP copies CONFIG.SYS to a duplicate file named CONFIG.BKP.

- ☛ To copy several files at once, use the DOS wildcards, * (which represents multiple characters) or ? (which represents a single character).

- ☛ To copy files from one directory to another, change to the source directory, then any of these examples:

  COPY JOE*.* \SALES
  COPY C:\MARKET\JOESALES.* C:\SALES
  COPY C:\MARKET\JOESALES.WK1 D:\SALES

  continues

continued

☛ To copy a file from a directory to a diskette, change to that directory, use either of these examples:

COPY DORPHIN.DOC A:
COPY C:\PROJECTS\DORPHIN.DOC B:

☛ To copy a file from a diskette to a directory, change to that diskette drive, then use either of these examples:

COPY DORPHIN.DOC C:\WORD
COPY A:DORPHIN.DOC C:\WORD

☛ To copy files from one diskette to another, change to the source diskette, then use either of these examples:

COPY SCOTTY.DOC B:
COPY A:SCOTTY.DOC B:

☛ To rename files, change to the directory that contains the files, then use any of these examples:

REN BUSH.WK1 CLINTON.WK1
REN APR??MEM.DOC MAY??MEM.DOC
REN *.BAK *.OLD

☛ Unless you have at least DOS version 6 something, to move a file to a new directory, you must copy it from the existing directory first, then delete it, as the following sequence shows:

CD\OLD
COPY JENNY.DOC C:\NEW
DEL JENNY.DOC

☛ If you have at least DOS version 6 something, you can move a file in one step, as in

MOVE C:\OLD\JENNY.DOC C:\NEW

Chapter 12
Spring Cleaning— Deleting Unwanted Files

In This Chapter

- Making a file disappear
- Evacuating all the files in a directory
- Deleting selected files
- Michael Jackson's secret love affair with the DEL command
- How to keep your job when you accidentally delete the wrong file
- Laying down DOS safety nets before you delete files

You use a PC to create things such as memos, reports, charts, and analyses. Unfortunately, PC's are not self-maintaining machines. They don't know when to take out the garbage. With the DEL command, you can clean out your PC's dust-bunnies—old files you no longer need. In this chapter, you'll learn how to use the DEL command to perform "spring cleaning" on your files. You'll also learn how to recover files if you delete them accidentally.

Things You Should Know About the DEL Command

Here's a quick review of some important concepts so you don't have to go running back to previous chapters (Isn't this awfully nice of me?):

Remember to press Enter to execute a command. Until you press Enter, nothing will happen. N-O-T-H-I-N-G. So press Enter after you type a command.

The DEL command is made up of two parts. The command itself (DEL), followed by the names of the files to delete.

The DEL command deletes files without asking. Okay, DEL will ask you if you're crazy when you tell it to delete all the files in the current directory—but in every other case, if you use DEL, your files are gone!

The DEL command erases files in the current directory or drive, unless you specify otherwise. Okay, you want to delete a file, but you don't want to get out of the directory you're currently in. No problem. Include the full path name to the file in the DEL command. For example, if you're in the WORD directory and you want to delete a file called FUN.TXT that's located in the PROJECTS directory, type **DEL C:\PROJECTS\FUN.TXT**. For more than you'd ever want to know about file paths, see the next section.

Beating a Path to a File

You can use a *file path* in any command (including the DEL command) to specify a file. The path tells DOS where to locate the file on the hard drive. If you don't use a file path with the DEL command, then the DEL command can only delete files in the *current directory*. It's a lot more typing to include a path name with the DEL command, but it's a lot less trouble than jumping back and forth between directories just so DOS can find the files you want to delete!

A path name to a file consists of three parts:

☛ The drive the file is located on followed by a colon, as in **C:**.

☛ A backslash (\) followed by the complete directory path to the file. Start with the parent directory, then add another backslash, and a subdirectory name if applicable. Finish up with a final backslash, as in **\123\WORK**.

☛ End the path name with a file name or file specification, as in **OLD.WK4**.

The completed path would look like this:

C:\123\WORK\OLD.WK4

To delete the OLD.WK4 file, you'd type DEL C:\123\WORK\OLD.WK4. With the path name included with the DEL command, DOS knows to look for the OLD.WK4 file in the \123\WORK directory on the C drive.

When Would You Ever Want to Use the DEL Command?

When it comes to collecting stuff, I'm the Queen. I just can't seem to throw anything away (like my complete set of grocery receipts from 1983—try to replace those at today's prices). If you're like me, the mere idea of deleting any file might send you into hiding, but there are many good reasons why it's worth your while. For example, with DEL, you can:

Make room for a new program. If you're out of room, you can copy seldom-used files onto diskettes and then delete them from your hard disk (see "When Everything Must Go!").

Clean up a diskette for reuse. If you have a diskette you want to recycle, you can use the DEL command to delete the files on it (see "Recycling Those Diskettes").

Get rid of files you no longer need. If a project is over, remove the files to make more room on your hard disk (see "When Everything Must Go!" and "Deleting, Single-File Style").

Clean up after programs. Many programs create working *backups* of your files. In case of a power outage, the programs use these backups to retrieve your data. These files usually end in .BAK, and they are not deleted. To make more room on your hard disk, you should periodically delete these space wasters. (See the Put It to Work project toward the end of this chapter.)

Remove an old directory. If you need to remove a program from your hard disk, you remove its directory. From time to time, you may also want to remove personal directories that you set up for special projects long since past. To remove a directory, it must be empty of files (see "When Everything Must Go!"). You'll learn how to remove the directory itself in Chapter 13.

Deleting, Single-File Style

To delete a file, you use the DEL command. For example, suppose you want to delete a file called 94PROD.CHT, located in the \CHART directory. Use these two commands (remember to press **Enter** after each command or DOS will do nothing):

    CD\CHART
    DEL 94PROD.CHT

The first command changes you to the \CHART directory, and the next command deletes the file—easy as pie.

TECHNO NERD TEACHES...

I prefer to change to the directory where the files I want to delete are stored, then use the DEL command to delete them. I find this much easier than trying to perform DEL in one step, which I could have done with this command:

DEL C:\CHART\94PROD.CHT

This command tells DOS to "Delete the 94PROD.CHT file, which is located in the \CHART directory on drive C." By including the path to the file, you can delete files in one step, although the command will be rather long (and pretty tiring on your fingers).

You might get the error message **Access denied** when using the DEL command. If you get this error message, it means that the file is protected, so you can't delete it in the normal way. Ask a PC guru to help you delete it (and to help you decide whether the file *should* be deleted—after all, it was protected for some reason).

When Everything Must Go!

If you want to remove a directory that's no longer needed, you must first delete all the files in it. Let's say that you had a directory called WALLS where you stored all the files for a big project. Now the project's completed, and you want to remove the directory. Just to be safe, copy all the files onto a diskette before you delete them, in case you ever need them again. So you don't have to return to Chapter 11 to remember how to copy files, here are the steps (press **Enter** after each command):

> **CD\WALLS**
> **COPY *.* A:**

These two commands copy all the files in the \WALLS directory onto the diskette in drive A (provided they will all fit).

Now, to tear the walls down (as it were), use these two commands (remember to press **Enter** after each command):

> **CD\WALLS**
> **DEL *.***

These two commands delete all the files in the \WALLS directory. The asterisks are *wildcards* which tell DOS which files to select (in this case, all of the files in the current directory). When you delete all the files in a directory by using *.* (asterisk period asterisk), DOS asks you to confirm that you haven't lost your mind and that you *really truly* want to delete everything in the directory. Press **Y** for yes, and the files are deleted. (Press **N** if you made a mistake and you don't want to delete the files.)

Now even though the directory is empty of files, there is still one more step before you actually remove the directory altogether. Jump on over to Chapter 13 for the how-to's on removing directories.

TECHNO NERD TEACHES...

Even after you delete all the files in a directory, when you use the DIR command to list files, you'll see something like this:

Directory of C:\WALLS
```
.          <DIR>     03-20-93   3:51p
..         <DIR>     03-20-93   3:51p
    2 file(s)        0 bytes
              16,957,440 bytes free
```

The . (dot) represents the address of this directory, and .. (double dot) represents the address of the parent directory (which in this case is the root). Think of these as "bread crumbs" that DOS uses to find its way back through the directory tree. These markers cannot be removed until the directory itself is deleted, so don't worry about them for now.

If you have *at least* DOS version 4, you can delete all the files in a directory in one step, as in **DEL C:\WALLS.** You'll see the message asking you if it's OK pretty please for DOS to delete all the files like you just asked it to do. Of course it is, so press **Y**, and then press **Enter** to delete all the files.

It's probably a good idea to actually reformat a diskette if you've been having trouble with it, because bad sections are marked as unusable during the formatting process. It's also a good idea to reformat a diskette (rather than simply deleting its files) whenever the data you want to place onto that diskette will eventually be your only copy.

Recycling Those Diskettes

Rather than buy new diskettes all the time, recycle them. Delete all the existing files on a diskette in drive A with these two commands:

```
A:
DEL *.*
```

The first command changes you to drive A (so there's no possibility that you'll delete files on your hard disk, make sure you always check your DOS prompt to be sure that you made it to drive A). The next command deletes all the files on the diskette.

Recycling diskettes in this way will only work if no one got fancy and placed directories on the diskette (it's pretty rare that you'll find directories on a diskette; they're relatively small compared to hard disks, so why bother?). If that's the case, just reformat the diskette—it's easier than trying to remove directories. See Chapter 6 for a refresher on how to format a diskette.

The DEL Command Goes Wild! (Deleting Selected Files)

You can use *wildcards* to delete selected files in a directory. DOS has two wildcards, the asterisk (which represents several characters within a file name, as in *.DOC) and the question mark (which represents a single character within a file name, as in PART??.DOC). Here are some more examples, using this sample file list:

SALEMAY.DOC
SALEJUN.CHT
BUDGET.DOC
SALEJULY.DOC
BADACCT.CHT
ALBERT.DOC

Wildcard pattern	Files it would delete
SALE*.*	SALEMAY.DOC, SALEJUN.CHT, and SALEJULY.DOC
SALE???.*	SALEMAY.DOC and SALEJUN.CHT
SALE*.DOC	SALEMAY.DOC and SALEJULY.DOC
*SALE.DOC	SALEMAY.DOC, BUDGET.DOC, SALEJULY.DOC, and ALBERT.DOC
B*.*	BUDGET.DOC and BADACCT.CHT
B*.CHT	BADACCT.CHT
*.CHT	SALEJUN.CHT and BADACCT.CHT
??????.DOC	BUDGET.DOC and ALBERT.DOC

TECHNO NERD TEACHES...

Notice what happened when the asterisk was used *in front of letters*, as in the *SALES.DOC example. It's the same as typing *.DOC. Be careful with the placement of an asterisk, because the letters after it are ignored (at least until you bump into the period).

For example, suppose you want to delete all your 1994 files from the SALES directory. All of the files begin with 94 something, as in 94JAN.DOC, 94SALES.CHT, etc. Follow these steps:

CD\SALES
DEL 94*.*

This command deletes all the files in the current directory that begin with the numbers 94. Use wildcards in place of filenames in any DEL command to delete multiple files at once.

How to be Sure You Delete Only the Files You Want

Using wildcards with the DEL command can be a bit scary. I mean, with one command, you can wipe out more files than North did during the Iran-Contra brouhaha. When using wildcards to delete files, use the DIR command first to verify that you will delete *the correct files*. For example, to delete all the files in the current directory that begin with an M and use an .XLS extension, use this command first:

DIR M*.XLS

With this command, you'll see a listing of all the .XLS files in the current directory. If you're satisfied that the listing contains all the files you want to delete, use the DEL command with the same wildcard pattern, as in:

DEL M*.XLS

If the wildcard pattern lists most of the files you want, you can request confirmation for each file before it is deleted. See the EZ in this section for details.

TECHNO NERD TEACHES...

If you have at least DOS version 4, you can train DOS to "sit up and beg" before it deletes a file. Going back to an earlier scenario, if you want to confirm the deletion of each 1994 file, use this command instead:

DEL 94*.* /P

The /P switch tells DOS to prompt for confirmation before deleting each file. You can use the /P switch whenever you use the DEL command, but it's especially helpful when you're deleting selected files with wildcards. As the name of each file appears, simply press **Y** to delete the file, or **N** to skip deletion.

Deleting Old Backup Files

A lot of programs create working backups of your files, which they use in case a power outage has damaged your original file and made it inaccessible. These files usually end in .BAK or .TMP, and they are never deleted. To make more room on your hard disk, you should periodically delete them. To delete backup files from a directory called WORD, use these commands (press **Enter** after each command):

```
CD\WORD
DEL *.BAK
DEL *.TMP
```

If you have at least DOS 5, you can search for all the backup files on your hard disk, and print out the listing, so you can go back and delete them (oh, goody.) Turn on your printer, then type this:

```
DIR C:\*.BAK /S >PRN
```

Oops, I Deleted the Wrong Files!

If you get trigger-happy with the DEL command, it's easy to accidentally delete the wrong file. Then what do you do? Well, if you have a copy of the file on a diskette, you can easily copy it back onto your hard disk. But what do you do if you don't have a recent copy of the file, and you're out of tissues?

If you have DOS 5, or one of the DOS 6 versions, you have something better than tissue; you have the UNDELETE command. Suppose you have just typed the command

DEL APR94.WK1

when your boss asks you to do a comparison between last month's sales (April) and this month's. How do you get that file back? Easy—just use this command:

UNDELETE APR94.WK1

How can you recover a *deleted* file? Well, DOS doesn't actually delete a file even when you tell it to. Instead, it marks a file as "deleted" by changing its name slightly on its internal file listing. What it does is replace the first character in the file name with a question mark, as in

?PR94.WK1

Think of putting an "X" through an old address in your address book. You know to ignore the address, and you may even reuse that address area by placing a label over it. When DOS marks a file with a question mark, it knows not to list that file when you use the DIR command. DOS also knows that it can reuse the space at any time. For all intents and purposes, the file is deleted, but in reality, it's still there—it's simply waiting to be overwritten by another file as soon as that file needs the space. That's why it's important to use the UNDELETE command as soon as possible, to ensure your best chances of a successful recovery.

When you use the UNDELETE command, you might be asked to supply the first letter of the file name, as in

?PR94.WK1
Please supply the missing letter:

Enter the missing letter (in this case, the letter **A**) and press **Enter**. If you don't really know what the missing letter is, it's okay, because neither does DOS. So type anything. The file should be recovered. I say should be, because this command works best *if you use it right after deleting the file.* Don't copy files onto your hard drive or use any programs until you've recovered the deleted file. In short, *if you accidentally delete a file, do NOTHING until you use the UNDELETE command.*

Recovering Several Files at Once

Okay, so you deleted not one, but several files. What do you do now? Use **UNDELETE /LIST.** The /LIST switch displays a listing of all the recently deleted files, along with their chances of a successful recovery. Once you see a list of the files that can be undeleted, you can use the UNDELETE command on any of them. To undelete several files at once, use wildcards with the UNDELETE command.

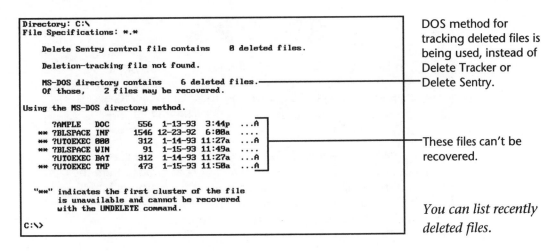

DOS method for tracking deleted files is being used, instead of Delete Tracker or Delete Sentry.

These files can't be recovered.

You can list recently deleted files.

To undelete several files, use wildcards, as in **UNDELETE *.BAK.** If you need help getting wild, see the earlier section in this chapter on wildcards.

Increasing Your Chances of a Successful Recovery

If you don't undelete a file right after accidentally deleting it, you may not be able to get that file back. You can *greatly* increase your chances by using one of these delete protection methods:

MIRROR   Use the MIRROR command with DOS 5. MIRROR keeps a list of recently deleted files, including the location of each part of the file.

Delete Tracker   Use Delete Tracker with DOS 6 something. Delete Tracker uses less disk space than Delete Sentry, and uses a method similar to MIRROR for tracking deleted files.

Delete Sentry   Use Delete Sentry with DOS 6 something. Delete Sentry creates a hidden directory called \SENTRY. When you delete files, they are moved to this directory before they are deleted by DOS. When you activate UNDELETE, they are moved back to their original directory. Files are saved in this directory until the \SENTRY directory has grown to 7% of your hard disk space, then old files are deleted to make way for new ones.

TECHNO NERD TEACHES...

Often DOS stores files by breaking them into chunks and storing them in the first available spots, all over the hard disk. If a file was stored in pieces, UNDELETE will have a harder time recovering the file unless you use MIRROR, Delete Tracker, or Delete Sentry.

When a file is deleted, DOS remembers where the starting piece of a file is located, but it may not remember where the rest of the pieces are. The delete protection methods listed here keep track of the exact location of each piece of a file and provide the missing information to DOS.

Delete protection is a little tricky, so have a friend help you place the appropriate command for MIRROR, Delete Tracker, or Delete Sentry in your AUTOEXEC.BAT file.

The Least You Need to Know

Deleting files is easy when you remember these things:

- ☞ To delete a single file, change to the directory that contains the file, then type **DEL** followed by the file name.

- ☞ To delete multiple files, use wildcards, as in **DEL MAR*.CHT**.

- ☞ To delete files without changing directories, include the directory in the file path, as in **DEL C:\HG\MAR*.CHT**.

- ☞ For added security, add the **/P** switch to the DEL command, so DOS will prompt you before it deletes a file (you must have at least DOS version 4 to use this).

- ☞ To recover a deleted file, use the UNDELETE command (you must have at least DOS 5). Type **UNDELETE** followed by the name of the file you want to recover.

- ☞ If you have DOS 5, increase your chances of recovering a file by using the MIRROR command in your AUTOEXEC.BAT file. If you have DOS 6 something, use Delete Sentry or Delete Tracker.

This page suitable for doodling.

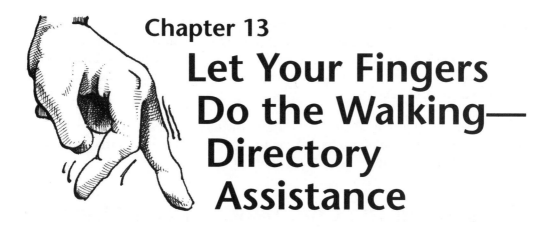

Chapter 13

Let Your Fingers Do the Walking— Directory Assistance

In This Chapter

- ☞ Jumping between directories
- ☞ In search of your directories
- ☞ Adding directories
- ☞ Chopping limbs off the old directory tree
- ☞ Renaming directories because you've got nothing better to do
- ☞ Grab the video, it's America's Funniest Directories
- ☞ Moving files from one directory to another

You use directories to organize your files, just as you might use shelves to organize books. Every program you buy, whether it's a word processor or a spreadsheet program, creates its own directory on your PC's hard disk. For example, if you installed WordPerfect, it would create a directory WP, and place all of its files into that directory.

But you should create your own directories, too. After all, you're the one who'll have to locate the files you create when you need them. For example, if you've just snagged the Bosco account, you could create a BOSCO directory, to put all the files that you generate for that account, such as memos, charts, spreadsheets, etc.

Why should you bother to organize your files? For the same reason that you organize other things in your life—so you can find them when you need them, and not after a time-wasting search. And when Mr. Bosco asks about that proposal, you won't have to avoid his questions while you search for the file.

This chapter is all about directories: how to create them and how to remove them. You'll also learn how to move files around, so that you can always locate whatever you need, when you need it.

Hints About the Commands in This Chapter

So you don't have to keep thumbing back to previous chapters, your mommy's provided a review of some important concepts:

Remember to press Enter to execute a command. Until you press Enter, nothing will happen.

Remember to brush your teeth after every meal.

When using the RD (remove directory) command, you might get the error message Invalid path, not directory, or directory not empty. In order to remove a directory, you must delete all of its files. If you get this error message, it means that the directory still has files or subdirectories in it. Follow the instructions later in this chapter for removing directories with success.

The MD (make directory) command creates a subdirectory off the current directory, unless you specify otherwise. If you want to create a directory somewhere else, just include a *path* in the MD (make directory) command. For example, if you are in the root directory, but you want to create a subdirectory under the \WORD directory and call it PROJECTS, you can include the path **C:\WORD\PROJECTS** in the MD command. See the next section for a more fully *evolved* explanation.

Running Down that Same Old Path

You can use a *path* in any command (including the MD command) to specify a file, or in this case, a directory. Used with the MD command, the path tells DOS exactly where to create the directory on the hard drive. If you don't use a path with the MD command, then the MD command creates the new directory under the *current directory*. And that's not always what you want to do.

It's a lot more typing to include a path name with the MD command, but it's also a lot more accurate. That way, you don't wake up with a mystery directory, wondering how it got there, and you don't start copying files into a directory you thought was there, but isn't.

A path name to a directory consists of two parts:

- ☛ The drive the directory is located on followed by a colon, as in C:.
- ☛ A backslash (\) followed by the complete directory path to the directory you want to create. Start with the parent directory, then add another backslash, then type the name of the directory you want to create, as in **\123\WORK**

The completed path would look like this:

   C:\123\WORK

The actual MD command, complete with its shiny new path, looks like this:

   MD C:\123\WORK

With this path name, the MD command creates a directory called WORK, and places it within the 123 directory for your computing convenience, and it does all this *regardless of the directory in which you might currently be located.*

When Should You Use the Commands in This Chapter?

Let's face it—all this talk about directories and paths is boring. So you're probably wondering, "Should I bother to organize directories?" Well, here are some reasons why you might like to:

The TREE command helps you become acquainted with a new PC. Find out what directories are out there on your PC's hard disk—and, by association, what programs are installed (see "Off to See the World: Finding Out What Directories You Have").

The MD (make directory) command organizes your files so you can work with them easily. By creating directories for your own files, you can easily locate them. For example, I have a directory called \PROJECTS, and I create a subdirectory for each book I write—for this book, I created the \PROJECTS\CIGD directory (see "Giving Birth to New Directories").

The RD (remove directory) command helps you reclaim your hard disk space. To remove a program from your hard disk, you remove its directory. From time to time, you may also want to remove personal directories that you had set up for special projects long since past (see "Deleting Unwanted Directories").

Getting things the way you like them. Whenever you move into a new office or cubicle, it's instinctive to put your "stuff" out first, to make the place "yours." Using a PC every day, you will want to customize it to the way you work. Part of that process entails creating directories that you need for your own projects and work habits, and renaming existing directories so they become meaningful (see "Giving Birth to New Directories" and "Renaming a Directory with DOS 6").

Subdirectory Actually, all directories could be considered *sub*directories, because all directories are subordinate to the one and only root directory. However, the term subdirectory is usually used to describe a directory within another directory (at least by me).

Changing Directories— A Review

Why do you need to change directories? Because each program is in its own directory, you change from one directory to another directory to use different programs. So you don't have to go running back to Chapter 7, here's a review on how to change directories.

To change directories, simply type the command CD followed by a backslash (\) and the name of the directory you want to change to. For example, to change to the WORD directory, use **CD\WORD**. To change to the DORPHIN directory, a *subdirectory* of the PROJECTS directory, use **CD\PROJECTS\DORPHIN**. To change to the root directory, don't enter a directory name at all: use **CD**.

Quick Trick for Changing Directories

Here's a trick I forgot to show you in Chapter 7 (aren't you glad now that you hung around?). You can move one level up the directory tree by using the command **CD..** (that's *CD dot dot*, or *CD period period*).

Let's say you were in the C:\PROJECTS\DORPHIN directory. If you used the command **CD..**, you would change to its parent directory, which in this case is C:\PROJECTS. If you used the command again, you would move up one more level, to the root directory (C:\>). Cool, eh?

Parent directory A directory above another directory in the directory tree. For example, the parent of the C:\WORD\DOCS directory is C:\WORD. The parent of the C:\WORD directory is the root directory.

Off to See the World: Finding Out What Directories You Have

When I was a kid and I wanted to see what was going on in my neighborhood, I'd climb a tree and I could see for miles. If you want to see what's going on in your PC's "neighborhood," you use the TREE command (there must have been some tree climbers at Microsoft too). The TREE command lists *all the directories* on a single drive, such as drive C.

The TREE command is useful when you're trying to organize files so you can locate them more quickly. At my old job, I inherited someone's old PC, so I used the TREE command to tell me what programs were on the PC (because each program gets its own directory, remember?) and to tell me what kind of directory structure had been set up for storing files. To display all the directories on drive C, use this command:

TREE C:\ | MORE

That's *TREE space C colon backslash space pipe space MORE*. The *pipe character* (|) in front of the MORE command may be a little tricky to locate. On my keyboard, it's above the backslash. In any case, on some keyboards, it looks like a solid line, while on others, it looks like two thin dashes one on top of the other. Just as a water pipe controls the flow of water, the pipe character controls the flow of information through it. In this case, it controls the display of directories down your screen.

This command translates to "Display all the directories on drive C, beginning with the root directory, one screenful at a time." The TREE command normally displays the directory listing and keeps on going, *unless you also use the | MORE command.*

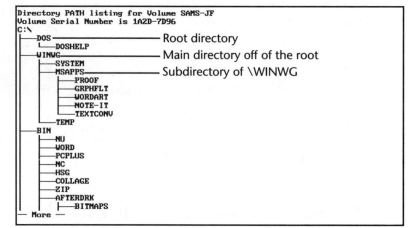

You can use the TREE command to list all the directories on a single disk drive, such as drive C.

The TREE command lists directories beginning with the current directory, unless you specify otherwise (as we did, by including the path C:\ , which means root directory of the C drive). Suppose you want to list all the subdirectories of your \PROJECT directory. Use a command like this one:

TREE C:\PROJECTS | MORE

By including the path, C:\PROJECTS, you tell the TREE command to start the directory listing at the PROJECTS directory, and not at the current directory.

What If I Want to See Files, Too?

The TREE command normally lists *only directories*, but you can also use it to *list files* (like the DIR command), if you want. For example, use this command to list all the files and directories on drive C:

TREE C:\ /F | MORE

That's *TREE space C colon backslash space forward slash F space pipe space MORE.* The /F switch tells the TREE command to list files in addition to directories. Such a list can be used for a thorough housekeeping of your hard disk or for locating an errant file.

You can't go back and forth through the list while it's displayed on-screen, so you may want to print it out by typing this command instead:

TREE C:\ /F > PRN

The greater-than sign (>) is the *redirection symbol*; PRN is DOS's name for your printer. The redirection symbol *points* towards where it wants the output of the TREE command to go, in this case to the PRN or printer. You may remember this little guy from Chapter 10, when you learned how to redirect the output of the DIR command and send it to the printer also.

Redirection symbol   Used to send the output of a command to another device (such as the printer or a modem), to a file, or to another command, instead of displaying the output on the monitor. The DOS redirection symbol is the greater-than sign (>), and it is placed in front of the name of the device, file, or command you want to direct the output to, like this:

TREE C:\ /F > PRN

or this:

TREE C:\ > TREE.LST

You can also send the tree listing to a file, so you can save it permanently or print it out later. Use a command like this one:

TREE C:\ > TREE.LST

By including a filename instead of PRN, you're telling the redirector to send the output of the TREE command to a file on the hard disk. Later, you can get someone to help you print it out, or you can look though it at your leisure with the help of the DOS editor, explained in technicolor detail in Chapter 16.

Giving Birth to New Directories

It's a good habit to keep your own files in directories other than the program directory. That's because doing so makes it easier to back up your files (copy them onto diskettes in case the originals get damaged) or to locate your files in a hurry.

For example, if your word processor is located in a directory called \WORD, you might want to create subdirectories for each project, such as \WORD\BERG and \WORD\CONFRNCE, or a single subdirectory for all the files you create, such as \WORD\PROJECTS or \WORD\WORK. After you create them, you could then save the memos, letters, and reports that you create with your word processor in one of these private directories.

Periodically (with the help you'll find in Chapter 14) you could back up your private files with a command that says, "Backup the files in the \WORD\PROJECTS directory, and don't bother with the other files." This saves you lots of time in backing up. You don't need to worry about backing up the program files for your word processor, because if something ever happens to them, you can just reinstall the program using the program diskettes.

SPEAK LIKE A GEEK

Backup   A process that copies your files onto diskettes in a special compressed format. If something bad happens to the originals, you can restore your backed-up files (a process that uncompresses the files and copies them back onto the hard disk).

To create directories, you use the MD (make directory) command. For example, let's say that you just got assigned a big account called MAYPRO, and you want to create a new directory within your WORD directory for it. Use these commands (remember to press **Enter** after each command):

    CD\WORD
    MD MAYPRO

The first command changes you to the \WORD directory. The last command creates a subdirectory called MAYPRO within the current directory, which, because you just changed to it, happens to be WORD. Notice that in the example, there is no backslash in front of MAYPRO. By leaving the backslash out, *the new directory is created as a subdirectory of the WORD directory, just like you wanted.*

If you had used a backslash, as in MD \MAYPRO, the MAYPRO directory would be created off the root directory, and not under the \WORD directory. That's because the MD command would see \MAYPRO as a *path*, and that path would override its natural inclination to create a directory under the current directory, and the path would force the MD command to create the directory where you specified, which in this was under the root. Oops.

Remember that you can also create directories in *one step* by including the complete path with the MD command, as in

MDC:\WORD\MAYPRO

Bottom line: choose one method or the other. Either use the two step process for creating directories, as in:

> **CD\123**
> **MD WORK**

Or use the one step method by including the complete path to the new directory with the MD command, as in:

> **MD \123\WORK**

It's your choice.

Deleting Unwanted Directories

After you are finished with certain projects, you may not want to keep their files on your hard disk. After all, they take up space that you'll need for new projects. Suppose you're finished with the MAYPRO account, and you want to delete its directory. To delete a directory, you must first delete all the files in it.

Make Sure You Save Those Files Before You Delete Them!

Before you delete files, you may want to copy them onto a diskette. To copy the files from our MAYPRO directory onto a diskette, type these two commands, pressing **Enter** after each one:

CD\WORD\MAYPRO
COPY *.* A:

The first command takes you to the MAYPRO directory. The last command copies all the files in the MAYPRO directory to a diskette in drive A (provided there's enough room—if there isn't, use the BACKUP command described in Chapter 14 instead).

Now Get Rid of That Old Directory

When your files are safely copied onto a diskette, you can feel comfortable deleting them. Assuming that you're still in the MAYPRO directory, use this command to delete the files:

DEL *.*

Press **Y** to confirm the deletion. Now that the directory is empty, you can remove it with the RD (remove directory) command. But first, you have to get out of the directory, too. (The directory has to be completely empty before it can be removed, which means that you can't be in it either.) Get out of the MAYPRO directory by changing to the root directory. Type **CD** and press **Enter.** Now, remove the directory with this command:

RD \WORD\MAYPRO

By including the directory path (\WORD\ MAYPRO) with the RD command, you specify exactly which directory you want to remove.

Why do you have to change from the MAYPRO directory before you can delete it? If you think of directories as rooms and files as boxes, then imagine that you want to remove a room of your house (maybe you're remodeling or you're just tired of your in-laws coming to visit). If everything in the room was boxed up, you'd remove the boxes first. Then when you were sure that everything was out of the room, you'd remove yourself, and release the wrecking ball. Removing directories follows this same sequence: remove the files, remove yourself by changing directories, then remove the directory (the empty room).

Recap: Deleting a Directory With No Subdirectories

Here's a step by step recap on how to delete a directory that *does not* have any subdirectories. Just type the name of your directory instead of the word OLDDIR:

☛ First, copy any important files onto diskette:

CD\OLDDIR
COPY *.* A:

☛ Next, delete the files in the directory:

CD\OLDDIR
DEL *.*
Y

☛ Then remove the directory:

CD
RD \OLDDIR

Deleting a Directory That Contains Subdirectories

Deleting a directory that contains subdirectories is not easy, unless you have at least DOS version 6 (see the next section). But for those of us who haven't upgraded to DOS 6 something yet, here's a step-by-step plan for removing a directory and its subdirectory.

Let's say that you have a directory called \OLIVE and it contains *one subdirectory* called \OLIVE\OIL. Removing the \OLIVE directory could get slippery, but here goes:

> **CD\OLIVE\OIL**
> **DEL *.***

These two commands move you to the subdirectory OIL, and delete its files. OK, so now the directory OIL is empty. Now try these two commands:

> **CD..**
> **DEL *.***

The first command moves you to the parent directory, which in this case is \OLIVE. The second command deletes all the files there. Great. Now both directories, OLIVE and OIL, are empty. Now type this:

> **RD \OLIVE\OIL**

This command removes the subdirectory OIL. Now the directory \OLIVE is completely free of *all subdirectories and files*, so you can remove it, too:

> **CD..**
> **RD \OLIVE**

The first command moves you to the parent directory, which in this case is the root directory. The second command removes the directory \OLIVE. Whew. Can we have a recap?

Recap: Deleting a Directory with One Subdirectory

Glad you asked. Here's a recap of the steps you need to follow to remove a directory *which has one subdirectory*. (If you're trying to get rid of a directory which contains multiple directories, see the tips at the end of this section.) Follow these steps, and **type the name of your directories instead of the words PARENT and OLDDIR:**

☞ First, delete the files in the OLDDIR directory:

> **CD\PARENT\OLDDIR**
> **DEL *.***
> **Y**

☞ Then remove the files in the PARENT directory:

> **CD..**
> **DEL *.***
> **Y**

☞ Now, remove the OLDDIR directory:

> **RD \PARENT\OLDDIR**

☞ Then remove the PARENT directory:

> **CD..**
> **RD \PARENT**

If the directory you wish to remove has lots of little subdirectories, it's going to take a few more commands to get rid of them. Repeat the first step to remove the files in each subdirectory, then repeat the third step to remove the directories themselves.

Deleting a Directory the Easy Way— With the DOS 6 Somethings

If you have one of the DOS 6 somethings (DOS 6, 6.2, 6.21, or 6.22), you can delete a directory in one easy step, by using the DELTREE command. The DELTREE command automatically removes all files and sub-directories in order to remove the directory specified. It's kind of like using a machete to trim your hedges—it gets the job done *real fast*. For example, if you want to delete the MAYPRO directory, copy the files onto a diskette (as explained earlier) and then use this one command:

DELTREE C:\WORD\MAYPRO

By specifying the directory path (C:\WORD\MAYPRO) in the DELTREE command, you specify exactly what you want to delete. After you press **Enter**, you'll be prompted to confirm the deletion. Press **Y** and **Enter**, and away it goes!

OOPS!

If you see the error message **Bad command or file name,** you need to set up a DOS path so that DOS can find the DELTREE or MOVE commands. For now, type **PATH=C:\DOS** and press **Enter**. See Chapter 4 for more details.

Renaming a Directory With the DOS 6 Somethings

There may be times when you'll want to change the name of a directory. Maybe you didn't get the name right and you keep forgetting what the directory is for, or maybe the purpose of the directory has changed. Unfortunately, the good folks at Microsoft didn't think to provide you with an easy way to do this (until the DOS 6 somethings, that is).

You might think that you could use the REN command to rename directories, just as you use it to rename files, but that would be *way tooooo easyyyy*. The good news is if you have at least DOS version 6, you can rename a directory with the MOVE command. For example, to rename a directory called \1993 to \1994, use this command:

>   MOVE C:\1993 C:\1994

That's *MOVE space C colon backslash 1993 space C colon backslash 1994*. The MOVE command works kind of like the REN command. You type the command MOVE, followed by the current name of the directory, followed by the new name of the directory.

What If I Don't Have One of the DOS 6 Somethings?

If you don't have at least DOS 6, don't give up hope. You can still "rename" your directory, but alas, there are a few steps involved in doing so. First, create the new directory:

>   MD \1994

Then copy all the files from the old directory to the new directory:

>   CD\1993
>   COPY *.* \1994

Now, delete all the files in the old directory:

>   DEL *.*
>   Y

And then, since the files are now comfortable and warm in their new directory, do the hokey pokey and shake yourself all about. And while you're at it, remove the old directory:

CD\
RD \1993

If the directory you are trying to rename contains subdirectories, it may not be worth your trouble to try to rename the directory, because it becomes more difficult to copy all the files and then delete them. Ask a pro to help you, or simply live with the current directory name.

The Least You Need to Know

I must confess, I love creating directories. When I was little, I had several cubbyholes where I'd stash my secret stuff. Now my treasure boxes are special directories I create for each project. You'll have no trouble creating and removing your own "treasure boxes" if you remember these things:

- To list all the directories on a drive, use the TREE command.

- To list all the files as well as all the directories on a drive, use the TREE command with the /F switch.

- To print the results of a command, add >**PRN** to the end of the command, as in **TREE C:\ /F >PRN**.

- To create a directory, type MD followed by the directory path.

- To delete a directory, if you do not have at least DOS 6, save any files you need onto diskette. Then change to the directory you want to delete, and delete all the files by using **DEL *.***. Next, change to the parent directory and use the RD command to remove the directory.

- If a directory contains a subdirectory, delete all the files in the subdirectory first, then remove the subdirectory by using the RD command. When all subirectories are removed, delete the files from the

continues

continued

parent directory, then remove it with the RD command.

☞ If you have at least DOS 6, use the DELTREE command to remove a directory and all of its subdirectories.

☞ If you have at least DOS 6, use the MOVE command to rename a directory.

☞ If you don't have at least DOS 6, rename a directory by first creating a directory with the new name. Then copy all the files from the old directory to the new directory. Finally, delete all the files from the old directory and remove it.

Part Three
Things Your PC Guru Never Told You

I hate when I'm having a computer problem, and someone says, "You mean you didn't do . . . ?" The hardest thing about using a computer is that there's always something that someone will forget to tell you. This section deals with the kinds of things you should know about, even if you don't want to do them yourself. With just a little light reading (I promise) you can prevent major, big-time problems later.

Chapter 14
Backing Up Your Hard Disk

In This Chapter

- Backing up all the files on your hard disk so you don't have to do any work today
- Backing up only the files you've created or changed recently
- Backups of the rich and famous
- How to con your kid brother into doing backups for you
- Using MS-DOS 6 something to perform backups

True story: One day I was sitting at a red light, minding my own business, and suddenly I found myself on the other side of the intersection. Someone was playing road hockey, and I was the puck. When the cops arrived, they said I was lucky; I had been wearing my seat belt.

Doing *backups* is something like wearing a seat belt: it's annoying, and you wonder why you bother doing it, until an accident happens and you're glad you did. (At least a backup won't wrinkle your clothes or break your bones.)

This chapter is divided into two sections: the first half is for users who don't have at least DOS 6, and the last half is for those who do.

If you don't know what your DOS version is, type **VER** and press **Enter**. If you have one of the DOS 6 somethings (DOS 6, 6.2, 6.21, or 6.22), the way you do backups is different from previous DOS versions, so read the next section, "If You've Skipped Ahead, BACK UP and Read This!," and then skip to the end of this chapter and read "Backing Up Your Hard Disk with the DOS 6 Somethings."

If you use Windows a lot and you have one of the DOS 6 somethings, you may want to use the Windows version of MSBACKUP. See Chapter 22 for the how-to's.

If You've Skipped Ahead, BACK UP and Read This!

The backup command that you use with the DOS 6 somethings is MSBACKUP. For earlier DOS versions, you use MRBACKUP, and a world of troubles go down the drain... (okay, I'm just being silly—earlier DOS versions use the plain old BACKUP command). Now before I get too carried away, here are some important concepts you should know.

Remember to press Enter to execute a command. Is there an echo in here? Anyway, it's really important, or I wouldn't keep mentioning it in every chapter. Until you press Enter, nothing happens.

A set of backup diskettes is like a multi-volume encyclopedia chronicling the contents of your hard drive at the time the backup was performed. During the backup process, DOS crams as many files as it can onto each diskette. When that diskette runs out of room, DOS asks you to insert a new diskette. DOS will keep asking for diskettes until there are no more files to back up.

Once you've chosen a few dozen or so diskettes for your backup set, don't use these diskettes for anything else. DOS gives your backup diskettes a special format that is incompatible (geeky word of the day) with the ordinary DOS format you use to store everyday files.

The backup commands are used to protect the files on your hard disk. You cannot use BACKUP or MSBACKUP to make copies of files on diskettes.

There's a difference between COPY and the backup process. When you copy a file to a diskette, the copy is immediately usable. When you back up a file, the backed-up version is unusable until you *restore* it. Another difference: when you copy a file to a diskette, existing files already on the diskette remain there. The backup procedure, on the other hand, takes control of the whole diskette and wipes out its previous contents.

There are different types of backups you can perform. You can back up all of your files or only selected ones. It's your choice, *full* or *incremental.* As a rule of thumb, perform a full backup once a week, and then perform an incremental backup at the end of each work day.

To format or not to format. Performing a backup uses a lot of diskettes. If you have at least DOS version 4, you don't have to preformat the diskettes used in a backup—just use them straight out of the box. BACKUP and MSBACKUP will just format diskettes as needed. However, using already formatted diskettes makes the backup process go much faster.

You should check for viruses before you perform a backup. One reason why you may need these backup disks in the first place is to restore your system after a computer virus has trashed it, so make sure your backups will be usable by checking for viruses on your hard disk first (see Chapter 18).

SPEAK LIKE A GEEK

Restore Backing up your files is a process that copies the files on your hard disk onto diskettes in a special compressed format. If the files on your hard disk get damaged somehow, you can *restore* them through a reverse process that decompresses the backed-up files and copies them back onto the hard disk.

Full backup A type of backup that copies every file on your hard disk.

Incremental backup A type of backup that copies only the files that have been changed since the last full or incremental backup. To restore a complete hard disk, you would need *both your full and all of your incremental backup diskettes.*

Any information already on the diskettes you use in a backup will be erased, so make sure that you don't need any of the files on the diskettes.

Why Worry? Backing Up the Entire Hard Disk

When I back up my entire hard disk, it gives me a feeling of euphoria. Because every file is safely copied onto a diskette, I can look my PC in the eye and say, "You can be replaced." If you have at least DOS 6, skip to "Backing Up Your Hard Disk with the DOS 6 Somethings" to find out what to do. If you have an earlier DOS version, you too can get that "Oh, what a feeling" by using this command (make sure that you already have enough diskettes formatted and on-hand—see the next section for help):

BACKUP C:*.* A: /S /L

That's *BACKUP space C colon backslash asterisk period asterisk space A colon space forward slash S space forward slash L*. Whew! Take a break; you deserve it after all that typing.

The command you just typed tells DOS to "Back up all the files on drive C, beginning with the root directory, and create a log of all the files that are backed up." You'll be prompted to place a diskette in drive A. Actually, you may already have placed one there. Good thinking. Press **Enter** and get on with the show.

As the backup progresses, you'll be asked to replace that diskette with other diskettes until the entire hard disk is backed up. The number of diskettes needed will vary, depending on the size of your hard disk and the capacity (density) of the diskettes you're using. While you're zoning out watching DOS do its stuff, wake up enough to label each diskette as you take it out of the drive. Nothing fancy here, just something like: FULL BACKUP DISK #1 will do.

Figuring Out How Many Diskettes You'll Need

Since it's a good idea to have your diskettes already formatted before you start a backup (actually, if you don't have at least DOS 5, you *must* already have your diskettes formatted), you might want to know how many diskettes you'll need for your full backup. Type this command and press **Enter:**

CHKDSK

Now, take the *bytes total disk space* minus the *bytes available on disk* to find the number of bytes being used by the files on your hard disk. Take this number and divide it by the number of bytes each diskette holds (yeah, I know, no one told you there'd be a math quiz):

	High-Density Diskette	**Double-Density Diskette**
5 1/4-inch	1,213,952 bytes	360 bytes
3 1/2-inch	1,457,664 bytes	720 bytes

For example, if my PC had a total of 168,132,608 bytes (160MB) and all but 14,598,144 bytes were used, then I'd have to back up 153,534,464 bytes worth of files (yech). If I used high-density 3 1/2-inch diskettes to perform the backup, the backup would take 105.3291 diskettes (better make that 106 diskettes). Some compression occurs during backup, so this is actually an overestimate (lucky me).

If the thought of sitting in front of your PC stuffing it with 106 diskettes makes you want to go back to pen and paper, don't think you're alone. No sane person wants to do it, yet if you don't, you take unnecessary risks with your data. If you've organized your files so the files you create are in their own directories, you may have other options than performing a full backup, but you should consult with a PC guru for advice.

What If I Have Another Hard Disk Drive?

If you have more than one hard disk drive, such as drive D, you'll need two complete sets of backups—one set for C, the other for D. *Don't reuse the same diskettes that you used to backup drive C.* Format a whole new set of diskettes for the backup of drive D. Use this command to do a full backup of drive D:

BACKUP D:*.* A: /S /L

If you have even more hard disk drives, check with your PC guru because you're really going to need an alternative to doing full backups if you want to keep your sanity. And besides, some of those extra disk drives might not be what you think. For instance, they might be connected to a *network*, in which case they are not your problem (yeah!), or they might be CD-ROM drives, or tape drives, or something else altogether. Anyway, it's time to call in the cavalry and get this figured out.

Network A network involves connecting several PCs together for the purpose of sharing information and printers. In a local area network (LAN), the connected PCs are located in the same building. In a wide area network (WAN), the connected PCs can be located thousands of miles apart, or in the same city.

The Lazy Way: Backing Up Only What's Been Changed

The problem with the full backup euphoria is that as soon as you change a document or create a new one, you need to do a backup again. That's because your backup diskettes no longer have a copy of everything that's on your hard disk. Instead of doing a complete backup all over again, do an *incremental* one. An incremental backup backs up only those files that have changed since your last backup. For the most part, these are the files you've changed, so there shouldn't be too many of them. First, dig out your set of full backup diskettes. Then use this command to perform an incremental backup of drive C:

BACKUP C:*.* A: /S /M /A /L

That's *BACKUP space C colon backslash asterisk period asterisk space A colon space forward slash S space forward slash M space forward slash A space forward slash L*. Wow, and you thought the other command was long!

By the time you're finished typing it, I'll have my explanation all finished. This command translates to "Back up all the files on drive C, beginning with the root directory, that have been modified since the last backup. Add this to the existing backup set, and update the log file." Dig out your full backup set and place diskette 1 in drive A. Press **Enter**. BACKUP will then go throu gh your hard disk, adding new files or changed files to your *existing backup set*. This process makes your backup set *current* with the files on your hard disk, and it doesn't take hardly any time to do.

Along the way, you'll be prompted for other diskettes in the backup set, as needed (aren't you glad you took the time to label them?). You won't be prompted for every diskette, only *the ones that need to be updated*, so don't be alarmed if BACKUP skips a few.

Backing Up Your Hard Disk with the DOS 6 Somethings

The backup program that comes with the DOS 6 somethings (DOS 6, 6.2, 6.21, and 6.22) is called MS Backup. MS Backup is graphical and easy to use, like the DOS Shell. This means that you'll select the drives, directories, and files to be backed up from menus and boxes, instead of typing long and nasty commands. In addition, these selections can be stored permanently in a *setup file*, so you can reuse them at a later date. MS Backup comes with a few setup files already created for common situations, such as a full backup.

When you perform a backup, DOS creates a *backup catalog*. A backup catalog is a file that contains information about what was backed up, and when. The backup catalog is copied to both the hard disk and the last backup diskette. The backup catalog is used when restoring files (see Chapter 15).

You can use the MS Backup program with either a mouse or the keyboard. If you've forgotten these common mouse terms, here's your roll call, mouseketeers:

Click To click with the mouse, move the mouse pointer over the selection and press the mouse button once.

Double-click To double-click with the mouse, move the mouse pointer over the selection and press the mouse button twice in rapid succession.

Backing Up the Entire Hard Disk

To perform a full backup, type **MSBACKUP** and press **Enter**.

The first time you run MS Backup, it performs some tests on your system so it can set itself up. You'll need two diskettes of the same size and density as the diskettes you'll use when you do real backups. Follow the on-screen instructions, and remember to save the configuration when the tests are over.

When the testing is done, press **Enter** to select Backup from the Main menu, and you'll see the screen where you'll make all your backup selections. Next time you use MS Backup, type **MSBACKUP** and press **Enter**, and you'll get to this screen right away, without going through the testing rigmarole.

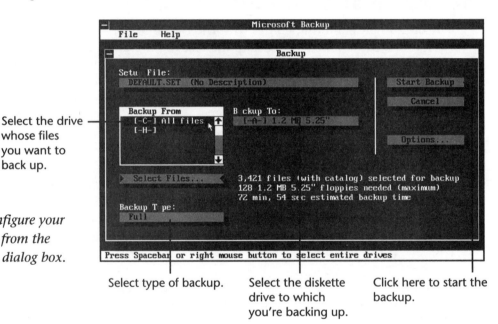

Select the drive whose files you want to back up.

You configure your backup from the Backup dialog box.

Select type of backup.   Select the diskette drive to which you're backing up.   Click here to start the backup.

1. Start by selecting the drive to back up in the Backup From box. Press **Tab** until the box is highlighted, use the arrow keys to highlight a drive, and then press the **Spacebar** to select it. If

you're using a mouse, click with the right mouse button on the drive to back up. MS Backup will display "All Files" next to the drive letter you select. Repeat for additional drives.

2. Change the drive to back up to, if necessary. If you are going to use diskettes of a different type or size than the one listed, change the drive letter in the Backup To box. Press **Tab** until the box is highlighted, and press **Enter** to display the selections. Use the arrow keys to select the drive, and then press **Enter**. If you're using a mouse, click on the box to display the selections, and then click on the drive you want to use. Click on the **OK** button when you are done.

3. When you're ready to go, select Start Backup by pressing **Tab** until it's highlighted and then pressing **Enter**. If you're using a mouse, click on the Start Backup button.

Performing an Incremental or Differential Backup

As you learned earlier in the chapter, DOS lets you do either a full or an incremental backup. When you do an incremental backup, MS Backup backs up the files that have been changed since the last backup (of any kind). That means that if you ever need to restore your entire hard disk, you not only need the diskettes from your last full backup, but the diskettes from every incremental backup you did after it. That can be a lot of diskettes!

Differential backup This type of backup, available with MS Backup, copies only the files that have been changed *since the last full backup*. To restore a complete hard disk, *you would need both your full and your latest differential backup diskettes*.

MS Backup provides an additional type of backup, called a *differential backup*. A differential backup saves you some disks by backing up all the files that have been changed since the last full backup, even if they were backed up already by an incremental or differential backup. This is cool because you don't have to keep the diskettes for each differential backup you do between full backups—only the most recent set.

Again, here's what you'd need:

Type of backup	What you'll need to restore data
Full	Full backup diskettes (the Full backup procedure updates the complete set of diskettes each time).
Incremental	Full backup diskettes and *each set* of incremental diskettes. Never reuse one set of incremental diskettes to perform another incremental backup. Keep the sets separate. When you do another Full backup, you can discard or reuse the incremental diskettes.
Differential	Full backup diskettes and the *latest set* of differential diskettes. When you do a differential backup, you update your original set of differential diskettes each time.

Performing an incremental or differential backup of your entire hard disk is easy. Start the backup process by typing **MSBACKUP** and pressing **Enter.**

Press **Enter** with the **Backup** box highlighted, and then follow these steps:

1. Start by selecting the drive to back up in the Backup From box. Press **Tab** until the box is highlighted, use the arrow keys to select a drive, and then press the **Spacebar**. If you're using a mouse, click with the right mouse button on the drive to back up. MS Backup will display "All Files" next to the drive letter you select. Repeat for additional drives.

2. Change the drive to back up to, if necessary. If you are going to use diskettes of a different type or size than the one listed, change the drive letter in the Backup To box. Press **Tab** until the box is highlighted, and press **Enter** to display the selections. Use the arrow keys to select the drive, and then press **Enter**. If you're using a mouse, click on the box to display the selections, and then click on the drive to use. Click **OK** when you are done.

3. Select **Incremental** or **Differential**. In the Backup Type box, select the type of backup you want. Press **Tab** until the box is highlighted, and press **Enter** to display the selections. Use the arrow keys to select the backup type, and then press **Enter**. If you're using a mouse, click on the Backup Type box to display the selections, and then click on the backup type to use. Click on the **OK** button when you are done.

4. When you're ready to go, select Start Backup by pressing **Tab** until it's highlighted and by pressing **Enter**. If you're using a mouse, click on the Start Backup box.

The Least You Need to Know

I was a horrible Girl Scout—whenever we'd go camping, my marshmallows would go up in flames, and I'd always come home with a case of poison ivy. But one thing about scouting stuck, and that's the motto, "Be prepared." You will be too, if you remember these things:

☞ Backing up your hard disk is a process that copies files onto a diskette or a backup tape in a special format. This process compresses the files so that more of them will fit on a diskette or a tape than would fit if you used the COPY command. By backing up important files onto a diskette or a tape, you can restore those files if the originals get damaged in some way.

☞ DOS versions prior to 6 support two different types of backups: full and incremental. In a full backup, all the files on the disk drive are copied onto diskettes. In an incremental backup, only the files that have been changed or created since the last backup are copied onto diskettes.

☞ To perform a full backup of drive C, type this command:

BACKUP C:*.* A: /S /L

continues

continued

☛ To perform an incremental backup of drive C, type this command:

BACKUP C:*.* A: /S /M /A /L

☛ To perform a full backup with DOS 6 something, type **MSBACKUP**, and press **Enter** to display the backup screen. Select the drive to back up, change the drive to back up to, and then select **S**tart Backup.

☛ To perform an incremental backup with DOS 6 something, type **MSBACKUP**, and press **Enter** to display the backup screen. Select the drive to back up, change the drive to back up to, and then select the backup type. Then select **S**tart Backup.

Chapter 15
Restoring Your Hard Disk

In This Chapter

- ☛ Restoring all your files when your hard disk goes belly up
- ☛ Restoring selected directories or files
- ☛ Restoring your sanity after your child's fifth birthday party
- ☛ Asking DOS to poke you before it restores a file
- ☛ Using the DOS 6 somethings to restore files

Okay, the worst has happened. You try to open an important document, and you're greeted with **Data error reading file**. Or worse yet, all the files on your hard disk have somehow been eaten by the latest computer virus. What do you do? Well, you thank your lucky stars that you read Chapter 14; then you just sit back, relax, and *restore* them. (Of course, if your PC has caught a virus, give it two aspirin, follow the directions in Chapter 18, and then restore the files.)

SPEAK LIKE A GEEK

Restore A process that copies files from a backup diskette or tape onto your hard disk. You perform the restore process when the files on your hard disk have been damaged in some way.

This chapter is divided into two sections: the first half is for users who don't have at least DOS 6, and the last half is for those who do. If you have one of the DOS 6 somethings (DOS 6, 6.2, 6.21, or 6.22), read the sections "This Section Should Not Be Removed Under Penalty of Law" and "Top 10 Reasons Why You'd Want to Restore Files," and then skip to the end of this chapter and read "Restoring Your Hard Disk with the DOS 6 Somethings." If you don't know what your DOS version is type **VER** and press **Enter**. Once you know what DOS version your PC is using, walk—don't run, to the appropriate section of this chapter.

This Section Should Not Be Removed Under Penalty of Law

Okay, here's the section that tells you all the stuff you could have learned in previous chapters but didn't, because why should you? I mean, that's what this book's for. Anyway, here's the usual list of things to know before preceding with this chapter:

With DOS 6 something, there's one command, MS BACKUP, that lets you both back up and restore. In prior DOS versions, backing up was done with BACKUP, while restoring was done with a separate command, called (quite appropriately) RESTORE.

Remember to press Enter to execute a command. Until you press Enter, nothing happens.

If you get the error message "Bad command or filename," you need a DOS path. See Chapter 4 for the complete lowdown.

The restore process restores files to a hard disk. You cannot restore files onto a diskette. If you think about it, there's no reason why you'd want to. Gosh, isn't it sorta comforting to know that DOS is capable of preventing you from doing those things you'd never want to do anyway. Now, if it would only prevent you from doing the things you shouldn't do....

Files are automatically restored into the directory from which they came. If a file is backed up from the \SALES directory, you can't restore it to the \MARKETG directory. (However, you *can* restore files onto a different drive, or onto a different computer.) Besides, after the files are restored, there's nothing stopping you from copying them to another directory. See Chapter 11 for details on the copying process.

There's a difference between COPY and the restore process. Backed-up files are compressed, so they're unusable until you *restore* them. Copied files are not compressed, so they are immediately usable wherever they are located. Also, you must restore backed-up files with the proper programs (RESTORE or MSBACKUP). You can't restore files using the COPY command.

You can perform different types of restore operations. You can restore all of your backed-up files, or only selected files or directories.

When you restore a file, it overlays the original on the hard disk. If the original file was unharmed and unchanged, and DOS overwrites it with the backup version of the same file, then no harm, no foul. You won't get any warning about this, so watch that you don't try to restore over top of a more recent version of your file—one that's been changed or amended with recent information since the time you performed your backup.

Top 10 Reasons Why You'd Want to Restore Files

David Letterman, look out, because here they come:

10. **Your hard disk is wiped out.** If human error or mechanical disaster trashes all your files, restore everything (see "When Your Hard Disk Kicks the Bit Bucket").

9. **A file becomes damaged and is unreadable.** When you pull up your file, instead of directions from the airport in Milwaukee, there are all these happy faces, arrows, and strange-looking U's.

8. **The power goes out while you're working on a document.** For example, if you were in the middle of an important save and a meteor suddenly struck your power lines, it would result in "a bit of a distraction."

7. **The boss changes his mind about the agenda and goes back from Plan B to Plan A.** You need to bring back Plan A from the depths. Lucky you made that backup.

6. **A bad spot develops on the hard disk where the file is located.** You can restore a single file or a whole directory (see "When Your Hard Disk Only Nicks the Bit Bucket" or "Restoring Selected Files and Directories").

5. **You have nothing better to do to kill time late on a Wednesday.** Face it, MSBACKUP is a far less violent activity for your computer than Mortal Kombat or Street Fighter.

4. **Windows messes up your files.** Please, you don't want to hear the full explanation; just accept the fact that it can happen.

3. **You buy a new PC and you want to transfer your files onto it.** Back up your files from one PC and restore them to another (see "When Your Hard Disk Kicks the Bit Bucket").

2. **Your new PC was a lemon and you need your files back on your old PC.** No real explanation needed here either, except the one that Uncle Dan's gonna have to give you on why he sold you that PC in the first place.

1. **Junior experiments with how many of those vinyl refrigerator magnets he can fit in the open drive bay.** Once you've salvaged your hardware, you'll want to perform an MSBACKUP restore *just in case* something's lost.

Well here it is, for what's it worth. Believe me, if your files are damaged, you're not going to need ten reasons why you'd want to restore them.

If you see the error message **Bad command or filename,** you need to set up a DOS path in order to use the RESTORE command. For now, type **PATH=C:\DOS.** For more info on paths, see Chapter 4.

When Your Hard Disk Kicks the Bit Bucket

Don't get me wrong: with utilities like Norton Utilities, PC Tools, and Mace Utilities, it's rare that your hard disk konks out so completely that you have to restore the whole thing. So before you attempt the whole process, get a PC guru to check your system first. Maybe the problem can be fixed without restoring everything.

However, this doesn't mean that you shouldn't perform backups and keep them current. Having a complete backup of your hard disk is like having accident insurance. When disaster strikes, you'll be glad you kept up your premiums. To restore your hard disk, use this command:

RESTORE A: C:*.* /S

That's *RESTORE space A colon space C colon backslash asterisk period asterisk space forward slash S.* This command tells DOS to "Restore all the files on drive C, beginning with the root directory." You'll be prompted to place the first backup diskette in drive A, so do that and press **Enter**. As the restore progresses, you'll be prompted to replace the first diskette with other diskettes until the entire drive is restored.

What If I Have Another Disk Drive?

If you need to restore a PC that has more than one disk drive, you'll need to perform two restore processes: one for C, the other for D. When you backed up your system, you created a second set of backup diskettes for the extra drive. To restore drive D using the second set of backup diskettes, use this command:

RESTORE A: D:*.* /S

and press **Enter**. Insert the first diskette in the second set of backups, and away you go!

When Your Hard Disk Only Nicks the Bit Bucket

If you accidentally break a finger, you don't amputate your hand—you just put a splint on it. The same thing's true of your hard drive; if only a single file has been damaged, you don't have to restore an entire hard disk, just the one file. Use this command to restore the file DAMAGED.DOC to your \WORD directory:

RESTORE A: C:\WORD\DAMAGED.DOC

That's *RESTORE space A colon space C colon backslash WORD backslash DAMAGED period DOC.* This command tells DOS to "Restore the file DAMAGED.DOC to drive C, into the \WORD directory." You'll need to dig out your full backup set and place the requested diskette into drive A. Because large files can be split onto several diskettes, you may be prompted for other diskettes in the backup set as well.

Restoring a Single Directory

If you're having problems with a particular directory, you may want to restore only that directory and any of its subdirectories. Use this command to restore the \PROJECTS directory and all of its subdirectories:

RESTORE A: C:\PROJECTS*.* /S

This command tells DOS to "Restore the directory \PROJECTS on drive C, and all its subdirectories, and while you're up, get me another beer."

When you use the /M switch with the RESTORE command, files that have been deleted since the last backup will be restored also.

Restoring Only the Files That Have Not Been Changed

Suppose you wanted to restore a directory, but not overlay any files that have changed since the backup was done. In other words, you don't want to overlay newer versions of your files with old ones stored on your last backup. Follow this command to restore only *unmodified* files to the \PROJECTS directory:

RESTORE A: C:\PROJECTS*.* /S /M

That's *RESTORE space A colon space C colon backslash PROJECTS backslash asterisk period asterisk space forward slash S space forward slash M.* Whew! The command you just typed tells DOS to "Restore only the files that *have not been modified since the last backup* to the \PROJECTS directory and all of its subdirectories." The /M switch limits the restore process to the files that have not been modified since the last backup. (In the original Sanskrit, this command meant, "All hail to the Daughter of His Royal Highness and Her Royal Hunting Poodles.")

Sometimes It's Nice to Be Asked

To have the most control over the restoration process, you can ask to be prompted before any file is restored. Using our \PROJECTS example, here's the command you would use:

RESTORE A: C:\PROJECTS*.* /S /P

This command translates to "Restore the \PROJECTS directory and all of its subdirectories to drive C, but please prompt me before restoring each file you dumb thing, or I'll cut off your legs, pretty please." The use of the /P switch causes a prompt to appear before any file is restored. Press **Y** to restore a file, or **N** to bypass it.

Restoring Your Hard Disk with the DOS 6 Somethings

As you may recall from the previous chapter (yeah, I'm sure you memorized it), the backup and restore program that comes with the DOS 6 somethings (DOS 6, 6.2, etc.) is called MS Backup. You can use the MS Backup program with either a mouse or the keyboard. To "restore" your memory of how to use a mouse, here's a quick refresher:

Click To click with the mouse, move the mouse pointer over the selection and press the mouse button once.

Double-click To double-click with the mouse, move the mouse pointer over the selection and press the mouse button twice in rapid succession.

Restoring the Hard Disk and Your Sanity

A full restore will restore all of the files from your backup diskettes to your hard disk. To perform a full restore, type **MSBACKUP** and press **Enter**.

If you see the error message **Bad command or filename,** you need to set up a DOS path in order to use the MSBACKUP command. For now, type **PATH=C:\DOS.** For more info on paths, see Chapter 4.

Select the diskette drive
from which to restore.

Click here to start the
restore.

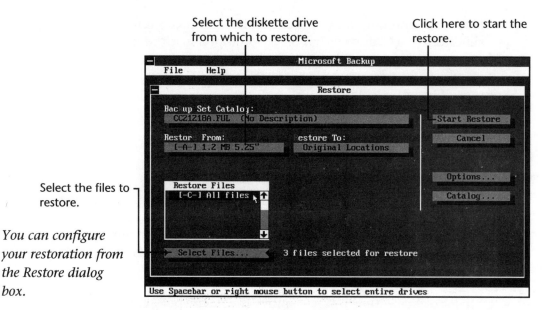

Select the files to
restore.

*You can configure
your restoration from
the Restore dialog
box.*

Click on the Restore button, or press **Tab** until it is highlighted, and
then press **Enter**. You'll see the screen where you'll make all your selections.

1. **Start by selecting the drive to restore in the Restore Files box.**
   Set this to the drive letter that the files were originally backed up
   from, regardless of whether you want to restore the files to another drive. Press **Tab** until the box is highlighted, use the arrow
   keys to select a drive, and then press the **Spacebar**. If you're using
   a mouse, click with the right mouse button on the drive to
   restore. MS Backup will display "All Files" next to the drive letter
   you select. Repeat for additional drives.

2. **Change the diskette drive to restore from, if necessary.** If you
   are going to use diskettes of a different type or size than the one
   listed, change the drive letter in the Restore From box. Press **Tab**
   until the box is highlighted, and press **Enter** to display the
   selections. Use the arrow keys to select the drive, and then press
   Enter. If you're using a mouse, click on the box to display the
   selections, and then click on the drive to use. Click on the **OK**
   button when you are done.

3. **Change the drive to restore to, if necessary**. Only if you want to restore files *to a different drive from which they were backed up*, use the Restore To button. Press **Tab** until the box is highlighted, and press **Enter** to display the selections. Use the arrow keys to select Other Drives or Other Directories, and then press **Enter**. If you're using a mouse, click on the box to display the selections. Then click either Other Drives or Other Directories. Click on the **OK** button when you are done.

4. **When you're ready to go, select Start Restore**. Press **Tab** until Start Restore is highlighted and press **Enter**. If you're using a mouse, click on the Start Restore button.

Restoring Selected Files and Directories

If only certain files or directories are damaged, you can restore only what you need. Start the restore process by typing **MSBACKUP** and pressing **Enter**.

Click on the Restore button, or press **Tab** until it is highlighted, and then press **Enter**. Follow steps 1–3 in the previous section to select the drive to restore and the diskette drive. Then follow these steps:

1. **Select the file(s) to restore**. Press **Tab** until the Select Files box is highlighted, and then press **Enter** to display the Select Restore Files dialog box. If you are using a mouse, click on the Select Files button. Select the files or directories you want to restore. Selected directories are displayed with an arrow. If all the files in a directory are not selected, the directory is displayed with a double-arrow. Selected files are displayed with a check mark.

   Using a mouse, click with the right mouse button on any file or directory to select it. To select multiple files or directories at once, press **Ctrl** as you click on them.

   Using the keyboard, press **Tab** to move between the directory and file sections. Move the highlight with the arrow keys, and then press the **Spacebar** to select an item.

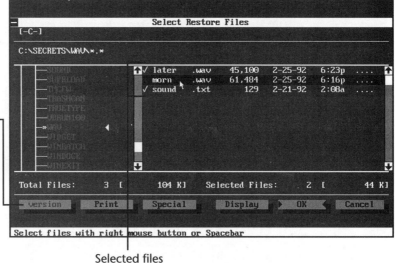

Selected directory ―

Restore selected files and directories with the Select Restore Files dialog box.

Selected files

2. Select **OK** to return to the Restore Window.

3. When you're ready to go, select **Start** Restore. Press **Tab** until **Start** Restore is highlighted and press **Enter**. If you're using a mouse, click on the **Start** Restore button.

The Least You Need to Know

When you've got a sick hard disk, you want to get it "well" as soon as possible—and you will, if you remember these things:

☞ When you restore your hard disk, DOS copies files from a backup diskette or tape onto your hard disk. You perform the restore process when your original files have been damaged in some way.

If you don't use at least DOS 6, follow these instructions to restore all or part of your hard disk:

☞ To restore a full backup of drive C, type this command:

   RESTORE A: C:*.* /S

☞ To restore a single file, such as GOODCOPY.DOC to the directory \WORD\DOCS on drive C, type this command:

**RESTORE A:
C:\WORD\DOCS\GOODCOPY.DOC**

☞ To restore a single directory, such as the \WORKS directory, and all of its subdirectories, use this command:

RESTORE A: C:\WORKS*.* /S

☞ To restore only files that have not changed since the last backup was done, use something like this:

RESTORE A: C:*.* /S /M

☞ To restore files after being prompted, use something like this:

RESTORE A: C:*.* /S /P

If you have one of the DOS 6 somethings, follow these instructions to restore all or part of your hard disk:

☞ To restore a full backup with one of the DOS 6 somethings, start by typing this command:

MSBACKUP

Select the **Restore** button to display the Restore screen. Next, select the drive to restore, change the drive to restore from, change the drive to restore to, and then select **OK**. Select **S**tart Restore.

☞ To restore only selected files and directories with DOS 6, 6.2, 6.21, or 6.22, start by typing this command:

MSBACKUP

Select the **Restore** button to display the Restore screen. Next, select the drive to restore, change the drive to restore from, change the drive to restore to, and then select the files or directories to restore. When you're ready, select **S**tart Restore.

"Look, another blank page!"

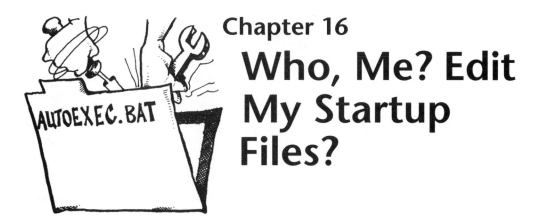

Chapter 16

Who, Me? Edit My Startup Files?

In This Chapter

- ☛ Easy ways to change your AUTOEXEC.BAT and CONFIG.SYS, I promise!
- ☛ Using EDIT or EDLIN without fear
- ☛ Exercising your editorial prerogative
- ☛ Saving your changes
- ☛ *Not* saving your changes
- ☛ Saving it for a rainy day

Just like a car, to help your PC run at its best, you have to do a little maintenance. This includes fine-tuning your PC's engine (adjusting the AUTOEXEC.BAT and CONFIG.SYS files) so your PC runs the way you want it to. Some changes to these files are necessary to make certain programs run at their best, and others are needed to make certain programs run at all. Some programs make their own changes to the AUTOEXEC.BAT or CONFIG.SYS automatically during installation, while others ask you to do it. (Can you believe the nerve?) Lastly, there are some changes you'll want to make for yourself.

The bottom line is this: at one point or another, you're going to be faced with the problem of editing either your AUTOEXEC.BAT, CONFIG.SYS, or some other file (unless you're lucky enough to always be able to find somebody else to do it). In this chapter, you'll learn the most painless ways to edit your startup files. After you start feeling a bit brave, continue on to Chapter 17, where you'll learn all about the kind of commands every AUTOEXEC.BAT and CONFIG.SYS should have.

If you have at least DOS 5, you can use EDIT, which is very simple and easy to use. EDIT is covered at the beginning of this chapter. If you don't have at least DOS 5, then you get to use a simple, but silly looking editor called EDLIN, covered at the end of this chapter.

If you don't know what DOS version your PC is using, type **VER** and press Enter. The DOS version will be displayed. If your PC is using DOS 4 or less, go to back of this chapter for help. Otherwise, read on.

Pssst! Before You Edit . . .

When you edit your configuration files, keep these things in mind:

☞ Do not edit CONFIG.SYS or AUTOEXEC.BAT without an emergency diskette handy. To create an emergency diskette, pop a blank diskette in drive A, then enter these commands, one at a time, pressing **Enter** after each command:

> **FORMAT A: /S /V**
> **COPY C:\AUTOEXEC.BAT A:**
> **COPY C:\CONFIG.SYS A:**

If you want to know more about this emergency diskette business, see Chapter 6.

☞ You'll find your CONFIG.SYS and AUTOEXEC.BAT (if they exist) in the root directory of your *boot drive*.

☞ If you make changes to a configuration file, make sure you reboot your PC (press the **Ctrl+Alt+Del** keys at the same time) to make those changes take effect.

Boot Drive   Your boot drive isthe drive which contains your operating system files, usually drive C.

Creating Your First File

So you can practice your editing without any fears, we'll start by creating a fake AUTOEXEC.BAT file for you to practice with. To do that, let me introduce you to a very old command called COPY CON. With this command, you can create a file by typing directly from the keyboard. So, type this, pressing **Enter** after each line:

```
CD\
COPY CON: FAKEEXEC.BAT
C:\DOS\SMARTDRV.EXE
SET PCPLUS=C:\PCPLUS
SET TEMP=C:\TEMP
```

After typing the text for the file, press **F6**, then press **Enter** to close the file and save it.

If you make a mistake, press **F6** and start over. While you're typing, you may notice that your DOS prompt seems to have disappeared. Don't worry—the prompt will come back when you press **F6** and **Enter** to save the file.

COPY CON works great to create a file, but it has two problems: you can't make changes to an existing file with it, and if you make a mistake, you have to start over. The two editing programs you'll learn about in this chapter, EDIT and EDLIN, overcome these difficulties by actually letting you *edit* (make changes) to what you type—what a concept!

Well, now that you have your practice file all nice and ready, let's tear it apart!

EDIT, the Cinemascope Editor

If you have at least DOS 5, you've lucked out because it comes with an easy-to-use, full-screen technicolor text editor called EDIT. As an added bonus, there's hardly anything you need to learn in order to edit simple files such as CONFIG.SYS and AUTOEXEC.BAT.

One of the most common commands you add to your AUTOEXEC.BAT file is the PROMPT command. The PROMPT command changes the default

DOS prompt from something boring like C>, to something fancy, like this one, which displays the current drive and directory:

C:\WORD\DOCS>

Let's add this command (and others) to our configuration file, using EDIT. We'll practice on FAKEEXEC.BAT (instead of the real AUTOEXEC.BAT); you can modify your real AUTOEXEC.BAT later, after you feel comfortable.

Let's Get Started

Because it's not a real configuration file, the changes you make to FAKEEXEC.BAT will not permanently change the way your computer runs (hint: that's a good thing). To start EDIT in order to make changes to FAKEEXEC.BAT, type this and press **Enter:**

EDIT C:\FAKEEXEC.BAT

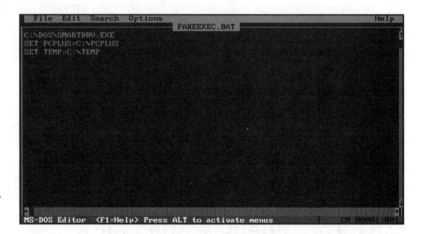

Our FAKEEXEC.BAT file is ready to edit.

This command tells DOS to "Start the EDIT program and open the file FAKEEXEC.BAT in the root directory of drive C." If you didn't create the FAKEEXEC.BAT file earlier, and you enter this command, DOS assumes you want to create a new file. EDIT opens with a blank screen titled

FAKEEXEC.BAT, in which you can type the file contents. (Turn back to the project to see what to type.)

EDIT Lets You Really Move

Once a file is open, you can make changes to it. Although there are many ways to move around the screen, we don't plan on being in this file long enough to care. Just to satisfy the overly curious, here are a few tips on moving around in a file:

To move:	Press:
Up, down, left, or right	Arrow keys
To the beginning of a line	Home key
To the end of a line	End key

When you start the DOS 6 something editor, you start out in *Insert mode*. This means that whatever you type is inserted at the cursor (that blinking box). To insert a new line, move to the beginning of an existing line *below* where you want to insert the new line and press **Enter**. The new line appears above the existing line you chose.

SPEAK LIKE A GEEK

Insert mode The default mode for word processors and text editors. Insert mode means that when you position your cursor and start to type, what you type is inserted at that point.

Overtype mode The opposite of Insert mode, as used in word processors and text editors. Overtype mode means that when you position your cursor and start to type, what you type replaces existing characters at that point.

If you want to type over existing characters, press the **Insert** key. You are now in *Overtype mode*. When you move the cursor to a point in the file and start typing, what you type replaces (overlays) the characters at that point. To return to Insert mode, press the **Insert** key again. If you want to delete some characters, position your cursor on top of any character, and press the **Delete** key.

Let's insert our two commands after the line **C:\DOS\SMARTDRV.EXE**. Move to the S in SET on line two by using the down arrow key, then press **Enter** to create a blank line. Move back up to the blank line by using the up arrow key, then type this line:

PROMPT PG

Press **Enter** to start a new line, and then type this:

PATH=C:\DOS

The first command, PROMPT PG, changes your prompt so that it displays the current drive and directory. The second command, PATH=C:\DOS, provides access to certain DOS commands such as EDIT.

If you accidentally create an extra blank line, move to that line and press **Delete**.

Now our practice file looks like this:

C:\DOS\SMARTDRV.EXE
PROMPT PG
PATH=C:\DOS
SET PCPLUS=C:\PCPLUS
SET TEMP=C:\TEMP

Now, for some more practice. Let's say you've re-installed the ProComm Plus program into a new directory called D:\UTILITY. You need to change the SET command to reflect this. Position the cursor to the *right* of the equal sign in SET PCPLUS=C:\PCPLUS, on top of the letter C. Press the **Insert** key, and you are in Overtype mode. Type **D:\UTILITY** *over top of* the letters C:\PCPLUS. Our finished FAKEEXEC.BAT file now looks like this:

C:\DOS\SMARTDRV.EXE
PROMPT PG
PATH=C:\DOS
SET PCPLUS=D:\UTILITY
SET TEMP=C:\TEMP

Good Idea #102: Saving All Your Hard Work

After making changes to your edited file, you must save it before exiting the editor (otherwise, you'll lose all changes to the file). If you don't want to save any changes at all, skip to the next section. To save your changes:

1. Open the File menu by clicking on it (press the left mouse button while the pointer is on the word File) or by pressing the **Alt** and **F** keys.

2. Select the Save command by clicking on it or by pressing **S**.

3. If you want to keep your original file intact (without changes) and save this file under a new name, click on the Save As command instead, or press **A**. Type the new file name and press **Enter**.

Exiting the DOS 6 Editor

After you've saved your changes, you can safely exit the editor.

1. Open the File menu by clicking on it or by pressing the **Alt** and **F** keys at the same time.

2. Select the Exit command by clicking on it or by pressing X. If you haven't saved your file yet, you'll be asked one more time if you want to save the changes (can't DOS take a hint?) Anyway, click on Yes to save the file, or No to lose the changes you've made to it.

You can run your FAKEEXEC.BAT file by typing these two commands, pressing **Enter** after each one:

CD
FAKEEXEC

The commands in the FAKEEXEC.BAT are real DOS commands, just like the ones you might want in your actual AUTOEXEC.BAT. By running the FAKEEXEC batch file, you may have changed some system parameters that were set up by your real AUTOEXEC.BAT, so reboot your PC (press **Ctrl+Alt+Delete** at the same time) to reset your computer to the way it was.

When you're done playing with it, delete the FAKEEXEC.BAT file so it won't cause any mix-ups by typing **DEL C:\FAKEEXEC.BAT** and pressing **Enter**. Goodbye file!

Meet Old Mr. EDLIN

If you don't have at least DOS 5, you get to use a simple—if a bit eccentric—editor called EDLIN to create and edit text files. But have no fear: There are only a few things you need to know in order to use old Mr. EDLIN to edit simple files, such as CONFIG.SYS and AUTOEXEC.BAT, and you can forget what you learn as soon as you're done.

One of the most common commands you add to your AUTOEXEC.BAT file is the PROMPT command. The PROMPT command changes the default DOS prompt from something boring like C>, to something fancy, like this, which displays the current drive and directory:

C:\WORD\DOCS>

Let's add this command to our configuration file using EDLIN. Use FAKEEXEC.BAT if you're a beginner, and then modify AUTOEXEC.BAT later, after you've learned the basic steps in editing a file.

Get Started with EDLIN

Having created our FAKEEXEC.BAT file earlier, we can now experiment without having to worry. If you didn't create the practice file, take two steps back to the beginning of this chapter, then come back here when you're done.

To start EDLIN in order to make changes to FAKEEXEC.BAT, type **EDLIN C:\FAKEEXEC.BAT.**

This command tells DOS to "Start the EDLIN program and open the file FAKEEXEC.BAT in the root directory of drive C." When you start EDLIN, the regular DOS prompt is replaced by an asterisk. You type commands at the asterisk to edit the file. Because you are editing an existing file, you will see this:

EDLIN C:\FAKEEXEC.BAT
End of input file
*

Oops, I Didn't Create the Practice File!

If you've created the practice file FAKEEXEC.BAT like you were supposed to, skip this section. If you didn't create the FAKEEXEC.BAT file earlier, and you enter this command, DOS assumes you want to create a new file.

EDLIN displays the words, **New file**, followed by an asterisk. Then to begin working on a new file, you must start in Insert mode. Type the letter **I** and press **Enter** and you'll see this:

1:*

Turn back to the project to see what to type. When you've typed the three lines, press **Enter** to start another line. Now, press **Ctrl** and **C** at the same time. You've now left Insert mode and returned to Edit mode, so you can proceed now with the rest of the class. You'll learn more about Insert mode in the sections "Inserting New Lines" and "Getting Out of Insert Mode."

When It's Time for a Change

Let's go back to editing the FAKEEXEC.BAT file. After the file is loaded, start by listing the file's contents. Type **L** and press **Enter**. EDLIN shows a line-by-line listing of the file's contents.

Edlin prompt

The L command causes the file to be listed line by line.

EDLIN lists a file's contents line by line when you use the L command.

With EDLIN, you edit files line by line, which is where EDLIN gets its name, "**Ed**it by **lin**e." Each line is assigned a number. This number becomes important, as we'll soon see.

Because the first part of the SET PCPLUS line was a repeat of the existing text (SET PCPLUS=), you could have pressed the right arrow key 11 times (or just held it down) to make EDLIN type the first 11 characters of the line for you.

Changing Your Mind Lines

Let's say you've re-installed the ProComm Plus program into a new directory called D:\UTILITY. You need to change the SET command on line 2 to reflect this. At the prompt (the asterisk), type **2** and press **Enter**. Line 2 appears, ready to edit:

```
2:*SET PCPLUS=C:\PCPLUS
2:*
```

EDLIN is waiting for you to type in the new line. Type this after the asterisk:

```
SET PCPLUS=D:\UTILITY
```

and press **Enter**. Now, list the contents of the file so you can see what's happening. Type **L** and press **Enter**, and you'll see this:

```
1: C:\DOS\SMARTDRV.EXE
2:*SET PCPLUS=D:\UTILITY
3: SET TEMP=C:\TEMP
```

By the way, the asterisk in front of line 2 means that it's the current line. If we're not specific about what line we want to edit, we could end up editing line 2 again. Oops!

Inserting New Lines

Now, let's add a couple of lines to the FAKEEXEC.BAT, at the top of the file. To insert a line, type the number that you want the new line to be, followed by the letter I. (The existing line with that number moves down.) We want to insert some commands above the SET PCPLUS=C:\UTILITY line, which is line 2. Type **2I** and press **Enter**. You'll see this:

```
2:*
```

Now, type these three commands after the asterisk, pressing **Enter** after each one:

```
PROMPT $P$G
PATH=C:\DOS
BOGUS COMMAND
```

The first command, PROMPT PG, changes your prompt so that it displays the current drive and directory. The second command, PATH=C:\DOS, provides access to certain DOS commands like EDIT. The last command is totally fake and it's there so you can practice deleting it. After typing these commands, press **Enter**, and you'll see this:

```
2:*PROMPT $P$G
3:*PATH=C:\DOS
4:*BOGUS COMMAND
5:*
```

Getting Out of Insert Mode

When you're done inserting lines, you must turn off Insert mode. With your cursor on line 5 (a blank line), press the **Ctrl** and **C** keys at the same time. You'll be returned to the asterisk prompt. You are now out of Insert mode. Let's list the contents of our file. Type **L** and press **Enter**. You'll see:

```
1: C:\DOS\SMARTDRV.EXE
2: PROMPT $P$G
3: PATH=C:\DOS
4: BOGUS COMMAND
5:*SET PCPLUS=D:\UTILITY
6: SET TEMP=C:\TEMP
```

All right so far? Good. Let's move on...

Deleting a Line

Let's delete the BOGUS COMMAND line. When we listed out our file, the BOGUS COMMAND was line 4. To delete a line, type the number of the line to delete, followed by the letter D. Type **4D** and press **Enter**. As soon as you

Insert mode is different in EDLIN than in EDIT. In EDIT, Insert mode means the existing characters move over to make room for what you type. Because EDLIN is line-based, Insert mode means that you're inserting entire lines; whole lines move down to make room for new lines you enter.

Always, *always* re-list the file after you have added or deleted lines. Line numbers shift when you add or delete, so the previous number assignments aren't accurate anymore, even though you may still see it on your screen.

If you were to type 3D for example, you could end up deleting the wrong line, unless you know for sure which line is number 3. And the only way to know that is to list the lines in the file with the L command.

delete a line of text, you should list out your file, because the remaining lines get renumbered. Type **L** and press **Enter**. You'll see:

    1: C:\DOS\SMARTDRV.EXE
    2: PROMPT PG
    3: PATH=C:\DOS
    4:*SET PCPLUS=D:\UTILITY
    5: SET TEMP=C:\TEMP

Saving Your File

When you're finished editing, you can save and exit both in one step. Type **E** and press **Enter**. The letter E means End, which saves your file and exits you from EDLIN. You are returned to the DOS prompt.

TECHNO NERD TEACHES...

You can run your FAKEEXEC.BAT file by typing

    CD
    FAKEEXEC

The commands in the FAKEEXEC.BAT are real DOS commands, just like the ones you might want in your actual AUTOEXEC.BAT. By running the FAKEEXEC batch file, you may have changed some system parameters that were set up by your real AUTOEXEC.BAT, so reboot your PC (press **Ctrl+Alt+Delete** all at the same time) to reset your computer to the way it was.

When you're done playing with it, delete the FAKEEXEC.BAT file so it won't cause any mix-ups by typing

    DEL C:\FAKEEXEC.BAT

Not Saving Your File

Sometimes, you make some mistakes in a file (especially with deleting), and you want to abort your changes and just get out of there. Type **Q** and press **Enter**. The letter Q means Quit. When you quit a file, you see the message, **Abort edit (Y/N)?**. Type **Y**, and your changes are abandoned (everything since starting EDLIN). Exit EDLIN and return to the DOS prompt.

The Least You Need to Know

Editing my configuration files used to give me chills until I learned these things:

☛ You should save your configuration files to your existing emergency diskette before editing them. Type

  COPY C:\AUTOEXEC.BAT A:
  COPY C:\CONFIG.SYS A:

☛ If you have at least DOS 5, you can edit files with EDIT. To start EDIT, type **EDIT** followed by the name of a file.

☛ To save a file in Edit, press **Alt** and **F** to open the **File** menu. Press **S** to save the file.

☛ To exit EDIT, press **Alt** and **F** to open the **File** menu. Press **X** to exit.

☛ If you don't have at least DOS 5, use EDLIN to edit a file. To start EDLIN, type **EDLIN** followed by the name of a file.

☛ To save a file and exit EDLIN, type **E** and press **Enter.**

☛ To abandon a file and not save the changes in EDLIN, type **Q.** When you see the message **Abort (Y/N)?,** press **Y.**

What a waste it is to lose a page.

Chapter 17

AUTOEXEC.BAT, CONFIG.SYS, and Other DOS Mysteries

In This Chapter

- ☞ The real secret of startup, revealed!
- ☞ Stuff to make life with DOS much easier
- ☞ Tim Allen's tips for making your AUTOEXEC.BAT and CONFIG.SYS scream to the extreme
- ☞ Ginsu tips for cutting through your configuration files
- ☞ Interrupting your PC while it's trying to start

Actually, I debated about including this chapter. I mean, no sane person wants to know more than they might need to *about anything*, especially AUTOEXEC.BAT and CONFIG.SYS. But then I thought, one of the scariest things about using a PC is *not knowing*. Not knowing what's going on, not knowing whether something's about to blow up in your face, not knowing how the last season of Star Trek is going to end.

So you can skip this chapter if you want; I won't be offended. Really. But if you stay, you'll learn the answer to the questions that have been puzzling mankind for generations, such as: What are all these things in my CONFIG.SYS and my AUTOEXEC.BAT? What are they doing there? And why would anyone pay good money to see Madonna in concert?

By the way, after you learn all these cool things about your PC's configuration files (CONFIG.SYS and AUTOEXEC.BAT), then you can go back to Chapter 16 and edit them (or bribe someone else to) if you want.

If you decide make any changes to either your AUTOEXEC.BAT or your CONFIG.SYS, then reboot your computer by pressing the **Ctrl+Alt+Del** keys at the same time. Your changes won't take effect until you do.

What Is the AUTOEXEC.BAT?

The AUTOEXEC.BAT is a special file that *automatically executes* commands when you boot (start) your PC. By placing commands in the AUTOEXEC.BAT, you can make changes to the way DOS works. Since DOS made changes to the way you used to work, this is only fair. With the right commands in your AUTOEXEC.BAT, you can even make your computer automatically start your favorite program (such as one that you use every day), while you go get some coffee. Just turn on your PC, and whatever commands are in the AUTOEXEC.BAT, DOS just carries them out, quick as you please. It's like having your own PC butler.

The AUTOEXEC.BAT is placed in the root directory of your boot drive, which is usually drive C. So you go to the root directory to locate your AUTOEXEC.BAT, view its contents, and edit it if you want.

Taking a Look Inside Your AUTOEXEC.BAT

Let's check out what your AUTOEXEC.BAT has in it. To view your AUTOEXEC.BAT file, type **TYPE C:\AUTOEXEC.BAT** and press **Enter:**

```
C:\>type autoexec.bat
LH /L:0,1,45456 /S C:\DOS\SMARTDRV.EXE
LH /L:1,13984 C:\DOS\SHARE.EXE /l:500 /f:5100

c:\windows\AD_WRAP.COM

SET PCPLUS=C:\PCPLUS
@ECHO OFF
PROMPT $p$g
PATH C:\DOS;C:\WINDOWS;C:\BIN\WORD;H:\NC;H:\COLLAGE
SET TEMP=C:\windows\temp


C:\DOS\MOUSE

C:\>
```

Here's what a typical AUTOEXEC.BAT file might look like.

Remember that the commands in your AUTOEXEC.BAT are listed *in the order in which they will be carried out.* So if you want something to happen before something else, you've got to place that command in front of the others in your AUTOEXEC.BAT. Here are some of the typical commands you might find in an AUTOEXEC.BAT, along with a brief explanation about what they do:

The ECHO Command

ECHO is not actually a command, at least not in the true sense of the word. You could type ECHO at the DOS prompt a million times, and it wouldn't do anything. ECHO has no purpose except within the AUTOEXEC.BAT (or other *batch files*).

You might see something like this in your AUTOEXEC.BAT file:

ECHO Welcome to the wonderful world of PCs.

Batch Files   A batch file has the filename extension of .BAT, so they are easy to identify. Batch files contain a number of commands *batched* together in one file. You create batch files to perform several commands in sequence for you, saving you the trouble of typing each command yourself.

The ECHO command causes its message to display on-screen, when DOS gets to that point in the AUTOEXEC.BAT file. You might also see this command, which is usually the first command in the AUTOEXEC.BAT:

@ECHO OFF

Why the @ sign? It tells DOS not to show the ECHO OFF command itself on the screen. Without the @ sign, the words ECHO OFF appear on-screen, and *then* the command turns ECHO to OFF mode.

This command tells ECHO *not* to display typical messages as the commands in the AUTOEXEC.BAT are carried out. With this command in place, you won't see what commands the AUTOEXEC.BAT file is performing, only the results of those commands. This makes your startup process look prettier, because a lot of junk is not being displayed.

TECHNO NERD TEACHES...

Even when ECHO is OFF, you can still use the ECHO command to type words on the screen. You just won't see the command to ECHO them; you'll only see the result. For example, when ECHO is ON, and you have the line:

ECHO Hello there!

in your batch file, here's what you'll see as the batch file executes:

ECHO Hello there!
Hello there!

If you set ECHO to OFF, then include the ECHO Hello there! command, you'll see this instead:

Hello there!

which is probably what you wanted in the first place, right?

The PATH Command

This is one command you should be familiar with by now. The PATH command provides DOS with a list of directories to search, when a command or a program is not located in the current directory. In Chapter 4 you learned that you need a PATH statement like this in order to access the external DOS commands such as FORMAT, DISKCOPY, MSBACKUP, etc.:

PATH=C:\DOS

Your actual path command may be a lot longer. That's OK. Your PATH command can include lots of additional directories, simply by separating them with a semi-colon ; (notice that I didn't say to add any *spaces*; you just run the list together like some long "path-worm"):

PATH=C:\DOS;C:\WINDOWS;C:\NU

The SMARTDrive Command

This command was discussed in Chapter 5, but since you may have slept since then, here's a review of what the SMARTDrive command does. First, the command itself is placed in your PC's AUTOEXEC.BAT by the DOS setup program, so you probably didn't put it there. Now, what does it do? Well, the SMARTDrive command creates a RAM *cache*, which basically makes your hard disk faster at getting files and/or saving them (*reading* and *writing*). Here's what your SMARTDrive command might look like:

C:\DOS\SMARTDRV.EXE

If you see something like this instead:

LH /L:0;2,45456 /S C:\DOS\SMARTDRV.EXE

then someone has run MemMaker to create the best memory-fit for SMARTDrive. The codes are harmless, but you *shouldn't try to change them*, since they mean a whole lot to MemMaker. By the way, MemMaker is a utility that gets the most out of your computer's memory, and you can look for it in Chapter 20.

RAM Cache   An area of RAM (memory) which stores copies of the most often requested files. Files in RAM are quicker to access than files on disk. By keeping often-requested files in RAM, your PC's hard disk can retrieve files a whole lot faster. A RAM cache can also be used to collect files that need to be written (saved) on the hard disk, so that it can be done in one step instead of lots of short trips to the hard disk to save one file, then another.

The PROMPT Command

As you learned in Chapter 7, the PROMPT command customizes the DOS prompt. Like Cinderella's godmother, it transforms the normal dusty DOS prompt:

> C>

into the beautiful star of the ball, such as something like this:

> C:\>

And just like Cinderella, the prompt changes back into its dusty old self, not at midnight, but when the PC is restarted. That is, unless you place the PROMPT command of your choice in your PC's AUTOEXEC.BAT file. This is one of the most popular variations of the PROMPT command which perhaps is already in your AUTOEXEC.BAT:

> **PROMPT PG**

The DATE and TIME Commands

You might see these commands in your AUTOEXEC.BAT:

> **DATE**

or

> **TIME**

They too, are pretty harmless. What are they doing? Well, when you start your PC, they cause something like this to display:

> **Current date is Thu 07-16-1994**
> **Enter new date (mm-dd-yy):**

If the date's correct, just press **Enter**; if not, type a new date. The purpose of these commands is to check to make sure that your PC knows the correct date and/or time. Most PCs keep track of this stuff automatically, but occasionally their batteries will wear down and they'll need replacing. Watching to see when your PC starts to get the date wrong will tell you when to replace the battery. So having these two commands in your AUTOEXEC.BAT file is pretty helpful.

TSRs or Terminate and Stay Resident Programs

TSRs are special utility programs which load into memory and then "go to sleep" until they are "awakened" by some event or a magic kiss. The virus detection program that you'll learn about in Chapter 18, VSAFE, is a TSR. When it's loaded into memory through the AUTOEXEC.BAT, it goes to sleep until it detects a bizarre change to one of your files, which might indicate a computer virus at work.

You might have other TSRs loading from your AUTOEXEC.BAT, and if you followed the instructions in Chapter 18 to load the DOS virus protection program, you might see these commands in your AUTOEXEC.BAT:

SPEAK LIKE A GEEK

Virus A computer virus is a program that vandalizes your system. The worst viruses destroy data and render your computer helpless. Other viruses are content with displaying strange messages, but they do no actual damage. A virus can enter your system through an infected diskette or an infected file that has been downloaded (received through a modem) from another computer.

```
MSAV /N
VSAFE
```

The first command scans for active viruses at startup, and the second command runs the TSR which maintains its constant (if sleepy) vigil over your PC.

Commands Which Load Programs for You

There are endless possibilities here for automation. You can place any regular sequence of commands which you normally type to start a program, into your AUTOEXEC.BAT instead. That way, the program is started for you when you turn on or reboot your PC. Under DOS rules, however, you can only start one application at a time, so pick the one you use every day. For example, if you use WordPerfect, you might add these two commands to your AUTOEXEC.BAT:

CD\WP51
WP

In addition, you might see this command, which loads a special program for your mouse:

CD\DOS\MOUSE.COM

If you have Windows, you might see this instead:

CD\WINDOWS\MOUSE.COM

This program does not use up your "one program at a time" allotment, because it's not really so much as a program, as a *device driver*. A device driver is a special program which manages data going to and from a special device, which in this case, is your mouse. Think of it as a traffic cop/interpreter for your mouse, taking care of the commands going to and from the mouse, and providing the necessary translation for your PC to understand it.

A device driver such as this one is needed because your mouse is an optional item, and your PC didn't come with the instructions on how to operate it. And there are way too many different kinds of mice out there anyway, so why program the computer for each and every one? Instead, they decided to make the manufacturer of your mouse provide the proper instructions to allow the PC to communicate with it. And this they do, in the form of the device driver.

If you don't find this command in your AUTOEXEC.BAT, and your PC uses a mouse, there may be a slightly similar command in your CONFIG.SYS instead, so don't panic. Just read the next section.

What is the CONFIG.SYS?

The CONFIG.SYS file is used to customize DOS for your own purposes. Some customization is necessary because the type of programs you're running may require it, while other commands are there to improve performance (make your PC run better). The CONFIG.SYS can also start special programs called *device drivers*.

When you boot (start) your PC, DOS checks to see if a CONFIG.SYS file exists. If it does, then the commands in the CONFIG.SYS are carried out, one by one. If there are any device drivers listed, those drivers are loaded into memory. If any changes are needed to the regular system parameters, then they are changed as requested. If no CONFIG.SYS file exists, the default values for the system parameters are used. That's okay, but it may mean that your PC won't run your specific programs as efficiently as it could if you'd simply change the system parameters to accommodate them.

Device Drivers Special programs which interpret commands for optional devices such as a mouse, network card, tape-backup, or a CD-ROM drive. Device drivers can also be used to configure memory (RAM) for special purposes.

Taking a Look Inside Your CONFIG.SYS

Like the AUTOEXEC.BAT, the CONFIG.SYS is placed in the root directory of your boot drive, which is usually drive C. To view your CONFIG.SYS file type **TYPE C:\CONFIG.SYS** and press **Enter**:

```
C:\>type config.sys
DEVICE=C:\DOS\SETVER.EXE
DEVICE=C:\DOS\HIMEM.SYS
DEVICE=C:\DOS\EMM386.EXE
BUFFERS=10,0
FILES=40
DOS=UMB
LASTDRIVE=H
FCBS=16,8
DOS=HIGH

STACKS=0,0

SHELL=C:\DOS\COMMAND.COM C:\DOS\ /p
DEVICEHIGH /L:1,38064 =C:\DOS\DBLSPACE.SYS /MOVE

C:\>
```

Here's what a typical CONFIG.SYS might look like.

Here are some of the typical CONFIG.SYS commands and what they do:

Device Drivers

As explained earlier, device drivers work as a go-between for DOS and some piece of equipment, such as a mouse. In addition, device drivers can also be used to configure memory (RAM). You'll learn more about memory in Chapter 20; don't forget to read all about it!

Here's one device driver which you might encounter:

DEVICE=C:\DOS\MOUSE.SYS

It's used to help your PC communicate with your mouse. Here's a command which loads a device driver for your PC's memory (RAM):

DEVICE=C:\DOS\HIMEM.SYS

This command is used by DOS to help it reach an area of memory called the *upper memory*. Without going into the gory details, suffice it to say that your PC's RAM is divided into different sections, most of which came along after DOS was invented. As a consequence of this pathetic oversight, DOS needs help getting to these different areas of memory. So what you'll find (that is, if your PC has more than 1 megabyte of memory, and most PCs today do) is that your CONFIG.SYS is full of these memory device drivers. Here's another one for your amusement:

DEVICE=C:\DOS\EMM386.EXE

Upper memory is typically used by DOS for keeping track of really strange stuff, but one thing you might use upper memory for is to get the biggest piece of DOS out of regular memory, leaving more room for your programs to play around in. Doing this does not affect DOS in any way, and it makes your programs real happy, so it's basically a win-win situation.

This device driver is used by DOS to access *extended memory*. For more info on this and other exciting areas of memory, turn to Chapter 20.

Lastly, you might find this little guy hanging around your CONFIG.SYS:

DEVICE=C:\DOS\ANSI.SYS

This command is used by DOS to access the extended DOS character set, whatever that is. Anyway, some old-style programs require it so they can display neat boxes and buttons and graphical menus on your screen (sort of like the DOS Shell, except that even the DOS Shell doesn't need ANSI.SYS). The kinds of programs which actually require the ANSI.SYS device driver are getting to be pathetically few, so if your CONFIG.SYS doesn't have this command, don't sweat it. You may need this command if you download an old game program from America Online or a similar BBS.

You might see this variation of the DEVICE command in your CONFIG.SYS. What it does is place the device driver into upper memory, which basically gets it out of regular memory. Doing this gives you more memory for your programs, instead of silly device drivers.

DEVICEHIGH=C:\DOS\DBLSPACE.SYS /MOVE

Actually, this particular device driver, DBLSPACE.SYS, is not quite so silly. It's used by the DoubleSpace program to give you more room on your hard disk for files (about double, in fact). You'll learn more about DoubleSpace and its cousin, DriveSpace, in Chapter 19.

The BUFFERS Command

Disk buffers increase the speed of your PC by storing frequently requested information in a handy spot in memory. Buffers, in a manner similar to a RAM cache, speed up your hard disk. Programs that you buy typically specify the number of buffers they require for peak performance. A database program may require 20 to 30 buffers, while a word processor may only need 10 to 15. Use a number that provides the best performance for all of your programs, by choosing a number that's high enough to accommodate everyone. In this example, you might select 25, because it's not too high and not too low that it fails to make the database and the word processor programs happy.

A typical BUFFERS statement looks like this:

BUFFERS=10,0

This command sets the number of buffers to 10, which may or may not be the right number for your system. Check the documentation for your programs to be sure.

The FILES Command

The FILES command helps DOS keep track of open files. Like BUFFERS, most programs that you purchase will specify the maximum number of files they need to keep track of at any one time. Again, pick a number which is not too low and not too high; a number which seems to fit between the conflicting requirements of your various programs. A typical FILES statement looks like this:

FILES=30

A command which is similar to the FILES command is the FCBS command. FCBS stands for File Control Block System, an area of memory where FCBS keeps track of open files. Hardly any programs use the FCBS command for tracking files, which usually looks like this:

FCBS=4,0

The STACKS Command

The STACKS command helps DOS tracks the number of *interrupts*. Interrupts are sent by the PC's various hardware components (keyboard, mouse, disk drives, etc.) in an attempt to get the CPU's attention. For example, when you press a key or click a mouse button, an interrupt is created—that is, an interrupt is sent to tell the CPU to stop what it's doing and pay attention to the keyboard or the mouse. Using the STACKS command would be like organizing all the interrupts you get in five minutes with your kids, and then processing them in the order in which they were received. If your STACKS command doesn't allow for enough interrupts, your PC can go into overload, running around like a chicken with its head cut off, screaming, "Internal Stack Overflow!" "Internal Stack Overflow!" The solution of course, is to increase the number of stacks.

A typical STACKS statement looks like this:

STACKS=9,256

This creates 9 stacks (usually plenty) of 256 bytes each. If you want to increase the number of stacks, change the first number here, in other words, change the 9 to something else.

If you run Windows, you could change it to this:

STACKS=0,0

Because Windows keeps track of interrupts in its own special Windows way.

The Shell Command

This command is *really dangerous* if you don't type it in correctly, so kids, don't change this without your parent's supervision. And parents, don't change this without a PC guru within spitting distance:

SHELL=C:\DOS\COMMAND.COM C:\DOS /P

What this command does is help DOS find itself. Or more specifically, it helps your PC find DOS. Without DOS, your PC is a real expensive paper-weight, capable of doing nothing, so you can see why you won't want to mess with this command. The reason it's there at all is because the DOS setup program puts it there. So just leave it alone and back away real slow...

The DOS Command

What is that doing there? Actually, the DOS command is real safe. What it's doing is pushing old DOS into upper memory (remember that discussion under "Device Drivers"?) Anyway, why would DOS want to go into upper memory? Why, to get to the other side.

Actually, it's to make room for more important things which use lots of regular memory, meaning *your programs*. If this makes no sense to you, that's OK. For more details, see Chapter 20. Oh, and by the way, the DOS command typically looks like this:

DOS=HIGH

or like this:

DOS=HIGH,UMB

Interrupting Your PC's Startup Procedure

After all that work trying to get your AUTOEXEC.BAT and CONFIG.SYS exactly suited for your needs, why would you ever want to mess with it? Why would you ever want to skip the commands in the AUTOEXEC.BAT or CONFIG.SYS? Good questions. Now for the answer: I don't know.

If you don't have at least DOS 6, you can still interrupt the startup procedure by placing a bootable diskette in drive A. Of course, if that diskette contains a version of your AUTOEXEC.BAT or CONFIG.SYS, the commands they contain will be executed. In any case, the configuration files on your PC's hard disk will be *ignored*.

I mean, I can't tell you when you might want to do that, but I can give you some good reasons. For example, suppose you're having problems with your PC. Big-time puzzling problems. You might want to avoid the CONFIG.SYS if you'd just made changes to it, and those changes caused your PC to do the mamba. Or maybe your AUTOEXEC.BAT always starts up your word processor, and today you feel like using a good spreadsheet program instead. Maybe it starts Windows instead, and you don't want it to.

If you do nothing during system startup, DOS looks around for the CONFIG.SYS file and executes the commands in it. Then it looks for the AUTOEXEC.BAT file and does the same thing. Well, if you've got DOS 6 or one of the DOS 6 somethings, you can do something about it.

Interrupt the processing of either the CONFIG.SYS or the AUTOEXEC.BAT by pressing **F5** at startup.

If you wish to bypass some commands but not others, press **F8** instead. You'll be prompted to bypass or execute each command. If at some point you wish to simply execute the remaining commands, press **Esc**. To bypass the remaining commands instead, press **F5**.

The Least You Need to Know

There isn't really a lot in this chapter that you *have to know*, but you can have a lot of fun with your configuration files if you remember these things:

- ☞ The AUTOEXEC.BAT and CONFIG.SYS are files which you use to customize how your PC is set up.

- ☞ The commands in both the CONFIG.SYS and the AUTOEXEC.BAT are automatically carried out when you start or reboot your PC.

- ☞ If you have at least DOS 6, you can bypass the commands in both the CONFIG.SYS and the AUTOEXEC.BAT by pressing **F5.**

- ☞ If you want to bypass selected commands, press **F8** instead, then select the commands you want executed.

Recycling tip:
tear this page out and photocopy it.

Chapter 18
Virus Got You Down?

In This Chapter

- What's a computer virus?
- Chemical-free virus prevention
- Starving a virus and feeding your cold
- Crazy Uncle Leroy speaks out
- How to use the DOS 6 something anti-virus protection program
- Shopping for an anti-virus program

This chapter is all about bad things that go bump in the night. Before your computer starts acting like crazy Uncle Leroy, you owe it to yourself to read this chapter. The information in this chapter won't do much to help Uncle Leroy, but it may save your computer and, more importantly, your data from self-destruction.

Lions, Tigers, and Viruses, Oh My!

A *virus* is a program that infects your computer in various ways, such as changing your files, damaging your disks, and preventing your computer from starting. Some viruses don't do any actual damage; they just display funny messages or pictures. But they are still annoying.

You can accidentally infect your system anytime you copy files onto your hard disk from some unknown source (such as a friend's mystery game diskette) or download files from some *bulletin board system* (BBS). You can also infect your system if you boot (start your system) with an infected diskette in drive A. If a file has been infected by a virus and it gets on your system, that virus can spread. For example, if a virus has infected one of your programs, when you start that program, the virus may go into action, destroying data hither and yon.

Bulletin board system   A BBS is an electronic bulletin board which can be accessed by multiple users at the same time through each user's modem. A BBS offers users a chance to communicate with each other with electronic messages, to exchange information, upload and download files, and to get help with computer problems.

Taking Your Vitamins (and Other Ways to Protect Your PC)

Although it's rare for a PC to contract a virus, you might as well be careful. You can protect your PC from serious damage by:

☞ **Maintaining a recent backup of your files** (a process that copies files onto diskette or backup tape in a special format). By backing up important files onto a diskette or a tape, you can restore those files if the originals get damaged due to some virus (see Chapter 15 for more information).

☞ **Checking diskettes for viruses before copying files from them.** Check any disk you get from any source that's not your own. *Also, be sure to check program disks before installing new software.*

☞ **Write-protecting program (installation) diskettes to prevent infection.**

☞ **Running a virus detection program (that works in the background) all the time.**

☞ **Never starting your computer with a diskette in a diskette drive.** (Make a virus-free bootable diskette for emergency purposes—see the next section.)

☞ **Running a virus removal program as soon as a problem occurs.**

I know, I know . . . but unfortunately, you can't afford to trust anyone these days. Even if your new software came in shrink-wrapped packages, it could have been infected at the software company (there have been several reported cases of this happening). So don't take any chances. Check all disks for viruses before using them.

Creating an Emergency Disk— Better Safe Than Sorry

If you haven't already, you need to create an emergency diskette now, before your system suffers from infection. You can create a virus-safe emergency diskette (as described in Chapter 6) by inserting a diskette in drive A and typing these commands, one at a time, pressing **Enter** after each one:

FORMAT A: /S /V
COPY C:\CONFIG.SYS A:
COPY C:\AUTOEXEC.BAT A:

Be careful about these commands; make sure you insert spaces in the proper place. The first command is *FORMAT space A colon space forward slash S space forward slash V*. The second command is *COPY space C colon backslash CONFIG period SYS space A colon*. The third command is similar: *COPY space C colon backslash AUTOEXEC period BAT space A colon*.

If you have at least DOS 6, you should also copy the Microsoft Anti-Virus program onto the emergency diskette. So type this command too:

COPY C:\DOS\MSAV.* A:

Now that your emergency diskette is complete, write-protect it (see Chapter 6 if you need help), and stick it in a safe place.

If you use DOS and Windows like I do, make sure you buy an anti-virus program that can run both from within Windows and from the DOS prompt. The Microsoft Anti-Virus program that comes with the DOS 6 somethings is such a program, and most anti-virus programs you buy today offer this feature.

If you make changes to your AUTOEXEC.BAT or your CONFIG.SYS at some later time, update your emergency diskette by first removing the write-protection, then repeating these commands:

COPY C:\CONFIG.SYS A:
COPY C:\AUTOEXEC.BAT A:

If you don't have at least DOS 6, read the next section, "Other Virus Protection Programs."

Other Virus Protection Programs

Frankly, there are many reasons to upgrade to one of the DOS 6 somethings (DOS 6, 6.2, 6.21, or 6.22), but the virus protection that's included with it is one mighty good reason. But if you're stuck with the DOS version you currently have, don't lose hope—there are many alternatives available:

Central Point Anti-Virus   This comes with the latest version of PC Tools, another Central Point product. The anti-virus program that comes with the DOS 6 somethings is a licensed version of this program.

Norton AntiVirus   Another sure winner—very dependable. I use this one myself.

McAffee Virus Protection Tools   This is an excellent shareware product (translation: it costs very little to buy, yet offers the same protection as the big guys).

Once you've acquired a good anti-virus program, copy it onto your emergency diskette as shown in the preceding section.

Starve a Virus, Feed a Cold

If you think that your computer is acting strange, don't assume that it's a computer virus. You may be using a program that's not installed properly, or your equipment may be going out. I've had weird things happen just because a cable was loose, so don't yell "The sky is falling!" until you're sure it is.

How do you know when you should panic? Well, if you own a good virus protection program, you can test your system for viruses before you call out the National Guard. When you suspect a problem:

1. **Stop whatever you're doing.** Return all tray tables and seat backs to their upright and locked positions, then exit all programs, including the DOS Shell or anything else you're running.

2. **Reboot your PC with your emergency diskette.** Now you'll find out why you created that thing in the first place. Put the emergency diskette in drive A and reboot by pressing the **Ctrl+Alt+Delete** keys at the same time.

3. **Use your anti-virus program to scan for viruses.** If a virus is detected, ask for it to be removed.

4. **If some of your files are damaged by the virus and can't be repaired, restore them from your backup.** Before backing up files, you should check for viruses on your system. Then if you need to use the backup to replace files that were infected after the backup was taken, you'll have virus-free files to restore. If you're not sure, run your virus detection program after restoring the damaged files.

If you have at least DOS 6, read the following section for detailed instructions on how to detect and remove viruses from your system.

Scanning for Viruses with the DOS 6 Somethings

If you have at least DOS 6, you can use its virus detection program to scan for viruses. After exiting all programs and rebooting with your emergency diskette (see the last section), follow these steps to scan your disk:

1. Start the Microsoft Anti-Virus program. Type **MSAV /A /C** and press **Enter** (if you're connected to a network, skip this and read the next paragraph). That's *MSAV space forward slash A space forward slash C*. The /A switch tells Microsoft Anti-Virus to scan all drives but A and B, and the /C switch tells it to remove any viruses it finds. The scan won't take too long—about 15 minutes or so, depending on the size of your hard disk.

If you are connected to a network, type **MSAV /L /C** *instead* (this limits scanning to local drives only).

2. When it's over, go home. The Microsoft Anti-Virus program scans all your drives and cleans them of any viruses found. After the scan is complete, press **F3** to exit.

You can stop the scan process at any time by pressing **F3**.

A Daily Anti-Virus Checkup

To perform a scan of your hard disk every time you boot your computer, add **MSAV /N** to your AUTOEXEC.BAT file (hey, didn't we learn how to edit our AUTOEXEC.BAT file in Chapter 16? I'd call that good timing!):

The /N switch tells Microsoft Anti-Virus to load itself into memory when you boot your PC, and to start scanning for viruses. If you are attached to a network, add **MSAV /N /L** to your AUTOEXEC.BAT instead.

With one of these commands in place, your hard disk will be scanned automatically at startup. If any changes to your files are detected, a dialog box appears, offering you several options (wait a minute, where's the Panic button?):

☛ Choose **Clean** to clean the virus from your system.

☛ Choose **Continue** to ignore the virus, but continue scanning. If you know that a file was changed legitimately, use this option. For example, if you know that you just changed your AUTOEXEC.BAT file yourself, choose this option.

☛ Choose **Stop** to stop the scanning process and go to the Anti-Virus Main Menu.

☛ Choose **Delete** to delete the infected file from your system. Use this option if the file has been destroyed by a virus and you want to prevent further infection.

Round-the-Clock Protection with the DOS 6 Somethings

Using the MSAV command at startup will detect only viruses that are active *at that time*. To have ongoing protection, run VSafe. VSafe is a program that runs in the background as you perform your normal computer tasks. VSafe will warn you of changes to your files that might be caused by viruses. To start VSafe automatically every time you boot your computer, add **VSAFE** to your AUTOEXEC.BAT.

If you need help adding the VSAFE command to your AUTOEXEC.BAT, see Chapter 16.

The Least You Need to Know

It's frustrating working with a sick computer, but you'll soon nurse it back to health if you remember these things:

- ☞ Don't panic if you suspect a virus—it could just be that soda you spilled on your keyboard last week.

- ☞ There are things you need to be doing now, before your PC gets a virus, like:

Creating an emergency diskette, and keeping it updated.

Always doing backups.

Checking diskettes for viruses before you use them—especially installation diskettes.

Write-protecting important diskettes so they don't contract a virus sometime in the future.

Never leaving a diskette in its drive.

Running a virus detection program all the time.

Running a virus removal program as soon as you suspect trouble.

continues

continued

☞ To create an emergency diskette, use these commands:

> **FORMAT A: /S /V**
> **COPY C:\CONFIG.SYS A:**
> **COPY C:\AUTOEXEC.BAT A:**

If you have a virus detection program, copy it onto the emergency diskette, too.

☞ To run the DOS 6 something virus detection program, type **MSAV /A /C**. If you are attached to a network, use this command instead: **MSAV /L /C**.

☞ To scan your hard disk with the DOS 6 something virus protection program when you boot your PC, add this command to your AUTOEXEC.BAT: **MSAV /N**. If you are attached to a network, use this command instead: **MSAV /N /L**.

☞ To continuously scan with the DOS 6 something virus detection program for viruses as you work, put this command in your AUTOEXEC.BAT: **VSAFE**.

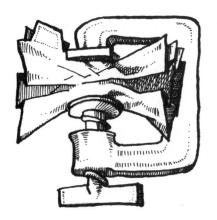

Chapter 19

Double Your Pleasure, Double Your Fun, Double Your Disk

In This Chapter

- ☞ Disk compression therapy
- ☞ Popular programs you can use to compress your hard disk
- ☞ New techniques for battling compression depression
- ☞ Using DoubleSpace or DriveSpace to compress a drive
- ☞ Compressing a diskette without pain or heavy objects
- ☞ Letting the air out of a compressed drive

Is It Getting Crowded in Here?

Disk compression programs store more information on a hard disk because they use a kind of "computer shorthand" that allows them to store data in less space than with DOS alone. If you use a disk compression program, your hard disk can increase its storage capacity by almost double.

Disk compression is not new; actually, the technology has been around for quite some time. The backup and restore programs that come with DOS use a compression technique similar to the kind used in disk compression programs. You can use a compressed drive the same way you would use any regular drive; the only difference is that the compressed drive will store more files than your hard disk normally would. One concern you may have is, "Will disk compression make my computer any slower than it already is?" Well, maybe a little, but we're talking computer time here (where things happen in the blink of an eye).

Popular Disk Compression Programs

If you have at least DOS 6 or 6.2, you're in luck; they come with a disk compression program called DoubleSpace. If you have DOS 6.21 or 6.22, then your compression program is called DriveSpace. (Actually, DOS 6.21 comes with a coupon which you must send in to get the DriveSpace program from Microsoft.) If you don't have at least DOS 6, you can up-grade or purchase a disk compression program such as Stacker, by Stac Electronics.

If you depend on utilities such as disk optimizers, disk repair utilities, memory managers, and anti-virus programs, make sure that they are compatible with your disk compression software. If you're not sure, con-sult the manual or call the manufacturer before you run these programs.

If you use DoubleSpace or DriveSpace, you can use any of the utilities that come with DOS (such as SMARTDrive) without any problem at all. If you want to use some other utility on your compressed drive, check the manual first.

TECHNO NERD TEACHES...

After you've installed a disk compression program, a huge file will eat most of your C drive. This huge file contains a compressed version of all of your files—think of that file as a trash-compacted version of your C drive.

Here's the tricky part. The disk compression program knows that you expect all the files that were on C: before to be accessible from C: now. But after disk compression, drive C is almost empty except for this huge file. So the disk compres-sion program tells DOS to re-assign the drive letter C: to the *compressed* file and to change the name of the *real* C: to something else (like H: or I:). That way you can still do everything from the C: prompt as you did before you com-pressed your hard disk.

Using DoubleSpace or DriveSpace to Compress a Drive

Okay, DOS 6 something users, it's time to compress. If you have DOS 6 or 6.2, you'll do your compression with a program called DoubleSpace. If you have 6.22, you'll do it with a program called DriveSpace instead. Six of one, half-dozen of the other, since they both work the same way. (What's different is the parts underneath that do the actual compression.) It takes roughly one minute per megabyte of data to compress your hard disk, so you might want to start the DoubleSpace or DriveSpace setup program at the end of the day and run it overnight. To set up DoubleSpace or DriveSpace, follow these steps:

1. Exit all programs, including the DOS Shell and Windows.

2. Change to the DOS directory by typing **CD\DOS** and pressing **Enter**.

If your disk drive was DoubleSpaced and you've upgraded to DOS 6.22, you can still use your hard disk as is, or you can convert it to DriveSpace compression. See the next section for details.

3. Start the DoubleSpace setup program by typing **DBLSPACE** or start the DriveSpace setup program by typing **DRVSPACE** instead.

4. Choose **Express** setup. If you want to compress a drive other than C: or to create an empty compressed drive, you'll need to use **Custom** setup. Grab some Oreos and get a guru to help you if you want to run the Custom setup.

5. A small section of your drive will remain uncompressed. If you want to change the default letter for the uncompressed drive, do so before pressing **Enter**.

6. A message will appear that tells you how long the compression process will take. This is a one-time process that takes about one minute per megabyte. Press **C** to Continue (which will complete the compression process) or **Esc** to exit (which will stop it).

7. After the disk compression is finished, a summary will display, showing information on the compressed drive. Press **Enter** and your system will restart with the compressed drive active and ready to play.

If you want to display information about your compressed drive, *change to that drive* which is usually drive C:, then type **DBLSPACE /INFO** or **DRVSPACE /INFO.** You'll see something like this:

DriveSpace is examining drive C.

Compressed drive C is stored on uncompressed drive H in the file H:\DRVSPACE.001.

Space used:	131.77 MB
Compression ratio:	1.6 to 1
Space free:	9.71 MB
Est. compression ratio:	1.7 to 1
Fragmentation:	21%
Total space:	141.48 MB

Converting a DoubleSpaced Drive to DriveSpace

If you've upgraded to DOS 6.21 or 6.22, and your hard disk is DoubleSpaced, you can leave it as is, or convert it to DriveSpace (recommended). The conversion process is pretty painless, as you'll soon see, and it doesn't take nearly as long as it did to DoubleSpace the hard disk originally (mine took about an hour, and my hard disk is about 160MB). Here's what you do:

Do a backup first. If something goes wrong, you can use it to restore your original hard disk. I didn't run into any problems, but doing a backup before a complex procedure like this one is always a good idea.

Check for free space. You're gonna need at least a half a megabyte free on the non-compressed drive (it's probably drive H:), and some free room to work on the compressed drive (probably drive C:). About 2 to 4 MB should be adequate.

Type DRVSPACE and press Enter. You'll see a message warning you to do a backup. Since you already have, pass go and collect your $200. Press **Enter** to continue.

DRVSPACE runs ScanDisk to check your disk first. Then it begins the conversion process. You can press F3 to quit at anytime, although I wouldn't do it. If you do run into problems and DriveSpace can't convert the entire drive, you won't be stuck because your PC will still work. But you should remedy the situation as soon as you can, and run DRVSPACE again to convert the rest of the drive.

When DriveSpace is done tinkering, it displays a message saying, "OK, that's done. Let's go for pizza!" Just press **Enter** to restart your system with a DriveSpace drive. From now on, the entire compression business will run automatically. You've done your part.

Now That I Have a Compressed Drive, What Do I Do with It?

You work with your compressed drive as you would with any other drive. The compression process remains invisible to you, the user. The DoubleSpace/DriveSpace maintenance program allows you to perform the compression functions listed here. You access the DoubleSpace maintenance program by typing **DBLSPACE**. Or, to access the DriveSpace maintenance program, type **DRVSPACE** instead.

From the DoubleSpace/DriveSpace maintenance program, you can:

- ☞ Increase the storage capacity of diskettes by compressing them. See the section coming up.

- ☞ Adjust the size of your compressed drive. See the section in this chapter.

- ☞ Display information about the compressed drive. See the previous section.

- ☞ Format a compressed drive. Get your PC guru to help you format your hard disk if you're really sure you want to.

- ☞ Defragment a compressed drive. See Chapter 5 for details.

Defragmentation When you modify a file, the changes often get written to a different spot on the disk than the original file. Files with pieces in more than one place are called fragmented. A defragmenting program rewrites data on the disk so that all the pieces of a file are in the same physical spot. Defragmenting can improve disk performance and efficiency.

☛ Check a compressed drive for lost clusters and chains with the ScanDisk command. See Chapter 5.

☛ Reverse the compression process and revert your drive back to a non-compressed drive. This option requires at least DOS 6.2, and a hard disk large enough to hold the uncompressed files. See the appropriate section in this chapter.

Adjusting the Size of Your Compressed Drive

After you compress your hard disk, you have what looks like two disk drives: H (which is a tiny uncompressed area of your physical hard disk) and C (which is the compressed portion).

If your compressed drive is starting to feel a little tight around its middle, you can increase the size of your compressed drive—that is, provided you have enough *uncompressed area* to expand into. Here's what you do:

1. Exit all programs, including the DOS Shell.

2. Change to the DOS directory by typing **CD\DOS** and pressing **Enter.**

3. Start the DoubleSpace maintenance program by typing **DBLSPACE**, or start the DriveSpace maintenance program by typing **DRVSPACE.**

4. Open the Drive menu by clicking on it or by pressing the **Alt+D** keys at the same time.

5. Select the Change Size command by clicking on it or by pressing **S.**

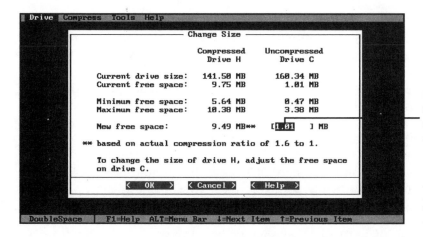

Enter the amount of space you wish to leave on your uncompressed drive

Adjusting the size of your compressed drive.

6. Enter the amount of space you want to leave in the uncompressed portion of your drive. The leftover space will then be assigned to the compressed drive.

7. Press Enter to start the resizing process.

This process will take awhile, so have a seat. When it's done, exit the maintenance program by opening the Drive menu and selecting the Exit command. (Press **Alt+D**, then **X**). Your compressed drive is ready to use.

Compressing a Diskette with DoubleSpace or DriveSpace

Once you've installed DoubleSpace or DriveSpace on your hard disk, you can use it to compress diskettes and improve their storage capacities. After a diskette has been compressed by DoubleSpace or DriveSpace, it will hold almost twice as much data as before. I don't want to throw you into a compression depression, but there is one drawback to using compressed diskettes: you can use a compressed diskette *only on a PC that is running DoubleSpace or DriveSpace.*

To compress a diskette with DoubleSpace or DriveSpace, insert the diskette in its drive, then type **DBLSPACE** or **DRVSPACE** and press **Enter.**

Then compress the diskette by following these steps:

1. Open the Compress menu. Click on the menu (press the left mouse button while pointing to the word Compress) or press the **Alt** and **C** keys at the same time.

2. Select the Existing Drive command. Click on the command with the mouse or use the down arrow key to highlight it, then press **Enter.**

3. If necessary, change the drive to compress. Use the arrow keys to select a drive to compress, and press **Enter.** Press **C** to continue.

4. After the disk is compressed, return to DOS. Open the **Drive** menu and select the Exit command by clicking on them with the mouse. If you're using the keyboard, press the **Alt** and **D** keys at the same time, then press the letter **X.**

Now that the diskette has been compressed, use the diskette as you would any other: copy and delete files to your heart's content.

TECHNO NERD TEACHES...

If you have DOS 6.0, do not remove your compressed diskette from its drive or reboot, or you'll have to "mount it" in order to use it again. Mounting is the process that a compression program goes through in order to make the compressed files available to DOS.

With DriveSpace and the DOS 6.2 version of DoubleSpace, the mounting process is automatic. What that means is anytime you insert a compressed diskette into a drive, your PC knows it and mounts it automatically for you. Now that's service!

Anyway, if you need to mount a compressed diskette in order to use it again, insert the diskette into its drive, then type:

DBLSPACE MOUNT A:

If you need to mount a compressed diskette in drive B, type this instead:

DBLSPACE MOUNT B:

Removing DoubleSpace or DriveSpace

If you want to, you can reverse the process and uncompress your hard disk. Of course, you need to have enough room on your hard disk for all of the uncompressed files. Also, if you're using DoubleSpace, you need the DOS 6.2 version of it. You can't uncompress a drive with the DOS 6.0 version of DoubleSpace.

Keep in mind that it will take approximately the same amount of time to uncompress a drive as it took to compress it (about 1 MB a minute), so you might want to wait and start this process at the end of the day, so it can run overnight.

To uncompress your drive:

1. Exit all programs, including the DOS Shell.

2. Change to the DOS directory by typing **CD\DOS** and pressing **Enter.**

3. Start the DoubleSpace maintenance program by typing **DBLSPACE** or start the DriveSpace maintenance program by typing **DRVSPACE.**

4. Open the Tools menu by clicking on it with the mouse, or by pressing the keys **Alt+T** at the same time.

5. Select the Uncompress command by clicking on it, or by pressing **U.**

6. Follow the additional instructions on-screen. When it's done, your drive will be uncompressed.

The Least You Need to Know

I never thought I'd find enough stuff to fill my new 240MB hard disk, but it was almost filled in a week. Until I used DoubleSpace and later, DriveSpace, I thought I'd have to invest in another computer. Now I've got plenty of room (at least 'til the end of the month). When using a disk compression program, remember these things:

- ☞ Disk compression programs store more information on a disk using a special "computer shorthand."

- ☞ Popular disk compression programs include DoubleSpace, DriveSpace, and Stac Electronic's Stacker.

- ☞ To install DoubleSpace, change to the DOS directory, and then type **DBLSPACE**. To install DriveSpace, type **DRVSPACE** instead.

Choose **Express** setup, then type the drive to compress, and press **Enter**. Press **C** to continue, and the compression begins.

- ☞ To display information about a compressed drive, type **DBLSPACE /INFO** or **DRVSPACE /INFO**.

- ☞ To compress a diskette with DoubleSpace, type **DBLSPACE**. To compress a diskette with DriveSpace, type **DRVSPACE** instead.

Open the **C**ompress menu by pressing the **Alt** and **C** keys at the same time. Press **E** to select the Existing Drive command. When the disk is compressed, press the **Alt** and **D** keys at the same time to open the **D**rive menu. Press **X** to select Exit.

- ☞ A compressed disk must be mounted in order to use it. After a disk is compressed, it is automatically mounted. However, if you're using the DOS version 6.0's DoubleSpace program, and you remove the diskette or reboot, it must be remounted in order to use it. To mount a diskette, place it in its drive, then type **DBLSPACE MOUNT A:** or **DBLSPACE MOUNT B:**.

Chapter 20

Pump Up the RAM!

In This Chapter

☞ Learning to express your true feeling about RAM

☞ RAM envy and what you can do about it

☞ Simple things you can do to improve your computer's memory

☞ Top techniques for improving memory, by Ronald Reagan

☞ Using MemMaker to improve your computer's use of memory—automatically

What Is RAM?

Random-access memory, or *RAM*, is the working area of your computer, in much the same way as your working area is your desktop. When you want to work on something, you get it out of a drawer (or off the floor) and place it on your desktop. DOS does basically the same thing; it retrieves files off of the hard disk (or a diskette or a CD-ROM), then places the files on its "desktop," which is called RAM. Once the files are in RAM, DOS can begin processing them. The amount of RAM your PC has determines how much "desk" space DOS has to work with. (Big clue: DOS needs a very *large* desk; the more RAM your PC comes with, the more room DOS has to work in.)

Why does DOS need so much RAM? When you start a program, the program files are loaded into RAM from a disk. Most of the graphic-based programs we use today are memory hogs (pretty pictures need lots of RAM). So by the time your program is loaded into RAM, a significant chunk of memory has been used up, and you haven't even done anything yet! As you use the program to create documents, those documents take up more space in RAM. If you run complex, memory-hogging programs—or create large documents—your PC is gonna need *lots of RAM*.

And Why Should I Care?

All programs need memory in order to run—some programs need quite a lot of memory. Not having enough memory affects the way your programs work and can even prevent some programs from starting.

Although your computer may have lots of RAM, the section your programs run in is very limited, as you'll learn later in this chapter. That's why it's important to make the most of each bit of memory. By managing this precious resource effectively, you can:

Have a faster, more efficient PC. How many of us plan our coffee breaks around the way we use certain programs, because we know they take so long to retrieve a file, perform calculations, or sort data?

Resolve "out of memory" problems. Everything your computer wants to use must go into memory: that includes any programs you want to start up, all the data files (documents) you want to work on, and even DOS. It's easy to see how this precious resource can get used up pretty quickly. Nothing is more frustrating than a program that won't start, or acts funny because your computer doesn't have room for all its "stuff."

Exploit memory usage to the fullest. I recently visited my husband's parents for Christmas—and we had to fit suitcases, presents, and half-finished Christmas projects into a trunk the size of a bread box. (My husband has a two-seater sports car.) Your computer's memory is like the trunk of a car. By helping your computer manage its memory better, you'll be amazed at what can fit into memory: a pop-up day planner, an anti-virus program, the DOS Shell, your word processor, and maybe even a spreadsheet program.

Tell Me More About Memory

RAM is divided into several sections. The area of RAM that DOS uses (the "main desktop," as it were) is called *conventional memory*. Conventional memory is the first 640 kilobytes of RAM in your computer's memory banks. *This is the only area of memory that DOS can use to store your applications when you start them.* The rest of RAM is useful only for system files, or for temporary data storage, such as the documents you create.

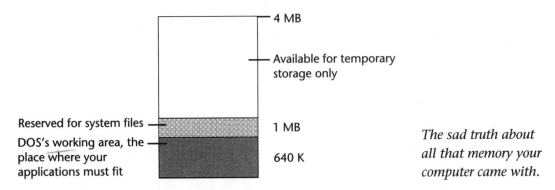

The sad truth about all that memory your computer came with.

The abbreviations *K* and *MB* in the figure stand for *kilobyte* and *megabyte*, two ways of measuring RAM. You'll learn more about them in the next section.

By now you may be thinking, "So what? Why should I care about memory? I only run my spreadsheet program." But that's not true. Your PC is actually running lots of stuff: DOS (of course—gotta have that one), your anti-virus program, your disk-compression program, the device driver for your mouse, your word processor, etc. And all these programs have to fit into that tiny area of RAM called conventional memory.

That is, *unless you can stuff them someplace else*. You see, only your *applications* (your spreadsheet program, for example, or your word processor) have to fit into conventional memory. Ordinarily you won't need to make direct use of DOS, your disk-compression program, your mouse device driver, etc.—as long as the system can get at them, there's no reason

NOT to put them in other sections of RAM. Stuffing these system files *someplace else* is what memory management is all about. And in today's RAM-hungry world, it's the only way to get your PC to do all the things you need it to do.

How Much Memory Does Your Computer Have?

Computers understand only two things: 1 or 0. (This makes computers much smarter than children, who understand only "Yes" and never such phrases as "No," or "Don't do that," or "Eat your food, don't play with it.") Each 1 or 0 in the computer is a *bit*, or **binary digit**. Place eight bits in a row, and you have a *byte*, which can be used to store any single character (such as the number 2 or the letter J) in your computer's memory. To store the sentence, "Learning all this stuff about memory really bytes," would take 49 bytes of RAM (well, okay, 51 if you count the comma and quotes).

A *kilobyte* (1K) is roughly a thousand bytes (1,024 bytes, to be exact). A *megabyte* (1MB) is roughly a million bytes (1,048,576 bytes). A *gigabyte* (1G) is roughly one billion bytes or way too much RAM.

Most new computers today come with at least 4MB of RAM, broken down like this: 640K of *conventional memory*, 360K of *upper memory*, and the rest in *extended memory*. Conventional memory is used by your applications. Upper memory is restricted for DOS to use; typically, system files are placed there. Extended memory can be used by applications to store the stuff you create *while you're using them* (such as a memo, a chart, or a 100-page report).

Some really smart applications shuffle things between conventional and extended memory all the time, in order to keep the "desktop" full of only those things the program needs DOS to work on right then. For example, if you decide to use the spelling checker in your word processing program, the application may switch it into conventional memory from extended memory (where it'd been kept in case of just such an emergency).

As you learned earlier in the chapter, only the first 640K (conventional memory) can be used to run applications. Now, here comes an even bigger kick in the pants: DOS keeps a part of that miserly 640K chunk of memory for itself. To check this out, exit all programs, then type **CHKDSK** and press **Enter**.

If you look at the bottom set of numbers in the listing, you'll see the horrible truth: of the total 655,360 bytes (640K), you have maybe 510,512 bytes left.

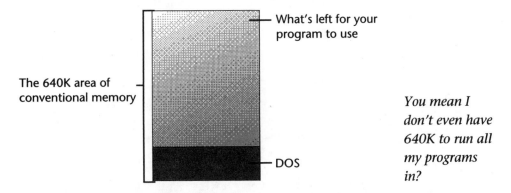

The 640K area of conventional memory

— What's left for your program to use

— DOS

You mean I don't even have 640K to run all my programs in?

Since you're not running any applications at the moment, what's taking up part of memory? The answer is DOS itself—it is loaded into memory. DOS needs a place to work (to interpret your commands and control information flow), so it grabs a piece of conventional memory for itself.

Using the MEM Command to See the Whole Picture

CHKDSK only displays information about the first 640K of memory. Bummer. If you have at least DOS 5, however, you can use the **MEM** command to see all about memory:

MEM tells you how much conventional, upper, and extended memory you have as well as how much is available at the moment. MEM also displays expanded-memory information if you have an expanded memory circuit board or if you've converted any of your extended memory into expanded memory. (What's this *expanded memory*? Well, it's actually just a cousin of extended memory, used for the same thing: to store data that you create using your programs. If you want to know the rest of the story—of course you do—read the following note.)

TECHNO NERD TEACHES...

There are four types of memory. The first 640K of RAM is *conventional memory*, and it is the only place where programs can run and where DOS can manipulate data. From 640K to 1MB is a wasteland called *upper memory*. Upper memory is reserved for special system files DOS uses: the programs for handling *input* (data coming into the computer) and *output* (data going out of the computer) are stored there.

If you have at least DOS 5, part of upper memory can be reclaimed for storing *device drivers* (special programs that help DOS use optional devices, such as a mouse) and *TSRs* (pop-up programs that run in the background, such as a calculator you can "pop up" while in your word processor or some other program). Storing drivers like this often frees up a small amount of conventional memory.

After the first 1MB of your PC's RAM, the rest of RAM is called *extended memory*. (This is that temporary data storage area we were just talking about.) Some programs can speed up their operations by stashing temporary files there (provided they're written specifically to do so) rather than writing them to a disk. As a matter of fact, Windows does this very thing, along with a number of other popular programs.

Expanded memory is extra memory that sometimes comes on a special circuit board, but it is more often converted from extended memory. Expanded memory serves the same purpose as extended—it just goes about its business in a different way. Some programs can use either extended or expanded memory, but most programs want one or the other. Lotus 1-2-3 for DOS is one famous program which uses expanded memory.

Simple Things That Improve Memory Usage

If you have DOS 5, you can add these commands to the *beginning* of your CONFIG.SYS file to improve your PC's memory usage right away (see Chapters 16 and 17). If you have one of the DOS 6 somethings, skip to the next section and save yourself the hassle of editing your own configuration files:

DEVICE=C:\DOS\HIMEM.SYS
DOS=HIGH

These two commands move DOS (or most of it anyway) out of conventional memory, into a nonconventional part of RAM that normally goes unused. This gives your programs more room in conventional memory to run.

If you have a PC that has a 386, 486, or Pentium CPU, and your PC has more than 1 MB of RAM, you can do some other things that improve your PC's memory management significantly. Accessing the other areas of memory can be kind of tricky, so ask a PC guru to help you.

SPEAK LIKE A GEEK

CPU   The CPU is the brain of your computer. Like your brain, this is the part of the computer that "thinks" or processes information. CPU stands for central processing unit.

Users of the DOS 6 Somethings: Just Sit Back and Relax

If you have at least DOS 6, you can thank your lucky stars. The DOS 6 somethings (DOS 6, 6.2, 6.21, and 6.22) come with a memory manager called MemMaker that is so simple it's virtually idiot-proof. MemMaker is designed to make changes that *optimize* (improve) your system's use of memory automatically, helping it "be all that it can be."

BY THE WAY

MemMaker is great, but it's not perfect. A PC guru who knows the tricks can optimize your system's memory usage much better than MemMaker can. If you want to know more about memory and how to make the most of it, read the *10 Minute Guide to Memory Management*, by the lovely and talented Jennifer Flynn.

MemMaker is very easy to use, and it provides fairly good results. To optimize your system with MemMaker, exit all programs, then type **MEMMAKER**.

Press **Enter** and a message appears, asking you to choose between Express (for real people like us) and Custom optimization (for confident users—such as geeks). To use Express, press **Enter**. To switch to Custom, press the **Spacebar**, then **Enter**. Let's assume you chose the easy way out— Express installation. Follow these steps:

1. A message appears, asking if you use any programs that require expanded memory. If a program requires this type of memory, it should say so on the box it came in. If you're not sure, pick **No**. You can always rerun MemMaker and change it later.

2. A message appears, asking you to press **Enter**. Do it, and MemMaker restarts your computer.

3. MemMaker analyzes your system, and changes your AUTOEXEC.BAT and CONFIG.SYS (your old files are saved with a .UMB extension). Press **Enter**, and MemMaker tests your new configuration.

4. A message appears, asking if your new configuration is OK. If you can see the message and nothing untoward happened during the reboot process (your PC didn't jam), then your new configuration *is* OK. Press **Enter** for Yes if the computer restarted okay, or press the **Spacebar** and then **Enter** to answer No (and continue testing different configurations).

5. A listing showing your system's memory usage appears. Press **Enter** to exit MemMaker.

The Least You Need to Know

Don't forget the following things about memory:

- ☛ RAM is the working area of the computer where information is processed.

- ☛ Conventional memory is the first 640K of RAM. Conventional memory is the most important part of

RAM; it is the only part where an application can run, and where data can be manipulated.

☛ Memory is measured in bytes. A byte stores a single character, such as the letter Q. A *kilobyte* (1K) is roughly a thousand bytes, and a *megabyte* (1MB) is roughly a million bytes. A *gigabyte* (1G) is roughly one billion bytes.

☛ If you have at least DOS 5, you can use the MEM command to display memory usage.

☛ If you have DOS 5, you can add these commands to the beginning of your CONFIG.SYS file, and free up some of the conventional memory your PC uses:

DEVICE=C:\DOS\HIMEM.SYS
DOS=HIGH

☛ If you have at least DOS 6, you can use MemMaker to configure the memory in your system for you. Type **MEMMAKER** to start MemMaker.

This page intentionally left blank.

Part Four
Now It's Back to the Real World

Someone somewhere decided that you needed a computer to get your work done faster and more efficiently. That person may even have provided some basic programs for you to use. Now you're sitting there thinking, "Great. They tell me this thing is going to save me a lot of time and trouble, and I just spent a half hour trying to turn it on!" This section deals with the trials and tribulations of learning to install, start, and use new programs—with or without the "help" of manuals.

Chapter 21
A Simple Guide to Software

In This Chapter

- ☛ This Old Program's exclusive guide to software
- ☛ How to install a program like a pro
- ☛ The "key" to starting a program
- ☛ How to navigate the great blue sea of menu systems
- ☛ Saving and printing a document with your new program

The one thing most beginners don't realize is how little they really need to know. (OK, so you're wondering, *why is this book so big?*) Once you've learned the basics in one program, you can easily wing your way through the next one, because most programs today follow the same basic format.

No automobile manufacturer would design a car so that the ignition key is inserted on the *left side* of the steering column. Why? Because if they did, they'd be faced with disbelief and dismal sales. No one enjoys having to "learn things all over again" so they wouldn't buy a car designed to be so different and difficult to operate.

One standard most programs follow is to use the same method to access their help files. In almost every program I can name, you press F1 to get help. If you remember nothing else from this chapter, remember that. Of course, there's no guarantee that a programmer will follow this standard—after all, it's not law—but maybe it should be. Anyway, I have no explanation why WordPerfect for DOS insists that F3 is the help key. (Actually even a big company like WordPerfect can get the hint; in their Windows version, F1 is the help key.)

Like car manufacturers, programmers (for the most part) design their programs to follow the same set of rules as everyone else. The benefit to you is obvious: once you've learned how to use one program, you'll spend less than half that time learning the next, and so on. In this one chapter, you'll learn probably *half* of what you need to know in order to use your programs. Really.

Get Your Programs Here!

A computer is no better than a boat anchor unless it has a *program* to tell it what to do. A program is a set of instructions written in a special "machine language" that the computer understands—the computer's way of saying, "Blah, blah, blah, blah." A program tells the computer to perform some particular task, such as acting like a typewriter or a calculator. Other programs tell your computer to act like a drawing pad, a stereo, a day planner, an Indy car driver, and many other things.

There are many types of computer programs you can buy. A program that tells the computer to act like a typewriter is called a *word processor*. To write a report or a family newsletter, use a word processor such as Microsoft Word, WordPerfect, or Ami Pro. If you want to balance a checkbook or last year's budget, use a *spreadsheet program*. Popular spreadsheet programs include Lotus 1-2-3 and Excel.

A program that organizes (and reorganizes) information in different ways is called a *database manager*. (A program that could reorganize my closets would be a *miracle*.) If you want to create an address book, or a customer list, or even a recipe file, use a database manager, such as dBASE, Q&A, FoxPro, or Microsoft Access. To create your own pictures for reports, presentations, or just for fun, use a *painting* or *drawing program*, such as PC Paintbrush, Corel Draw!, or Windows Draw.

Desktop publishing programs let you combine text and graphics into a finished page. This book was assembled in a desktop publishing program. With a simple desktop publishing program, you can create banners, signs, and calendars. More complex programs can be used to create anything that combines text and pictures, such as newsletters, brochures, and reports. Popular desktop publishing programs include Publish It!, Express Publisher, PageMaker, and Corel Ventura Publisher.

Utility programs are actually several small programs sold together that perform you-never-know-when-you'll-need-it tasks like undeleting files and recovering from system problems. Don't leave home without one of these. Popular utility programs include PC Tools, Norton Utilities, and Mace Utilities. Several utility programs come gratis from Microsoft in the DOS 6 somethings.

A program that helps your computer talk to another one through a *modem* is called a *communications program*. If you need to send data to other offices, or if you want to connect to an on-line information service, such as CompuServe or GEnie, you'll need a modem and this type of program. Some popular communications programs include ProComm Plus, Smartcom, and Crosstalk. Nearly all major on-line services now utilize their own software to provide users with graphical (picture-oriented) access. CompuServe has CIM for this purpose, GEnie has Aladdin, Delphi has (or will have by the time of this printing) D-LITE, Prodigy Services has, well, PRODIGY...

SPEAK LIKE A GEEK

Modem A modem converts computer data into beeping noises that can be transmitted through an ordinary telephone line. At the receiving end, a modem converts the beeping noises back into computer data.

If you are tired of starting your applications by typing a series of mysterious commands, get yourself a *menu program*, and all you have to press is a number. Popular menu programs include Direct Access and Automenu. If you're looking for something fun, try a *game program*. Many popular games such as poker, backgammon, and chess have been computerized. Action-adventure games and flight simulators are also popular. (Don't use this type of program at work—unless you're the boss!)

SPEAK LIKE A GEEK

Burn-in is what happens when the same image is displayed too long on a PC monitor. When other images are shown, the burnt-in image is still there, like a ghost on-screen.

Ever seen a burned-out Pac-Man machine? Have you noticed, when you walk up to the screen, even though it's not plugged in any more, you can still read "GAME OVER CREDITS: 0" as though it were written in charcoal? Old console video games never cared much about screen burn-in. *Screen savers* blank out your own screen or replace it with pretty pictures whenever you leave your PC unattended for a few minutes. Programs like these prevent *burn-in*, which leaves a ghostly image of a program permanently etched into your PC's monitor. Popular screen savers include After Dark and Intermission.

With a *DOS shell*, you can perform all the same wonderful things you can with DOS, but without the headache of remembering exactly what to type. Shells get their name because they protect you (like a shell) from the hassles of using DOS. Don't think that using a shell will make you a DOS turtle—using a shell is easy, *fast*, and fun. Some popular shells include the DOS Shell (which comes with DOS versions 4, 5, and 6, later versions of DOS require that you send off for a copy of the Shell), PC Tools Desktop (which comes with PC Tools, a utility program), Norton Commander, and Windows (which is much more than a shell, and a whole lot of fun to use). If you want to know more about using these types of programs with DOS, see Chapter 23. For information on specifically how to use the DOS Shell, see Chapter 8.

Don't worry that you won't be able to find the right program for your needs. There are so many software programs on the market these days that the right program is as easy to find as a rerun of "It's a Wonderful Life" during Christmas season (which starts, in case you didn't know it, in April). If anything, you may be overwhelmed by the sheer number of choices. Ask the clerks at the software store for their recommendations.

Deciding on What Programs to Buy

After you buy a new PC, don't go anywhere near a computer store. If you do, some mysterious force will reach out and suck you into the store, totally against your will. Believe me. I know.

If you find yourself sucked into a computer store accidentally, there's nothing else to do but to *buy something*. Then they'll let you out. Believe me. I know.

But how do you decide what to buy? Well, here are some tips:

Start with the basics. You'll need at least a word processor, and probably a good spreadsheet program. With the word processor, you can write letters to your parents asking for more money (since you've just spent it all on software). With the spreadsheet program, you can track monthly expenditures on your new toy. From there, get the programs that interest you, such as a drawing or painting program or maybe a game.

Find out if the program will work on your PC. Read the back of the program box. Does your PC come with the mouse that the program requires? Does your PC have enough RAM (see Chapter 20 for help determining how much memory your PC has)? Does your PC have enough hard disk space available? (Type **DIR** and press **Enter**, and it will show you.) Does your PC have the minimum DOS version required? (Type **VER** and press **Enter** to find out.) Does your PC have the minimum CPU needed? Is Windows required?

Ask for advice and shop around. Ask friends and co-workers if they've used the program, and if they liked it. If they haven't used it yet and they bought it a year ago, maybe you can do without it too. Read reviews in magazines, but take each with a grain of salt. Keep in mind that *big* companies pay *big* bucks to advertise in the magazine, and they wouldn't be too happy to get a *big* stinker of a review.

If you decide to buy, pick up a version that contains the right size diskettes. If your PC has a 3 1/2-inch diskette drive, then make sure the program box includes 3 1/2-inch diskettes. Also, since your PC uses DOS (or you wouldn't be reading this), don't get the Macintosh version of a program.

Installing Programs like a Pro

Installing is a process which gets the program you just bought copied from the program diskettes, and onto your PC's hard disk. If you're a beginner, you may want to ask someone else to install your programs for you. It's easier, and since it's something you only have to do once, why bother to learn how? But if you need it done *now*, you're the best person to do it, so here goes:

1. **Open the box, unwrap the diskettes, and check them for viruses.** If you have at least DOS 6, type **MSAV A:** and press **Enter**. If not, use a virus-protection program such as Norton Anti-Virus or Central Point Anti-Virus.

2. **Make copies of the diskettes.** Making copies of installation diskettes will provide you with a backup should something happen to the originals. (If you think this is a step you can skip, think again. Right now, your chair is just itching for a chance to roll over a helpless diskette, if only you'd drop it.) Before you copy the original diskettes, *write-protect* them. Then use DISKCOPY (see Chapter 6) to copy each diskette.

Write-protect When a disk is write-protected, it can be read, but not changed. On a 3 1/2-inch diskette, slide the tab up so the hole is exposed. On a 5 1/4-inch diskette, stick a black tab (included with the labels) over the side notch.

3. **Find out some basic information about your PC before you try to install.** The installation program will ask you lots of silly things that no sane person could know, such as what type of monitor you have and what type of printer. Look for names or other trademarks. If you have the owner's manuals for your PC and each of its components, check there. If all else fails, ask a co-worker. Most companies buy in quantities, so you might have the same system as the person next to you.

4. **Read the program manual.** I know, I know... but even I read the manual just to be sure I know what to do before I try to install some strange new software. Look for a separate Installation Guide, or look under "Setup" or "Installation" or "Read me first" in the user's manual.

5. **If you've misplaced the manual or it's unclear,** start by placing the first of the installation diskettes in drive A, then type these commands, pressing **Enter** after each command:

    A:
    SETUP

    If you this doesn't work, try these commands:

    A:
    INSTALL

6. **If you're given a choice, choose Express or Easy installation.**
This type of installation installs your program with the least
amount of fuss. Answer any questions that the installation
program asks, and whenever possible, choose the defaults by
pressing **Enter** (the choices that are already highlighted for you).
If you need to choose something from a list, use the arrow keys to
highlight your selection, and then press **Enter**.

If you type in the command to install your program, then
you see an error message that says Windows needs to be
running, you should start Windows first, *then* install your
application. Type **WIN** and press **Enter**. Once Windows is
started, open the **File** menu in the Program Manager by
clicking on it (or by pressing the **Alt** and **F** keys at the same
time). Select the **Run** command by clicking on it, or by
pressing **R**. Now retry the installation by typing the same
command you did before, such as

    A:INSTALL

or

    A:SETUP

*Do not attempt these commands from the temporary DOS
prompt that Windows provides,* unless of course, it's July 4th
and you want to add to the fireworks.

Running Programs Like a Pro

Now that you've installed your program, let's see how you might start it if
there's no one around to help. First, check the manual for the proper
command to start the program (I know—"Duh!") If you can't find it, go
exploring by typing **DIR C:*. /P**. That's **DIR** *space* C *colon backslash
asterisk period space forward-slash* **P**. This command lists all the main directories on your C drive (along with any files that don't have extensions;
ignore these). Look for a directory with a recent date. If you find one, it
must be a new directory, so that's probably your new program. Let's say
you find a new directory called FASTACTG. Type something like this:

CD\FASTACTG

This command takes you to the FASTACTG directory. Now search for a file to start the program by typing this command:

DIR *.EXE /P

What are you looking for? Well, something obvious. For example, if you just bought a program called Fast Accountant, you might see FA.EXE or FAST.EXE, or something similar. (Clue: It'll be a file which ends in .EXE.) Type the name you see (not the whole thing, just the part *in front of the .EXE* thing), and you'll probably start the program:

FAST

If you didn't find anything appropriate, try this command:

DIR *.COM

or this command

DIR *.BAT

Still not in the program? Well, it was a good effort, but now it's time to go find a PC guru to help you.

Learning How to Use Your New Program

Once you make it inside the program, you're stuck with the boring job of learning how to use it. Yech! Oh well, one good thing to keep in mind is that a lot of this stuff you'll only need to learn once. Once you know how to do some of the basics, use a mouse, select a command, save a file, you can apply what you learn to just about any new program you might buy.

If there's a tutorial program built into your application, by all means *use it.* If the thing gets too boring or too confusing, you can always bail out. Take notes on whatever the tutorial shows you, so you can use it later.

To start the tutorial, you probably need to open the Help menu. What's a menu? Read on...

Menu Mania

After you get your program started, the first thing you will probably see are some menus. What's a *menu*? See the next figure for a picture of one. Menus present lists of commands to choose from, so you don't have to memorize a lot of key combinations.

Menus are usually tucked away in a menu bar at the top of the screen. The menu bar lists the main menu names, such as File, Edit, and Help. Under each of these menus, there are additional selections, but you can't see them until you *pull down* (open) the menu.

Pull down   A *pull-down* menu contains commands you can select. This type of menu, when activated, is "pulled down" from the main menu bar, the way a window shade can be pulled down from the top of a window frame.

The Annual Menu System Convention(s)

Most menu systems make use of these *conventions*:

A dialog box appears when you choose any command followed by an ellipsis.

The command you select is highlighted.

Pull-down menu

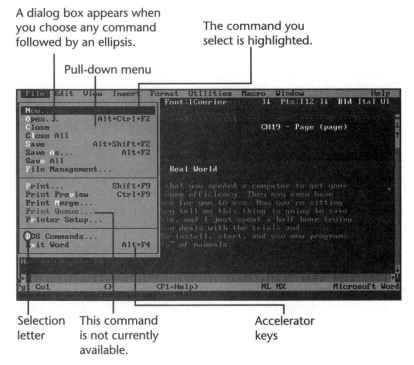

Selection letter

This command is not currently available.

Accelerator keys

Most menu systems follow the same conventions.

Grayed text   Commands that are currently unavailable are grayed to prevent you from selecting them, and to let you know that these selections are normally available but this time, they are just not. (I've often suspected that grayed text is just there to tease you.) For example in the figure, the Print Queue command is currently greyed because nothing is printing, so there's no "queue" or list of printing documents to look at.

Selection letter   A single letter of a menu command, such as *x* in Exit, that can be used to activate the command with the keyboard when the menu is open. Selection letters appear as underlined or bold letters on the main menu.

Dialog box   A dialog box is a special window that appears when the program requires additional information before executing a command. It generally asks you a question, like "Should I save this file first?" and then gives you a simple choice of "Yes," "No," and "Help" buttons. The Help button is generally there when you don't know what choosing Yes or choosing No would really do.

Accelerator keys   Like selection letters, these can be used to activate the command with the keyboard. Unlike selection letters, however, accelerator keys work without opening the menu. Usually a function key or key combination, such as Alt+F2, accelerator keys are displayed next to the menu command. To use an accelerator key, press the first key (in this case, **Alt**) and hold it down, then press the second key (in this case, **F2**). (They're called "accelerator keys" because great sci-fi-sounding names make them sound fast, and help sell the programs that use them.)

Ellipsis   An ellipsis consists of three periods after a menu command, such as the File Save As... command. An ellipsis indicates that after you've chosen this command, a *dialog box* appears, requiring you to provide more specific information before the command is executed.

Take Your Pick: Selecting Menu Commands

It's easy to select menu commands using either the mouse or the keyboard.

To select a menu command with the mouse, click (press the left mouse button) while pointing to the menu name. For example, click on the word **File**. While the menu is open, click once on any menu command to select it.

To select a menu command with the keyboard, press **Alt** plus the **selection letter** at the same time. For example, to open the File pull-down menu, press **Alt** and **F** at the same time. While the menu is open, use the arrow keys to highlight any command, and then press **Enter** to select it. Alternatively, you can press the selection letter for the command. For example, with the **File** menu open, you can select the **Save** command by pressing the letter **S**.

Talking to Your Computer Through Dialog Boxes

When you select a menu command that requires additional information, a dialog box appears. Commands that result in the display of dialog boxes appear on menus with an ellipsis, as in the File Save As... command.

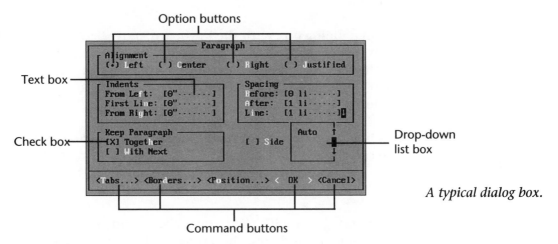

A typical dialog box.

There are a few standard components of dialog boxes:

List box   Presents a list of items to choose from, such as a list of files.

Text box   Enables the user to type in (or edit) information, such as the name of a file.

Drop-down list box   Like a normal list box, except that the list does not display until activated. The list displays under the main list item, like a window shade.

Check boxes   Check boxes are used to indicate options that can be turned on or off, such as Read Only.

Option buttons   Option buttons are used to select mutually-exclusive options, such as Right, Center, or Left alignment.

Command buttons   Perform some specific command, such as Start or direct the program to carry out or ignore the dialog box selections with OK or Cancel.

Making the Right Choice

In some dialog boxes, you'll be presented with many different components, such as list boxes and option buttons, that you use to make your choices. You can use either the mouse or the keyboard when making these choices in a dialog box.

To move around in a dialog box with the keyboard, move between dialog components by pressing **Tab** to move forward, and **Shift** and **Tab** to move backward. Alternatively, you can press **Alt** plus the highlighted letter of the dialog component. For example, to move in a dialog box to a list box named **Directories**, press **Alt** and **D**.

To make choices in a dialog box with the keyboard, use the arrow keys. (In a list box, you can also use the Home, End, PgUp, and PgDn keys.) To select an option button or check box, use the **Spacebar** to toggle the option on or off.

To move around a dialog box with the mouse, click on any item (point to it with the mouse pointer, and press the left mouse button). To select an option button or check box, click on it to toggle the option on or off.

You'll meet some of these players while using dialog boxes: select **Cancel** to cancel the choices you have made in the dialog box and return to your program. Select the **Close** button to retain the choices you made and close the dialog box without executing those choices. If you want to close the dialog box and execute your choices, use the **OK** button.

A Special Look at the Lotus Menu System

Some programs use what is known as the Lotus menu system, made popular by the spreadsheet program Lotus 1-2-3. The Lotus menu bar appears at the top of the screen like most menu systems, but when a main menu is selected, the menu commands appear across the screen instead of on a pull-down menu.

These are the commands
on the File menu.

```
A:A1: 'INCOME STATEMENT 1992: Sloane Camera and Video
        Save  Combine  Xtract  Erase  List  Import  Dir  New  Open  Admin
Replace the current file with a file from disk
  A
      INCOME STATEMENT 1992: Sloane Camera and Video

                     Q1         Q2         Q3         Q4         YTD

      Net Sales  $12,000.00  $19,000.00  $16,000.00  $22,000.00  $69,000.00


      Costs and Expenses:
        Salary      2,000.00    2,000.00    2,000.00    2,500.00    8,500.00
        Int         1,200.00    1,400.00    1,600.00    1,600.00    5,800.00
        Rent          600.00      600.00      600.00      600.00    2,400.00
        Ads           900.00    2,000.00    4,000.00    4,500.00   11,400.00
        COG         4,000.00    4,200.00    5,000.00    8,000.00   21,200.00

        Op Exp      8,700.00   10,200.00   13,200.00   17,200.00   49,300.00

      Op Income   $3,300.00   $8,800.00   $2,800.00   $4,800.00  $19,700.00


INC10S.WK3
```

Lotus uses a horizontal menu system that works differently from the standard pull-down menu.

This is a description of
the highlighted
command, Retrieve.

Although you can select Lotus commands with a mouse, most people don't—it's too easy just to use the keyboard. To select a menu command with the keyboard, press / (the forward slash) to display the menu. Then use the left or right arrow keys to highlight a menu, and press **Enter**. Use the left or right arrow keys to select a command.

You can also select a menu or a command by pressing the first letter of its name. For example, to select the **File** menu with the menu displayed, press **F**. To select the **Save** command on the File menu, press **S** with the File menu displayed. The entire sequence to select the File Save command consists of three keystrokes: **/**, **F**, and **S**.

Saving and Printing

One of the first things you must learn in order to use your program safely is how to save what you create. Remember, your computer has a *really* short memory: if you turn off your computer before you save your work, it's erased. (How rude.)

To save your work, open the File menu and select the Save command. (Click on the menu to open it, or press **Alt+F**, then press **S** to select the Save command.)

You'll see one of those dialog boxes, asking you for more information. You'll see a lot of confusing bells and whistles that you can just ignore. Type a filename and press **Enter**. That's it—your document is saved!

As you type the filename, make it something descriptive to help you identify your document later on. In a show of overwhelming generosity, DOS allows up to *eight whole characters* for this filename. The filename can contain letters or numbers, but no spaces; for example, SALES94 or LETHOME or TAXFIG93. And that's not all! The filename may contain !, @, #, &, (, or) *absolutely free!* (You're still limited to eight characters, though. Offer void where prohibited.)

Once your work is saved, it's left on your screen so you can continue making changes if you want (if you want to leave the program, exit stage right, to the last section of this chapter). Don't let them get you on this one—if you make more changes, you've got to save them too. Open the **File** menu and select **Save** again. This time you won't need to enter a filename, since by now, even silly ol' DOS remembers what you called it. Your document is saved again under its original name. This more recent version overwrites your original document, easy as pie.

To print your document, you may be able to get away quick by clicking on an *icon*, a button representing the action you want performed. In this case, look for a tiny picture of a printer. If you find it, click on it with your mouse. If you can't find it (or a cute picture was not provided) open the **File** menu by pressing **Alt+F**, then select the **Print** command by pressing **P**.

Another one of those nosy dialog boxes will probably appear. If it does, just ignore the darn thing and press **Enter**. Your document should now print.

Getting Out of There

Well, you've had some fun, but now it's time to exit your program. First, save whatever you're working on. (Take one step back to the last section.)

To exit, open the File menu and select the Exit command. Click on the **File** menu to open it, or press **Alt+F**. Click on the **Exit** command, or press **X**. When you see the whites of DOS' eyes (the good ol' DOS prompt), you can safely turn your computer off, or start the whole process again by starting up another program.

The program may ask you if you're crazy, because I mean, why would you ever want to leave? Anyway, answer Yes by pressing **Enter** (who's it going to tell?).

The Least You Need to Know

You won't need AAA to jumpstart your applications if you remember these basics:

- ☞ In most programs, you access help by pressing **F1**.

- ☞ To install your new program, place the first installation diskette in drive A, then type something like **A:SETUP** or **A:INSTALL**.

- ☞ To select a command from a menu with the keyboard, press **Alt** plus the shortcut key at the same time. While the menu is open, use the arrow keys to

continues

continued

highlight the command you want, and then press **Enter** to select it.

To select a menu command with the mouse, click (press the left mouse button) while using the mouse pointer to point to the menu name.

☞ To select a command in a program that uses the Lotus menu system, press /, the first letter of the menu, and then the first letter of the command.

☞ Move between dialog box components by pressing **Tab** to move forward, and **Shift** and **Tab** to move backward. You can also press **Alt** plus the highlighted letter of the dialog component.

☞ To make choices in a dialog box with the keyboard, use the arrow keys. (In a list box, you can also use the Home, End, PgUp, and PgDn keys.) To select an option button or check box, use the **Spacebar** to toggle the option on or off.

☞ To move around a dialog box with the mouse, click on any item. To seiect an option button or check-box, click on it to toggle the option on or off.

☞ To save your document, open the File menu and select Save. Type a filename with no more than eight characters, then press **Enter**.

☞ To print your document, open the File menu and select Print. Ignore the dialog box and just press **Enter**.

☞ To exit your program, open the File menu and select Exit. If it asks you if you're sure, select Yes by pressing **Enter**.

Chapter 22
It's a Windows Wonderland

In This Chapter

- Tour of the Windows winter landscape
- Opening and closing Windows
- Playing with windows while no one's looking
- Why washing Windows is not a good idea
- Using Windows to start programs instead of doing DOS

If you've just recently purchased your computer, chances are you own Microsoft Windows. You may not have asked for it, but it's there anyway. (The modern definition of a "popular" product: Everybody owns it, whether they want it or not, like those automatic shoulder-strap seat belts.)

It's quite possible you may end up preferring to use Windows rather than DOS for some of the everyday file-management chores. You may also find that Windows programs and applications seem more sensible than DOS programs. This doesn't mean you have to abandon DOS, and forget everything the last 21 chapters told you. In fact, you'll find that Windows and DOS work pretty well together (a bit like sending a message simultaneously by telephone and smoke signal, but in all, a workable arrangement). If you're familiar with Windows, but not with using DOS within Windows, skip to Chapter 24.

Icon   A graphic image that represents a command, such as saving or printing. An icon can also represent an object, such as a file on a disk.

So What is Windows?

Windows is the "microwave" version of DOS: fast, hot, and safe from a distance of five feet. It's just easier to get things done with Windows than by using DOS alone, which is a good reason most computers sold today come with Windows. So why is Windows easier? Windows is full of pictures called *icons*, which represent stuff you want to do, or things you want to work with. Drag a picture of a piece of paper over to a picture of a hard disk, and you've just copied a file. Select a picture which looks like Word for Windows, and start it.

Another nice feature of Windows: it can run more than one program at a time. That means you can start your word processor to write a letter to the boss asking for more money, then—without having to exit—jump over to a calculator program to figure out a nice percentage to ask for. Handy.

Some programs require Windows in order to work. These programs are called, cleverly enough, *Windows programs*. Some of the popular Windows programs include Word for Windows, Excel, and Lotus 1-2-3 for Windows. When you go shopping for software, just look for the Windows logo to tell whether the software requires Windows or not. Windows can run more than just Windows programs, however. It can run your DOS programs too, and do a better job of it. So don't think you're stuck if you have mostly DOS programs.

Although I can't teach you everything you'll want to know about Windows in this one little ol' chapter, you'll learn what you need to know in order to use Windows to perform DOS tasks, instead of that ugly DOS prompt. If you're just dying to know more, pick up another one of our cute orange books: *The Complete Idiot's Guide to Windows*—available where all orange books are sold.

Starting Windows

When you turn on some computers, Windows starts by itself. If you can talk some guru into doing the work, you can get your computer to do that too. (If you want to attempt this little bit of automation yourself, it's actually not that difficult—see Chapter 16 on how to add the WIN command to your AUTOEXEC.BAT startup file.) If you see the DOS prompt when you start your PC, then type **WIN** and press **Enter** to start Windows. Away it goes. When Windows has started, you'll see a screen that looks something like this:

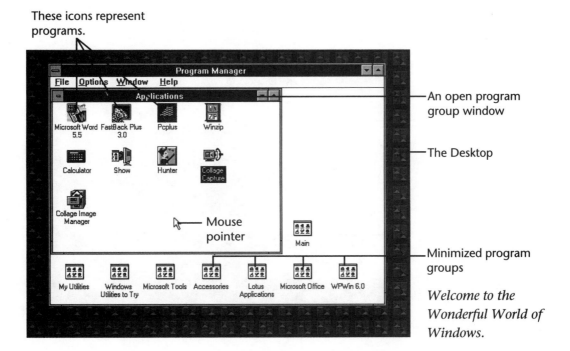

These icons represent programs.

An open program group window

The Desktop

Mouse pointer

Minimized program groups

Welcome to the Wonderful World of Windows.

DO NOT REBOOT or restart the computer while Windows is running. That's a *big* No-No. Depending on how many programs you're running at the time, it could mean wholesale slaughter for your files. To shut down safely, see the section called, "Quitting Windows" later in this chapter.

A Walking Tour of Windows

The Program Manager is like a butler who greets you in Windows. True to its name, it manages all programs you want to run. The "floor" underneath Program Manager is called the Desktop. Windows' programs hang out in program groups, instead of at the mall. Each icon (picture) you see represents a program which you can run for fun or profit.

The Desktop is where all your active programs sit, in boxes called, well, *windows*. Actually, Program Manager itself is just another active program, waiting around in its box for someone to ask it do something. You can put your programs away temporarily by "minimizing" them, which you'll learn how to do in a moment. A minimized program is still running, in a kind of "suspended animation."

Each program runs in its own window.

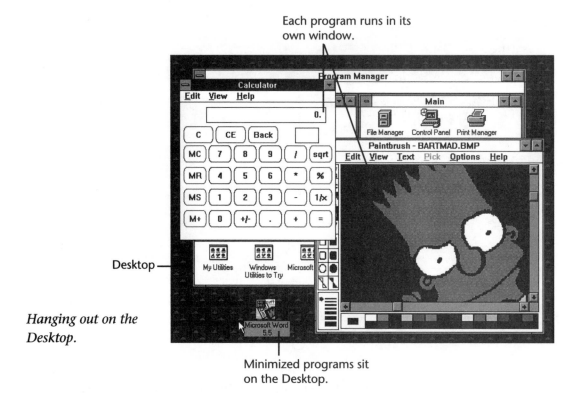

Desktop —

Hanging out on the Desktop.

Minimized programs sit on the Desktop.

That Mighty Mouse

Windows is easier to use when you've got a mouse. Not those white things that prance around in laboratories, high on the drug du jour, but a mechanical one that helps you point to things on-screen. With a mouse, you click, double-click, or drag (usually with the left mouse button) to get things done quickly—so save yourself the hassle of fumbling with the keyboard and get a mouse to use with Windows.

Moving Windows

Every time you start a program, it's placed in its own window. If you look back at the last figure, you'll see two programs, each running in its own window. You can move these windows around the screen, just as you move stuff around on your desk to reveal things you should have done yesterday. Just click on a window's *title bar* (that bar across the top of each window that shows the name of each program), hold down the mouse button, and drag that critter wherever you want. A rectangle in the shape of the window will follow your mouse as you wrangle it around the desktop like a steer in a rodeo. Release the mouse button to "drop" the window.

Minimizing, Maximizing, and Resizing Windows

Point To move the mouse pointer over top of an object on-screen.

Click To click with the mouse, press the left mouse button once.

Double-click To double-click with the mouse, press the mouse button twice in rapid succession.

Drag To drag with the mouse, first move the mouse pointer to the starting position. Now click and hold the left mouse button. Drag the mouse pointer to the ending position and release the mouse button.

You can resize a window so it fills the screen, or takes up less room. Windows can also overlap each other in a kind of patchwork quilt. To minimize a window (shrink it down to an icon), click on the down arrow—that's the *Minimize button*. Minimizing a program window doesn't stop the program, but instead it puts it into a kind of suspended animation until you wake it up by double-clicking (clicking two times really fast) while the mouse pointer is over the minimized icon.

To *maximize* a window so it fills the entire screen, click on the up arrow—that's the *Maximize button*. When you maximize a screen, the up arrow transmutes into a two-headed arrow called the *Restore button*. If you click on it, the window returns to whatever odd size it was before you maximized it.

Title bar   Minimize button   Maximize button

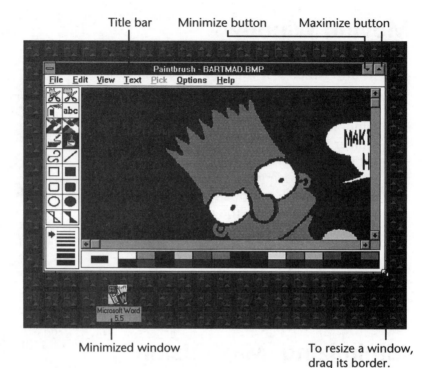

*The Windows
Grapefruit Diet plan.*

Minimized window   To resize a window,
                                     drag its border.

To resize a window to any size you want, click on the window's edge. Hold down the mouse button and drag the border outward to make the window bigger, or inward to make it smaller. You'll see a ghostly outline of the window border to make this easier to do. Release the mouse button when the window's the right size.

Your Butler, Program Manager, Awaits Your Command

As I said earlier, Program Manager is like a butler, waiting patiently for you to tell it to run some program. To start a program, you open the program group window in which it's stored. For example, if you look back at the first figure in this chapter, you'll see that there's one group window already open: the Applications group window. Once a program group window is open, you can start any program inside.

Starting a Program with Program Manager

To open a program group window, double-click on it. Double-clicking is like snapping your fingers to get attention. By clicking two times quickly with the mouse button, you're telling Windows to pay attention 'cause you want it to do something *now*.

To start a program, double-click on its icon. For example, if you're still looking at that first figure, you'd double-click on the icon for Microsoft Word to start that program.

General Stuff All Windows' Programs Share

Windows is more fun than a day at an amusement park: lots of stuff to drag, slide, or poke at. All Windows' programs share the same basic cast of characters, which makes using Windows fun (there's less stuff to learn with each new program). You've already met the title bar and the Minimize and Maximize buttons; let me introduce you to the rest of the crew.

When you start a DOS program from Windows, that DOS program takes over the entire screen, as if you started it from the DOS prompt. If you need to switch between it and several other programs quickly, you can force a DOS program to fit into a resizeable window. But be warned: this will make the DOS program look very weird. Press **Alt+Enter**, and as long as the DOS program is currently not using any graphics, it will shrink to fit into its own window, like its been left in the dryer too long. Press **Alt+Enter** again to switch things back to normal.

Scroll Bars

A window can only display so much information on-screen. In the same way a window on your house shows you a portion of the world, a window in Windows shows you a portion of your *document*. The windows in Windows allow you to look at another part of your document by *scrolling*.

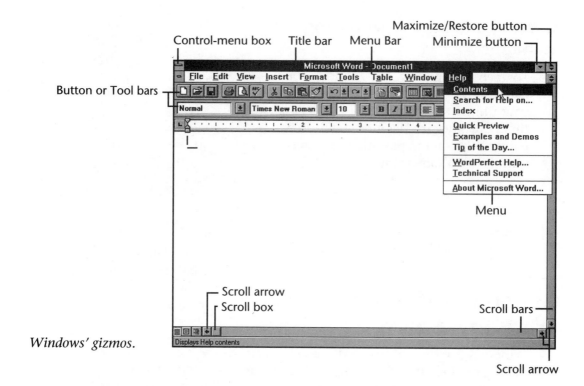

Control-menu box   Title bar   Menu Bar   Maximize/Restore button
Minimize button

Button or Tool bars

Menu

Scroll arrow
Scroll box

Scroll bars

Windows' gizmos.

Scroll arrow

If you cut a square hole in the center of a piece of paper, then held this page under the hole, and then slid the book up and down or left and right beneath the hole as you read the text, you'd get the idea of what scrolling a window's all about (however, you'd probably miss some of this great comic banter).

There's a *horizontal scroll bar* along the bottom of a window, and a *vertical scroll bar* along the right-hand side. Inside each of these bars is a small box. One way to move a different section of the document "beneath" the viewing window is to scoot one of these boxes. While the mouse pointer is over the scroll box, you click and hold the left mouse button, drag the box to another location, then release the button.

Another way to change your view of the document is to scroll. Click on the scroll arrows at either end of the scroll bar. The scroll box itself moves along the scroll track a proportionate amount, so you can always tell what portion of the overall picture you're seeing. I think of the scroll box as a kind of elevator car that shows me what floor I'm on. For example, if you were looking at the first lines of a document, the scroll box would be all the way at the top of the vertical scroll bar (on the top "floor"). If you were looking at page 12 of a 20-page document, the scroll box would be about halfway down on the scroll bar. You get the picture.

Menus

Windows' programs present commands in lists called *menus*. The main menus are arranged from left to right along a menu bar. Click on the menu name (such as **Help**), and the menu falls down in front of you to reveal all the commands inside. Click once on a command to select it. Some commands are not always available, so they are grey and lonely. Clicking on them has no effect.

Button or Tool Bars

Most programs have button bars or toolbars, or whatever they're called this week, which are filled with little buttons. Each button contains a picture (an *icon*) which represents some command, such as saving a document, or printing. Decipher what the pictures mean, click on the right button, and the program will dutifully carry out your request.

Control-menu Box

At the left-hand edge of the Title bar is the *Control-menu box*, which contains a list of commands that affect the window itself (such as moving and resizing). Double-click on this guy to close a window, which stops the program. (More on stopping programs in just a minute.)

BY THE WAY

Windows works like us humans—it can focus on only one program at a time (even if it does so almost as fast as a speeding bullet). It attends to the one program, then switches to the next one when the first one's needs are met. The program Windows is attending to is called "the active program."

Which window is the active one? Just look at the title bar. The brighter-looking one contains the currently active program. If you haven't changed the Windows default colors, then the active window is the one with the blue title bar. The inactive windows have a grey-white title bar.

Switching Between Programs

What's the use in running twenty programs at once if you can't switch between them? It would be like trying to use a 120-channel TV without a remote. Luckily, Windows has seen to it that you have a way to switch between programs whenever you want. In Windows (unlike in DOS), you don't have to exit one program completely to start using another.

For example, I might start up Word for Windows (a word processor I use to write this stuff—see? I'm not entirely to blame), Collage Plus (a program that takes a picture of what's on my screen so I can illustrate what I'm writing about), Excel (a spreadsheet program like Lotus 1-2-3, which I use to keep track of how much I've written, which is usually not enough), and File Manager (a program that comes with Windows, which I use to copy my finished documents onto a diskette so I can give them to my editor, who removes the really bad jokes). Throughout the day, I jump back and forth, moving from one program to another as my needs change.

There are three ways to switch among programs:

☞ **Quickest method:** If you can see the program on-screen, just click inside its window to activate it.

☞ **Almost the quickest method:** If you want to get a program out of the way, minimize it by clicking on that down-arrow-thing. (Remember that minimizing a program only "puts it to sleep" temporarily.) Just double-click (click twice fast) on its icon to reactivate that program. Once your programs are minimized, you should be able to see the program you want to switch to—just click inside that program's window, or double-click on its minimized icon to switch to it.

☛ **The-not-so-quick-but-it-works-every-time-method:** Press **Ctrl+Escape** at the same time to bring up the Task List, the TV listing of what's currently running. Double click on a program's name to switch to it. You can also press **Alt+Escape** to switch to the next program in line, without having to go through the Task List. As if that wasn't enough to remember, you can also press **Alt+Tab** at the same time and see the name of the next program in line. Keep pressing **Alt+Tab** until you see the name of the program you want, then release both keys, and Dorothy, you're not in Kansas anymore.

Stopping Programs

Learning to stop programs (exit, quit, say Sayonara, baby) safely is probably the most important things you can learn. Mess this up, and you might lose that letter home asking Mom to send more money. So first, save that precious letter. There might be a funny-looking button to click on (such as the miniature image of a diskette), or you might have to click once on the **File** menu name (located at the top of the window), then click once on the **Save** command. If you haven't saved your letter before, type a name with 1 to 8 letters, such as **LETHOME**, then press the **Enter** key. OK. Now that you're hard work is saved (and your future monetary concerns have been taken care of), go ahead and stop the program.

To stop a program, you click once on the File menu name, then click on the Exit command. You can show off your newly acquired Windows skills with this quickie method: just double-click on the Control-menu box (that's the box with the big minus sign in it, located in the upper left-hand corner of the window—see the last figure if you need help ID-ing it).

Quitting Windows

If you quit Program Manager, you quit Windows. So to exit Windows, just click on Program Manager's **File** menu and select **Exit**. You can also double-click on the Program Manager's Control-menu box if you're in a hurry. Just be sure to close down (exit, quit) all your other programs first, before you try to leave Windows. Once you're out of Windows, you'll be returned to the Land of the Dull DOS Prompt (which looks something like **C>** or **C:\WIN>**), at which point you can turn off your computer.

The Least You Need to Know

☛ Get a mouse to use with Windows.

☛ Clicking is pressing the mouse button one time. Double-clicking means you press it twice, in quick succession. Dragging is done by clicking on something, hold the mouse button down, then dragging that something on-screen to wherever you want, and releasing the mouse button to drop it.

☛ Type **WIN** and press **Enter** to start Windows. Double-click on the Program Manager's Control-menu box (the minus sign in the upper left corner) to exit Windows.

☛ An icon is just a pretty picture that represents some command, or some file. Deciphering what the picture means can be confusing, but clicking on it can be fun.

☛ Each program you run is placed in its own window that you can move around on-screen, resize, maximize (stretch to fill the screen), and minimize (shrink down to an icon). To move, drag a window by its title bar. To resize, drag its border. To maximize, click on the up arrow in the right-hand corner of the window. To minimize, click on the down arrow. When a window's been minimized, double-click on the icon to open it back up.

☛ To start a program, double-click on its icon. To stop a program, click on the File menu and then click on Exit. Be sure to save your file if asked.

☛ Windows can run several programs at one time, and you can switch between them by pressing **Alt+Esc, Alt+Tab,** or **Ctrl+Esc.**

Chapter 23
Managing (Not Mangling) Files in Windows

In This Chapter

- ☞ Copying and moving files with File Manager
- ☞ Deleting files just for the heck of it
- ☞ Adding and deleting directories
- ☞ Special DOS tools just for Windows

If Program Manager is the Captain of the *SS Windows*, then File Manager is its first mate, Gilligan. File Manager helps you take care of all those common DOS chores such as copying, moving, or deleting files. Like other Windows' programs, File Manager has lots of icons and neat stuff that makes it easier (or at least more fun) than plain ol' DOS.

Unlike Gilligan, File Manager usually does things exactly like you want. If you're careless with the mouse however, File Manager can quickly turn in to *File Mangler*. But have no fear, for the most part, File Manager is harmless fun, and much more entertaining than DOS.

I usually leave my Main group open so I can get to File Manager more quickly. To do that, just leave it open when you exit Windows. When you start Windows up later, the Main group will still be open and ready for your immediate enjoyment.

Starting File Manager

To start File Manager, open the Main program group window by double-clicking (clicking twice fast) on its icon (the little picture with the word "Main" underneath it). Once the Main group window is open, double-click on the File Manager icon (looks like a miniature file cabinet).

Once File Manager is running, you can use it to copy files from one directory on the hard disk to another, or to copy them onto a floppy diskette. You can delete, move, or rename files too. You can also create and delete directories. In File Manager, you get most things done by dragging icons (cute pictures of file folders and document pages) from one place to another on-screen.

Listing Files

File Manager lists the files for only one directory or drive at a time. You can open multiple file windows to display two or more directories/drives at once. You can even minimize these windows down at the bottom of the screen to get the extra ones out of the way.

Each window is pretty much the same: the directories are listed on the left, and the files for the currently selected directory are listed on the right. Various drive icons are listed at the top. Each window also includes the common Windows gizmos (such as Minimize and Maximize buttons, scroll bars, and the like). File Manager also has a menu along the top of its window, full of commands. If you're on unfamiliar ground here, jump back a few pages and review the section called "General Stuff All Windows' Programs Share."

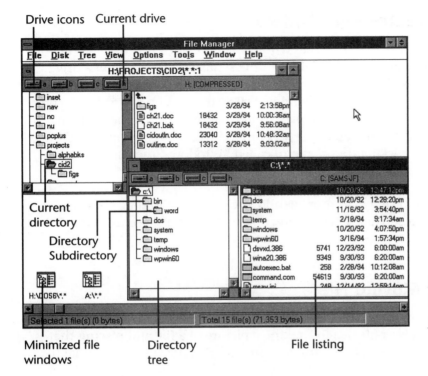

Drive icons   Current drive

Current directory

Directory
Subdirectory

Minimized file windows

Directory tree

File listing

Directories on the left, files on the right, please.

Changing Drives and Directories

To change the file listing so it shows you the files on a different drive, just click on the drive thingamajigs at the top of each window. Clicking on the A drive button gets you a floppy drive; clicking on the C drive button gets you your hard disk. If you've DoubleSpaced or DriveSpaced your drive as I have (see Chapter 18 for more "double" talk), you'll see a drive H or I. That's where most of your stuff is. Also, if someone installed DOS 6, 6.2, 6.21, or 6.22 on your PC, chances are you have a special Tools menu like mine. You'll learn what's behind that door at the end of this chapter.

To change to a different directory, click on one of the file-folder-thingies on the left-hand side of the window. This area is called the Directory Tree, because it lists all your directories and subdirectories (branches). When a directory's selected, the file folder opens. The title bar changes too, to show the name of the currently-selected drive and directory.

Creating an Extra File Window

If you want more than one files window (a good idea if you're moving or copying files between directories or drives), just double-click on a drive icon. For example, you can double-click (you know, click twice) on the A drive icon, and create a new window listing the files on the A drive. You can then drag these new windows around, or minimize some of them them (as I did for the figure), or split up the screen evenly among all open windows (by clicking on the menu called "Window," then selecting the **Tile** or the **Cascade** command).

Once you have two or more windows open, you can drag file-thingies from one place to another to reorganize your hard disk, or to copy files onto a diskette.

Copying or Moving Files

Copying and moving files are the main reasons you'll use File Manager. When you copy a file, it's like taking a picture of a file and placing that extra copy in a new place. Moving a file simply relocates the original file.

Copying a file is easy. Let's say you wanted to copy the file WIN.INI from your \WINDOWS directory on the C drive, to a diskette in drive A. Change to drive C by clicking on the icon. Change to the \WINDOWS directory by clicking on its folder. Click on the WIN.INI file, and hold the mouse button down as you drag the file over to the A drive icon. A file icon will follow along as you drag. Release the mouse button. If you see a box asking you if it's OK to do what you want, click on **Yes** and then you're done.

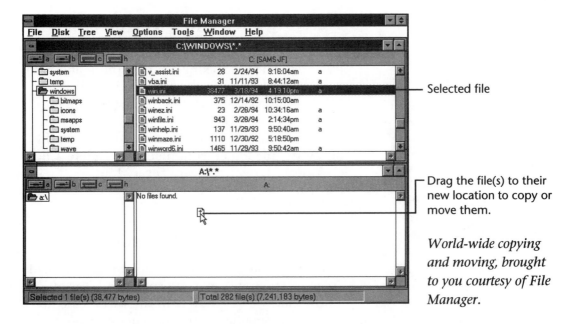

Selected file

Drag the file(s) to their new location to copy or move them.

World-wide copying and moving, brought to you courtesy of File Manager.

To move files instead, select the file, then press and hold the Alt key. Drag the file and release the mouse button, and it's moved. If you want to move or copy a file to a different directory, just drag the file to that directory on the left, instead of dragging it to a drive icon.

To copy or move more than one file at a time, press and hold the Ctrl key as you click on each file. Each file you select is highlighted. Once you've selected your last file, grab 'em by clicking over one of the selected files (still holding that Ctrl key), then drag them as a group to a new drive or directory. The icon following your cursor will look like multiple pieces of paper, so you'll know you've got more than one file.

To copy or move a file (or files), open two file windows. This will make it easy for you to reorganize your files without making a mistake. Once you have two windows open, set one to the drive and directory where the file is stored, then set the other to the drive and directory where the file is to be moved or copied. All set? Now copy or move your files by dragging them between the windows (as the figure shows).

If you got a little trigger-happy and deleted an important file, you may be able to get it back with the Undelete utility for Windows (included with the DOS 6 somethings). See the end of this chapter for emergency instructions. If you don't have at least DOS 6, see your PC guru for help. Bring lots of cookies.

Deleting Files and Directories

If files or directories make you mad, delete them! Just select files by clicking on them (press and hold the Ctrl key if you want to select more than one file), then fire away with the Delete key. You may see a box asking you if this is OK, so just click on **Yes**. To delete a directory (remove it), click on the directory's file-folder icon, then press **Delete**. Click on **Yes to All** (which means "everything must go!"), and the directory's a goner.

Renaming Files and Directories

Sometimes you get it wrong. It might have seemed OK to call your memo about smoking in the office simply MEMO.DOC, but now that you've got to write another memo, it seems silly. Well, don't worry, just rename the file to something more meaningful like NOSMOKE.DOC. Here's what you do: select the file, then click once on the **File** menu to open it. Click on **Rename**. Type a new name *in the bottom box*, then press **Enter**.

You can rename directories the same way: select one, open the **File** menu, select **Rename**, then type a new name *in the bottom box* and press **Enter**.

Special Stuff You Get With the DOS 6 Somethings

The DOS 6-somethings (DOS 6, 6.2, 6.21, and 6.22) come with a grab bag of goodies designed for Windows. They were placed in a special group window called Microsoft Tools, so keep an eye out for it. Inside you'll find three utilities: Anti-Virus, Backup, and Undelete. You've met the DOS versions of these utilities in previous chapters: Anti-Virus was in Chapter 17, Backup in Chapter 14, and Undelete in Chapter 6. Turn the pages back in time if you need a quickie update.

To get to the tools, you have to be in Windows of course. Switch to Program Manager and double-click on the program group icon called Microsoft Tools. Then double-click on the utility du jour.

When DOS 6.x ("6.x" is techno-nerdspeak for "6 something") was installed, the Windows versions of these utilities were installed for you—provided you told the program to copy both the DOS *and* WIndows versions to your hard disk. If you know you have at least DOS 6, but you can't find the utilities in Windows, ask a guru to help you install them.

Microsoft Windows Anti-Virus

An anti-virus program protects your system from infection by over-zealous (and extremely unofficial) programs—often created as pranks or outright sabotage, then disguised as mild-mannered reporters—that can take over your system and destroy your files willy-nilly. To prevent the foolishness and bad language they cause, use the Anti-Virus utility.

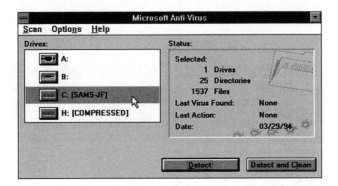

Microsoft Anti-Virus on the prowl.

Start the program by double-clicking on its icon in the Microsoft Tools group window. Click on a drive letter, then click on **Detect** and **Clean**. This will take awhile, so sit back and watch the display. If anything out of the ordinary is detected, you'll hear a beep and see a box asking you what to do. Pick an option and get on with your merry life: **Update** tells

Anti-Virus to update its files, that the file was changed deliberately. **Clean** tells Anti-Virus that you don't know why the file was changed, and to see if it can fix it. Close down the program like any other; click on the **Scan** menu and then click on **Exit Anti-Virus**.

MS Backup for Windows

The Windows version of MS Backup is remarkably similar to the DOS version. So similar in fact, that there's very little to tell, other than what you already learned in Chapter 14. Here's a quickie review: to back up the entire hard disk, double-click on the drive icon. The information at the bottom of the window will show you how much time you'll spend changing diskettes and staring at the walls while the backup is going on.

Change the floppy drive shown in the Backup To box (if you want) by clicking that down-arrow-thingie and clicking on a new drive. You can perform an *incremental* or *differential* backup by clicking on the down arrow in the Backup Type box, and selecting a different option. Click on **Start Backup** to start the show. When the show's over, click on the **File** menu and click on **Exit**.

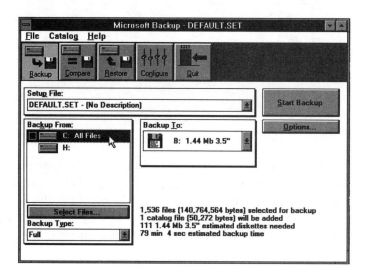

Back up and take another look at the Windows version of MS Backup.

TECHNO NERD TEACHES...

You won't be able to back up any files currently being used by Windows, so for a complete backup of your system, you're better off using the DOS version of MS Backup. By the way, if you do a backup in Windows, you can restore it using the DOS version, and *vice versa*.

To restore a backup, click on the **Restore** button. Double-click on the drive you want to restore, then click on **Start Restore**. If you've done lots of previous backups, you can use an old one if you want. Just dust it off and select it from the **Backup Set Catalog** list.

Microsoft Undelete

Undeleting is probably the most fun I have in Windows (other than playing with my screen saver). It gives me such power, knowing I can act like an idiot and delete any file I want, then say "Oops," act real cute, and get it back.

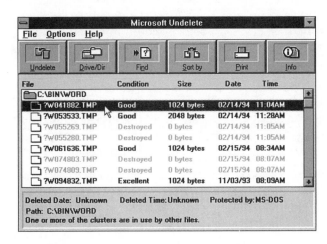

On a salvage expedition.

Start the Undelete utility just like all the others: double-click on the **Microsoft Tools** program group icon to open that window, then double-click on the **Undelete** icon to start the program. Now, click on the **Drive/Dir** button-thing, and click on the directory which contains the file you accidentally zapped. Click on the **OK**ey-dokey button.

TECHNO NERD TEACHES...

If you don't see the directory you want, you'll have to wander the directory halls. Double-click on [..] to go up in the directory tree, or double-click on a directory name to go down (find a subdirectory). Double-click on a letter thing-a-mabob (such as [-h-]) to change to that drive. Click on the directory you want, and then click on OK.

You'll see a bunch of files listed, some of which won't be salvageable. (A *salvageable* file in this instance is one that DOS hasn't yet overwritten with new files.) Click on the name of a salvageable file, and then click on the Undelete magic button. If you zapped several files, click on each one while holding down the Ctrl key, then click on Undelete. After performing surgery on your files, click the File menu and click on Exit.

The Least You Need to Know

☞ To change to a different drive in File Manager, click on the drive icon. To change to a different directory, click on the directory folder on the left-hand side of the window. To create an extra window for working, double-click on the drive icon.

☞ To copy a file in File Manager, click on it and drag it to wherever you want to place the copy. To move the file instead, press and hold the Alt key as you drag. To copy or move more than one file, press and hold the **Ctrl** key as you click on filenames.

☞ To delete a file or directory in File Manager, click on it and press **Delete**. To delete more than one file at a time, press and hold the **Ctrl** key as you click on each filename, then press **Delete**.

☞ To rename a file in File Manager, click on the file, then click on the **File** menu. Click on **Rename**. Type a new name in the lower box and press **Enter**.

☛ To use Microsoft Windows Anti-Virus, start the program and click on a drive to check. Click on **Detect** and **Clean**.

☛ To backup a hard disk, start the MS Backup program then double-click on a drive. Click on **Start Backup**.

☛ To restore an accidentally-deleted file, start the Microsoft Undelete program and then click on the **Drive/Dir** button. Click on the directory containing the deleted file, and click on **OK**. Click on the file you want to undelete, then click on the **Undelete** button.

This page unintentionally left blank.

Chapter 24

Using DOS from Within Other Programs

In This Chapter

- ☛ A DOS prompt can be such a temporary thing
- ☛ Commands you should not use while at a temporary prompt
- ☛ Capabliities you'll "shell" out for
- ☛ Getting back to your program from a shell

Some programs (Windows being a very famous example) allow you to sneak out to DOS to perform some command, then sneak back to the main program, without having to really exit the main program at all. They do that by providing you with something called a *temporary DOS prompt*, otherwise known as a *shell*, thank you very much. Before I get into how they became known as shells, let's consider something more immediate, such as why would you want to do this? And, why should I read this chapter about shells when I don't collect them? Well, consider the following scenario:

Suppose you were working madly away in your spreadsheet program, and you decided to save an important document onto a diskette, but you weren't sure if there was enough

A temporary DOS prompt is also known as a *shell*, because it provides this nice safe environment from which you can do DOS. Meanwhile, your application is totally unaware of what you're doing (in its shell).

room. Before you tried to save the file, you could use this command, if only you could get to a DOS prompt:

DIR A:

The DIR command would tell you what files were present on the diskette, and how much space was left. While you were at the DOS prompt, you could even delete some files from the diskette to make more room, as in:

DEL A:OLD.DOC

With access to DOS, you could even format a new diskette if necessary:

FORMAT A: /V

The possibilities are endless, but the problem is simple: you gotta get to DOS, but you don't want to quit your spreadsheet program just to save your file. I mean, you're not done working yet.

If your spreadsheet program provides a temporary DOS prompt (a shell), you could shuffle out to DOS without actually exiting. Not all applications provide this service, but to learn how to use one, read on . . . .

A Side Note on Windows

The previous example might make sense when you're running a DOS program such as a spreadsheet program, or a word processor (such as Word for DOS or WordPerfect for DOS). I mean, when you're in a DOS program, you're stuck in it until you exit. That means you can't get to DOS, unless the DOS program you are running is nice enough to provide a temporary DOS prompt for you.

The benefits of a temporary DOS prompt within a DOS program are obvious, as you saw in the example at the beginning of this chapter. But what about using a temporary DOS prompt within Windows?

If you read Chapters 22 and 23, you know that Windows helps you deal with DOS in a friendly way (without throwing books at your computer—I mean, can you imagine?) Anyway, with Program Manager and File Manager, why would you ever want a temporary DOS prompt? Maybe for some of these reasons:

You don't like File Manager. Maybe its graphical approach is just not your style, or maybe you feel more comfortable following the directions in this book when dealing with DOS.

You want to do some DOS task that File Manager doesn't provide for. Maybe you want to check memory usage with the MEM command, or maybe you want to check out your system with the MSD utility (see Chapter 28), or maybe you want to use wildcards with a DOS command (instead of selecting those files with the mouse).

You bought this book, and you're determined to use it. Granted, it does include steps for using File Manager in Chapter 23, but what the hey, you've learned all about the DOS prompt, so why change now?

Getting to DOS and Back

When you "exit" to the temporary DOS prompt, you're working in a protected environment that keeps your main application "safe" while you perform various DOS commands.

Windows believes you'd want a temporary DOS prompt, for these reasons or others. Anyway, you'll learn how to get to the temporary prompt in just a little bit.

To find the temporary DOS prompt in your application, try looking under the FIle menu for a command called DOS Commands, or DOS Prompt, or some such. You may also find the command lurking under the Utilities or Tools menus. The command you use to access a temporary command prompt (a shell) will vary by application (assuming the application even includes one). But it goes something like this:

1. From within the application, select the command that gives you access to the temporary prompt. Look for commands like "Command Prompt" or "DOS Commands" or "Shell" or some such.

If you want to use the temporary DOS prompt from within Windows, simply double-click on the Main program group to open it, then select the MS-DOS Prompt icon by double-clicking it.

2. Type your DOS command as usual. Nothing special—just type the command as you normally would. There are some commands you should avoid using; these are explained in the next section.

3. Return to your application when you are through. Regardless of what application you're using, once you reach the temporary DOS prompt, there's one command that always gets you back. Just type **EXIT** and press **Enter**.

What You Shouldn't Do While Using a Temporary DOS Prompt

Remember that even though you are typing commands at a temporary DOS prompt, your application is still running. You should take care *not to use* certain commands:

DEL   Be sure you don't delete any important files accidentally—especially those your program is currently using, such as a backup file for your document (which will end in .BAK).

CHKDSK or SCANDISK   Don't use the /F parameter with CHKDSK; it can change file information that your program may be using. If you use SCANDISK, don't let it delete any files.

BY THE WAY

If you use DOS programs from within Windows as I sometimes do, don't try to access their temporary DOS prompts; use the one provided by Windows. It might work anyway, but it's really confusing.

REN   Don't rename any files your program may be using.

FORMAT   Formatting a diskette is okay, but if you replace a diskette that the program was using with another one, make sure you put the original diskette back into its drive before you return to your application.

FASTOPEN, SHARE, APPEND, JOIN, and SUBST   If you don't know what these commands are for, that's okay; just don't use them while in a shell.

DoubleSpace or DriveSpace or some other disk compression utility   Because these change the way files are stored, they could really mix up your application.

DEFRAG or any other disk optimizer   Because these rearrange files on the hard disk, they'll make your application think it's on drugs. Don't use them while in a shell.

Any command that starts a program   Starting a program within another program is usually not a great idea. Return from the temporary DOS prompt and exit your application *before* you start another program.

The Least You Need to Know

Before the age of temporary DOS prompts, working in an application was like trying to take a shower (that DOS phone was always ringing). You won't "slip on the soap" getting in and out of an application if you remember that:

☞ A temporary DOS prompt is a special part of an application (such as a word processor) that allows the user access to DOS without having to exit the main program.

☞ A temporary DOS prompt is also known as a *shell*.

☞ After using a temporary DOS prompt, type **EXIT** to return to your application.

☞ There are some commands you should be careful about using while in a DOS shell: DEL, FORMAT, APPEND, CHKDSK, SCANDISK, FASTOPEN, JOIN, REN, SHARE, SUBST, DBLSPACE, DEFRAG, and any command that starts another program.

Recycling tip:
tear out this page and photocopy it.

Chapter 25
It's a Portable PC World!

In This Chapter

- ☞ Saving power on your laptop so it doesn't poop out at 20,000 feet
- ☞ The information super-sidewalk
- ☞ Transferring files from your desktop to your laptop
- ☞ Transferring files the other way
- ☞ Laptops from Mars invade Earth!

As if it weren't bad enough that PCs are practically everywhere—at work, home, glued to shopping carts, etc.—they had to go and make *portable PCs*. I carry mine everywhere I go, including the bathtub—just in case I have *some computing to do*, such as writing an opening paragraph for my next chapter, which of course can't wait until I'm someplace where there's decent lighting, a comfortable chair, with no possiblity that I might electrocute myself accidentally. (It's the danger that draws me to writing in the first place.)

If you've got one of those portable wonders, and at least DOS 6, stay tuned. In this chapter, you'll learn how to suck more life out of your laptop's battery—so while you're putting the finishing touches on that proposal that's due in ten minutes, the computer won't *run out of power.* Useful stuff like that.

You've Got the POWER!

The DOS 6 somethings (DOS 6, 6.2, 6.21, and 6.22) come with a command called POWER which helps your portable PC conserve battery strength when programs are on coffee breaks, hanging out at the copier or not doing anything special. How much battery life you actually end up saving depends on your portable, and whether it follows some standard called the APM or Advanced Power Management—but it could be as high as 25% (or as low as 5%). Bottom line: the POWER command won't change your life, but using it could give you that critical 10 minutes you need to finish a big project and then save it.

To get this potentially whopping benefit, you're going to have to do a little bit of work. I *know*—but that's life. What you're going to have to do (unless you and a quart of Ben & Jerry's New York Super Fudge Chunk can convince your local computer geek to do it for you) is to edit your CONFIG.SYS file. Instructions for doing that are in Chapters 16 and 17. Just open the file and add this on a separate line (it doesn't matter where):

    DEVICE=C:\DOS\POWER.EXE

Type the whole thing, no spaces. Make sure you use backslashes (\) and not regular ones (/). Close the file and restart your portable. From now on, the POWER command will conserve power automatically anytime you're using your portable and a program's sitting idle.

Now, Let's See What We've Got Here...

Whenever you're running your portable on batteries, you can type **POWER** and press Enter, and see a listing showing you what's what:

    Power Management Status
    ————————————

    Setting = ADV: REG
    CPU: idle 45% of time.
    AC Line Status: OFFLINE
    Battery status: High
    Battery life (%):
    100

That last line's the critical one; it tells you the equivalent of "You're about to run out of gas 40 miles from the nearest gas station." If you see a number under 35%, you should probably shut down, because power will start dropping off pretty rapidly.

Going From Desktop to Laptop

So you've got two computers! Now you can get twice as much work done, if only someone would show you how to get these stupid files off your PC and onto your laptop computer so you can make that flight to Denver to see the client who doesn't like the new commercial.

If you don't see anything at all, you're probably not running on batteries (oopsie!) or your PC doesn't conform to the APM standards.

Well, you're in luck, because with the help of the DOS 6 somethings and a cable connecting your two PCs, you can transfer files with the greatest of ease, and even print them out on your desktop PC without transferring them from your laptop.

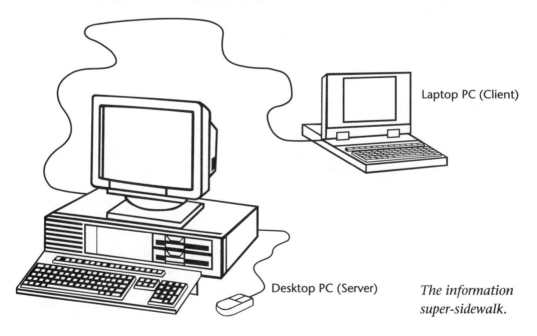

Laptop PC (Client)

Desktop PC (Server)

The information super-sidewalk.

Connecting the Two PCs

Step One: get the proper cable. What you're going to need is something called a *null modem cable*. Make sure that your computer store doesn't try to foist an ordinary modem or serial cable on you; a null modem cable is different. (There's also a new product called a LapLink cable, which will work just as well.) There are several types, so be sure to get one with the proper connectors for your PCs. (Also be sure you have a free connector available on the back of each PC into which you can plug this cable; the two connectors should look alike—i.e. they should both have *holes*, not pins.)

Step Two: make sure your desktop PC—henceforth (I always wanted to use that word) called the *server*—has at least DOS version 6.0. To find out, go over to the desktop, type **VER**, and press **Enter**. If you don't see good news (version 6.0 or above), go out and get a DOS upgrade (believe me, it's worth it for more reasons than just this one) when you get your cable. Then you can bribe someone into installing both for you.

Setting Up the Laptop (Client)

The laptop in this scenario is called the *client* because it uses the stuff the desktop has. The desktop PC is called the *server*, because it gives and gives and gives, while the laptop just takes and takes and takes. The server/client relationship is in some ways like a lawyer/client relationship, with some exceptions. One, most notably, is that the server feeds the client; in the lawyer/client relationship, well . . . (insert your favorite lawyer joke here).

Anyway, to get the laptop all set up so it can leech off of the desktop, you're going to have to do some rather complicated stuff, so do yourself a favor and beg, borrow, or steal someone else to do it for you. But if you're stuck, you're stuck, so here's the low-down:

If the client (laptop) doesn't have at least DOS 6, then go back to the desktop and type this command to copy a file onto a diskette (oh yeah, get a diskette first, and place that in drive A):

COPY C:\DOS\INTERLNK.EXE A:

Note that the only two spaces are just after the word **COPY** and just before the **A:**. Note also that you need to type backslashes (\) and not regular ones (/). Press Enter, and (with any luck) you'll see **1 File(s) copied**. OK so far. Now, trot back to the laptop, insert your diskette, and type this:

COPY A:INTERLNK.EXE C:\DOS

Same warnings as before—be careful about spaces and backslashes and things that go bump in the night. Press **Enter**.

Now the fun part. You've got to add this line to your CONFIG.SYS. Details are in Chapters 16 and 17 if you want to attempt this on your own. Just open the file and add this as a separate line *at the end of your CONFIG.SYS*:

DEVICE=C:\DOS\INTERLNK.EXE

Save your changes, and restart the client (laptop).

Testing . . . The Moment of Truth

Here's the moment you've been waiting for: the part where we connect the two computers and test this out. Here's what you do:

1. With the power OFF on both computers, connect them with the cable. Plug the linking cable into connectors on the back of both PCs.

2. On the server (desktop PC), type **CD\DOS** and press Enter. Now type **INTERSVR**. Press Enter again.

3. Restart the client (laptop) PC, and you should see something like this:

Microsoft Interlink version 1.00

Port=COM1
Drive letters redirected: 3 (D: through F:)
Printer ports redirected: 2 (LPT1: through
LPT2:)

This Computer (Client)		Other Computer (Server)
D:	equals	A:
E:	equals	B:
F:	equals	C:
LPT1:	equals	LPT2:
LPT2:	equals	LPT3:

Well, if you see this message, everything is working just fine. If not, go back and recheck the connections and what you typed.

Using the Connection

Now that you have your desktop and laptop linked together, you can do all sorts of stuff:

Copy files from your laptop to your desktop. Sit at the laptop and type **COPY A:***FILENAME* **F:***DIRECTORY*. Replace the *FILENAME* part with the real filename(s) you're trying to copy over, and replace *DIRECTORY* with the name of the directory on the desktop PC to which you're trying to copy the files. F: is now the name of the desktop's C: drive. For more help with the COPY command, see Chapter 11.

Copy files from your desktop to your laptop. To copy some files from the desktop's hard drive onto your laptop's hard drive, try this:

COPY F:*DIRECTORY**FILENAMES* C:*LAPDIRECTORY*

Replace *DIRECTORY* with the name of the directory on the desktop PC where the files are kept. Replace *FILENAMES* with actual filenames to copy. Replace *LAPDIRECTORY* with the name of the directory on the laptop to which you want these files copied. (Remember that F: refers to the desktop's hard disk, normally called drive C:.)

Print files on your laptop with your desktop's printer. First, on the desktop computer, type this:

> SET LPT1:=LPT2:

Just go into whatever program you've got on your laptop (such as WordPerfect or Lotus 1-2-3), then select the **File Printer Setup** command (or some such).

Breaking the Connection

When it's time to say goodbye, don't prolong the agony; make a clean break of it by walking over to the server (the desktop PC) and pressing these two keys at the same time: **Alt** and **F4**. (Be sure that you're not interrupting anything important on the laptop computer first.) When that's done, restart the laptop computer.

BY THE WAY

If you just need the printer that's hooked up to the desktop computer and nothing else from that computer, you could simply disconnect the parallel printer cable from the desktop computer, and hook it up to the laptop computer. Note: If you do this with the power turned *off* for both computers, this should work fine.

The Least You Need to Know

☛ To conserve power on your portable computer, add **DEVICE=C:\DOS\POWER.EXE** to your CONFIG.SYS file.

☛ You can connect your desktop PC to your laptop if you have at least DOS 6 and a null modem cable. Add **DEVICE=C:\DOS\INTERLNK.EXE** to the CONFIG.SYS of the client (laptop) PC. On the server (desktop) PC, type:

> **CD\DOS**
> **INTERSVR**

Restart the laptop PC and you're in business.

☛ Use this connection to copy files back and forth, or to "borrow" the desktop's printer so you can print files on your laptop.

This blank page thing is really getting out of hand.

Part Five

Problems That All of Us Have, and How to Fix Them

Contrary to popular opinion, computers are really very hard to break. Computers don't always understand exactly what you want them to do, so you might think they're broken when they're really just being stupid. The information you'll find in these special sections will help you get over the rough spots when your computer refuses to understand.

Chapter 26

Help! What Does This Message Mean?

There are few things more cryptic than DOS error messages (except maybe a tax form, the meaning behind a Calvin Klein commercial, or my hand-writing). Even veteran users can't always tell what DOS means when it issues an error—but don't worry—in this section, you'll find the cures for what ails you. Here you'll find a listing of the most common DOS error messages, complete with a list of what happened and what you should do now.

Abort, Retry, Fail?

See *General failure error reading (or writing) drive x. Abort, Retry, Fail?*

Access denied

What happened:

You tried to delete or edit a file that's protected.

What you should do now:

Don't *do* that! You should probably not delete or edit this file, because files are usually protected for a reason. If you feel that you need to delete or edit this file, ask a PC guru for advice.

Bad command or filename

What happened (1):

You mistyped the command.

What you should do now:

Check the spelling of the command and any filename. Verify that you did not enter extra spaces where they are not needed.

What happened (2):

The command you tried to use is an external command, and DOS didn't recognize it.

What you should do now:

Type **PATH=C:\DOS**. See Chapter 4 for more information on setting up a PATH for DOS to follow.

What happened (3):

You might have tried to start a program that lives in a directory DOS can't find. Or the directory might not exist anymore.

What you should do now:

Move to the program directory by typing something like this: **CD*PROGRAM*.** If you use this program a lot, you may want to add the program's directory to your DOS path. See Chapter 4 for more information on how to set up a PATH for DOS to follow.

Bad or missing command interpreter

What happened (1):

You've just exited a program that you started from a diskette.

What you should do now:

You should not remove a diskette that a program is still using. First, try sneaking the diskette back into the drive, and pressing **R** for retry. If that doesn't work, reboot the computer (press **Ctrl+Alt+Delete**), and it should be okay.

What happened (2):

Your PC lost its "brain." The COMMAND.COM file that is normally in the root directory of your C drive has been deleted accidentally, or—while copying all the files from a diskette—you've copied an older version of the COMMAND.COM file onto your drive.

What you should do now:

Click your heels three times, then reboot the computer (press **Ctrl+Alt+Delete**) with your emergency diskette in drive A, then type this: **COPY A:COMMAND.COM C:**.

Bad sectors

What happened:

After you've formatted a diskette, a number of bad sectors may be displayed. The diskette may be damaged, or you may have formatted the diskette to the wrong density.

What you should do now:

Verify that you formatted the diskette to the proper density. If the diskette appears damaged, don't use it for anything but a frisbee.

Current drive is no longer valid

What happened:

You jumped the gun and removed a diskette before a function was complete, or you were trying to use a diskette drive that didn't have a diskette in it.

What you should do now:

Well, Fast Fingers, put that diskette back in the diskette drive. If you want to make drive A the current drive, type **A:** at the prompt. If you want to return to drive C, type **C:** at the prompt.

Data error reading drive x

What happened:

A file was damaged and your PC is having a tough time making heads or tails of it.

What you should do now:

Press **R** for Retry. If that doesn't work and the message returns, press **A** for Abort. Try to locate another copy of the file (say, on a backup), and use it instead. If the file is on a diskette, try reinserting the diskette in its drive. If you have any disk utilities (such as Norton Utilities), you might be able to repair a damaged diskette.

Divide Overflow

What happened:

The program you were just running tried to divide something by zero, causing your PC to scratch its head and finally give up.

What you should do now:

Restart the program and try again. Chances are good that you'll never see the error again. If you see it repeatedly, call the technical support for the program, and tell them to send out the goof squad.

Duplicate filename or file not found

What happened:

You used the REN command to rename a file, but the new filename already exists.

What you should do now:

Try the command with another name, as in:

REN OLDFILE.DOC NEWFILE.DOC.

Errors found, F parameter not specified

What happened:

You used the CHKDSK command, but did not include the /F switch. Errors on the hard disk were found, but without the /F switch, the PC can't do anything about it, even though it's probably itching to do so.

What you should do now:

Retype the command as **CHKDSK /F**. When asked, type **Y** to convert lost clusters and chains to files.

Error reading drive x

See *General failure error reading drive x.*

File cannot be copied onto itself

What happened:

You just tried the COPY command, but you left out some important stuff, such as a new directory or drive for the file or a new name.

What you should do now:

If you typed something like **COPY JENNY.DOC**, DOS didn't know what to do. Copy JENNY.DOC where? If you want to copy the file into the current directory, do you want to give it a new name? Be sure to specify complete paths when copying a file, as in **COPY JENNY.DOC A:** or **COPY JENNY.DOC NEWJENNY.DOC.**

File not found

What happened (1):

You mistyped the filename in the command.

What you should do now:

Retype the command with the correct filename. If necessary, type **DIR /P** to verify the spelling of the filename.

What happened (2):

You mistyped the path leading to the file.

What you should do now:

It's probably that backslash thing again. Verify the path you are using, and make sure that you type a backslash (\) to separate the parts of a path, as in **C:\PROJECTS\DRU\CHAP01.DOC**.

What happened (3):

The file you referred to in the command does not exist.

What you should do now:

Try the command again, with a different file.

General failure error reading (or writing) drive x. Abort, Retry, Fail?

What happened (1):

In your big rush to do something with DOS, you forgot to format your diskette.

What you should do now:

Press **F** for Fail, then format the diskette to its proper density by typing something like **FORMAT A: /V**. See Chapter 6 for more information.

What happened (2):

The diskette in the drive you referred to was damaged, and could not be read or written to.

What you should do now:

Replace with another diskette and press **R** for Retry, or press **F** for Fail, and reformat this diskette.

What happened (3):

You used the wrong type of diskette, such as a high-density diskette in a double-density drive.

What you should do now:

Reformat the high-density diskette as double-density, or use a diskette of the proper type.

What happened (4):

The diskette in the drive you referred to may not be placed in the drive properly, or you left the drive door open.

What you should do now:

Remove the diskette from its drive, and verify that it is placed properly in the drive. If necessary, tap the diskette on the side to make sure the diskette material has not shifted in the sleeve. And for gosh sakes, close the door—there's a draft!

What happened (5):

There is a possibility that the drive you referred to is having problems. If you were trying to use the hard disk, this could be the first indicator of some major problems.

What you should do now:

Have a PC guru help you test your hard disk.

What happened (6):

> If you were trying to start a program, this could indicate a problem with the program files. If you get this error with a variety of programs, the problem is more likely your hard disk.

What you should do now:

> Again, have a PC guru help you test your hard disk. They may recommend re-installing the program.

Insufficient disk space

What happened:

> There's no room at the inn. You tried to copy a file onto a diskette, and there was not enough room.

What you should do now:

> Delete some files from the diskette to make room for the files you want, or reuse the COPY command with another diskette.

Insufficient memory

What happened:

> If you were trying to start a program, and you got this message, you have too many things in memory (RAM), and you need to unload some of them.

What you should do now:

> Exit as many programs as possible, then retry the command. If necessary, reboot the computer; rebooting (pressing **Ctrl+Alt+Delete**) causes a computer's memory to clear. You might want to take steps to improve memory usage; see Chapter 20 for more information.

Internal Stack Overflow

What happened:

Your PC's been interrupted by too many keypresses or too many mouse clicks, or too many requests from your program. Anyway, it got so busy, it just blew its stack.

What you should do now:

You'll need to increase the size of the stack with the STACKS command. See Chapter 16 for help on adding the command to your CONFIG.SYS.

Invalid directory

What happened (1):

You tried to change to a directory that does not exist, or you misspelled the directory name.

What you should do now:

Check the spelling of the directory. If you have at least DOS 5, type **DIR C:*. /S** to display a listing of directories on your hard disk.

What happened (2):

You forgot to place a backslash between a directory and a subdirectory name.

What you should do now:

Remember to use a backslash (\) to separate the parts of a path name, as in **C:\WORD\DOCS.**

Invalid drive specification

What happened (1):

You referred to a drive that exists only in your vivid imagination.

What you should do now:

Type a valid drive letter.

What happened (2):

You referred to a network drive *before* you logged onto the network.

What you should do now:

Log on the network drive, then repeat the original command.

Invalid filename or file not found

What happened (1):

You used the TYPE command with wildcards, as in TYPE *.BAT.

What you should do now:

You can only use the TYPE command on a single filename, as in:

TYPE AUTOEXEC.BAT.

What happened (2):

You tried to rename a file with an invalid filename.

What you should do now:

Try renaming the file to something else. If you need to review the list of valid filenames, refer to Chapter 7.

Invalid media or Track 0 Bad

What happened:

You tried to format a diskette to the wrong density, or the diskette was badly damaged.

What you should do now:

Verify the density of the diskette, and try formatting it again.

Invalid parameter or Invalid switch

What happened (1):

You used a parameter or switch that's invalid for this command.

What you should do now:

Check the appropriate chapter in this book, and follow the examples carefully.

What happened (2):

You entered a space between the forward slash and the character when entering a switch.

What you should do now:

If you want to enter a switch for a command, such as the /W switch for the DIR command (which tells the DIR command to display files in a wide format), do not type a space between the forward slash (/) and the W. Type the command like this: **DIR /W** and not like this: DIR / W.

What happened (3):

You used a backward slash when specifying a switch.

What you should do now:

Use a forward slash for switches, as in **DIR /W** and not DIR \W.

What happened (4):

You used a forward slash when specifying a filename path.

What you should do now:

Use a backward slash (\) when specifying the path to a file, as in **C:\WORD\NEW.DOC.**

Invalid path

What happened:

You specified an incorrect path to a file, or you mistyped a directory name.

What you should do now:

Verify the path and retype the command.

Invalid path, not directory, or directory not empty

What happened (1):

You used the RD command to remove a directory, and that directory contained subdirectories or files.

What you should do now:

Delete the files and subdirectories first, then repeat the RD command. If you use DOS 6, you can use the DELTREE command instead. See Chapter 13 for more information.

Non-system disk or disk error

What happened:

You left a diskette in drive A while you booted the computer.

What you should do now:

Remove the diskette and press **Ctrl+Alt+Delete** at the same time. Do *not* press "**any key to continue,**" as the screen suggests, because you run the risk of transmitting a virus to your system if the diskette is infected.

Not ready reading drive x. Abort, Retry, Fail?

What happened (1):

You typed a command that referred to a diskette drive, and there was no diskette in that drive.

What you should do now:

Place a diskette in the drive, then press **R** for Retry. If you no longer want to execute the command, press **A** for Abort.

What happened (2):

You didn't close the diskette drive door.

What you should do now:

Close the door and press **R** for retry.

Overwrite xxxxxxxx.xxx (yes/no/all)?

What happened:

You have DOS 6.2 something, and you tried moving or copying a file on top of an existing version of that same file.

What you should do now:

Press **Y** to overwrite the file, or **N** to skip it.

Press any key to continue...

What happened:

This is not an error message. DOS is pausing while it waits for you to do something, such as switch diskettes in a drive, or read the display.

What you should do now:

When you are ready to continue, you can press any key on the keyboard, such as the Enter key. Do not look for a key called "Any." Although it sounds as if there should be a specific key you should press, you can actually press any key you want.

Required parameter missing

What happened:

You left out some required part of a command.

What you should do now:

Refer to the appropriate chapter in this book, and follow the examples closely. Also, "A DOS Command Reference That Even My Mother Would Love" includes the most common DOS commands and several examples of how to use them.

Source diskette bad or incompatible

What happened:

When using the DISKCOPY command, you specified two diskette drives of different densities.

What you should do now:

Don't do that. If the two diskette drives are different densities, you'll have to use one drive to do your disk copying, as in **DISKCOPY B: B:**.

Specified drive does not exist or is non-removeable

What happened (1):

When using the DISKCOPY command, you specified a hard disk drive.

What you should do now:

Use only diskette drive letters with the DISKCOPY command, as in
DISKCOPY A: A:.

What happened (2):

When using the DISKCOPY command, you specified a nonexistent
drive.

What you should do now:

Make sure you specify valid drive letters from this universe.

Warning: all data on non-removable disk drive x: will be lost! Proceed with Format (Y/N)?

What happened:

You used the FORMAT command and did not specify a drive, or you
specified a hard disk drive.

What you should do now:

Press **N**, then retype the FORMAT command with a diskette drive
specified, as in **FORMAT B:**.

Write protect error writing drive x

What happened:

You tried to copy data onto a protected diskette.

What you should do now:

If you really want to do this, remove the write-protect tab (if it's a 5 1/4-
inch diskette) or move the write-protect switch to cover the "hole" (if
it's a 3 1/2-inch diskette), and then press **R** for Retry. If you don't want
to copy the file, press **A** for Abort.

Something clever this way comes.

Chapter 27

Before You Call the PC Doctor

When your computer starts acting up, there are some easy things you can do, such as run away. If that's not an option, this part of the book contains a list of common situations and possible solutions you can try.

My Computer's Acting Weird

What do you mean, weird? That's pretty vague. But then, computers can do a wide variety of weird things—beeping, flashing, odd characters scrolling across the screen, uncontrollable mouse pointer movement, nothing on the monitor—the list is endless. Don't panic. But before you call for help, check these things first:

- ☛ Check the cables and make sure none of them are loose. If they are loose, look to see if anyone's watching, then just plug 'em back in. Get a small screwdriver and nail those puppies in place so this doesn't happen again.

- ☛ Turn the power off, and then back on. Sometimes resetting the computer is all it needs—especially if you leave the power on all the time. Remember, turning off the power clears out the gunk. It's like applying Drano.

- ☛ Think about what is happening. Do you notice any trends? Ask yourself these questions:

Does the weirdness start when you use a particular program? If so, reinstalling the program or checking its setup may help.

Does the weirdness happen when you use the mouse? Are there strange characters on the screen, or does the mouse pointer go where no mouse has gone before? If so, try cleaning your mouse. Open the bottom latch that holds the trackball, and use a toothpick to clean all the gook off the rollers. Check the mouse cord to be sure it isn't pinched. Disable the mouse for a few days or borrow one (if it's the same brand), and see if the problems go away—if so, you may need a new mouse.

Has anything changed lately? Have you installed a new program or added any hardware? Did you make any changes to your CONFIG.SYS or AUTOEXEC.BAT files? If you have old versions of each of those files, try copying them onto your hard disk, and see if the problem goes away.

Can you duplicate the error? Is this a one-time thing, or does it happen whenever you do a particular task?

Are you typing too fast? Sometimes an older computer just can't keep up. Try going slower and paying more attention to what you're doing—maybe you're using the wrong commands.

☛ Check for viruses. Most computer weirdness has nothing to do with viruses, but to be sure, you should check. Refer to Chapter 18 for more information.

☛ There are some disk utilities you can purchase that can diagnose—and even fix—most problems with hard disks. Try Norton Utilities, PC Tools, or Mace Utilities.

My Computer Won't Start at All

This one can be real scary, but don't panic until you've checked these things:

☛ Check the cables and make sure they are not loose. If they are, well, plug them back in.

☛ Make sure that the computer is getting power. Check the power strip/surge protector; it may need resetting. If necessary, plug a lamp into the socket the computer normally uses, to verify that it works. Most computers make a humming noise when they are on.

☞ Is the monitor on? I've lost track of how many times I forget to turn this stupid thing on and begin to panic. If the monitor is on, is it dimmed? Play with the brightness and contrast knobs for a while. Go ahead. It feels good, and it's cheaper than throwing a brick at the PC.

☞ Can you boot from a floppy disk? To check, place a system disk in drive A, turn the computer off, and then on again. If your computer starts this way, see the next section.

My Hard Drive's Gone

If your computer starts okay from a floppy disk, but you can't use your hard disk, think about these things:

☞ Has your hard drive been acting up for the last few months? (For example, have you been getting Access, Search, Read, or Write errors?) If so, then your hard disk may have some real problems. Best to get a guru to help you, and be sure to mention what's been going on.

☞ Have you recently made changes to your AUTOEXEC.BAT or CONFIG.SYS? If so, you may have accidentally deleted commands that load a driver file that the computer uses to initialize a disk drive. These driver files are necessary if you are using a disk-compression utility, or if you have a large hard disk (over 32MB) and a DOS version prior to DOS 4. Boot your disk with your emergency diskette, and copy the AUTOEXEC.BAT and CONFIG.SYS files back onto the hard disk.

☞ If you've changed your PC battery or the computer's hardware recently, you may need to run your computer's SETUP program. Get a PC guru to help you.

☞ Yes, it's true: there are some disk utilities that you can purchase that can diagnose and even fix most problems with hard disks. Try Norton Utilities, PC Tools, or Mace Utilities.

Although I love and use all three of these utilities, the Mace Emergency Room program is my particular favorite; it helped me one time when I thought I'd never see my hard disk again.

My Computer's Locked Up

This is not a hard one to notice: you're running a program, when suddenly you realize your computer isn't paying any attention to you. Don't bang helplessly on the keyboard! Here are some more productive things you can try:

☞ Try pressing **Esc**. This is the simplest and least damaging thing to do.

☞ If Esc doesn't work, try pressing **Ctrl** and C at the same time (or **Ctrl** and **Break**). This sends a signal to DOS that says, "Hey, I'm here—pay attention to me!"

☞ In Windows, try pressing **Ctrl+Esc** to access the Task List. Highlight the program that's been acting crazy (or not responding), then click on **End Task**.

The easiest way you can recover from problems is to save your document often while you're working on it. Some programs contain an automatic save feature that is quite nice—use it if your program has one. I set mine to save every 10 minutes. That way, I never lose any more than 10 minutes worth of stuff if I have to reboot.

☞ As a last resort (in or out of Windows), reboot by pressing **Ctrl+Alt+Delete** at the same time. (If your computer has a reset button, this does basically the same thing, except that sometimes the reset button works when Ctrl+Alt+Del won't.) You can pretty much expect to lose some data with this method. When you get your program started again, check the document you were working on for missing pieces.

My Mouse Has Gone South

If you've just bought one of these plastic rodents, you may need to perform these simple steps before you can get it to work:

☞ Is the mouse connected? You need to stick that tail thing (the cable) into the appropriate socket at the back of your PC. Make sure that it hasn't come loose.

☞ Did you install the mouse program? A mouse uses a device driver program that enables DOS to understand its signals. This device driver is loaded with a command to your CONFIG.SYS. Get the manual out again and make sure you installed the driver correctly.

☛ Did the installation program ask you to select a COM port? If so, perhaps you selected the wrong one; your computer can have as many as *four*. Try running the install program again and selecting another one. MSD, a diagnostics program that comes with the newer DOS version, may be able to help here. See Chapter 28 for help.

☛ Are you using a program which supports a mouse? For example, don't expect to see a mouse pointer at the DOS prompt. Go into a program that uses a mouse and look for it there.

☛ Is you mouse hiding again? Move the mouse around on the mouse pad and see if it comes out of its corner.

I Just Spilled Something on My Keyboard

Oops! Follow these steps:

1. Turn everything off.

2. Dab up what you can, using a clean cloth.

3. Let everything dry out. I'd recommend waiting a day before you use the keyboard.

4. Don't spray anything on the keyboard to clean it! This can damage it.

5. If necessary, you can remove the keys to clean underneath them. It's okay—they are built to snap off and on—but be careful.

6. Once everything is working again, don't keep any drinks in the work area. I know, I know—I just can't function without my morning tea—but it's a good idea if you can do it.

My Diskette is Unreadable

If your PC is having trouble reading your diskette, try this:

☛ Did you insert the diskette correctly? For example, is the label facing the ceiling, and is the opening (or metal door) of the diskette facing away from you?

☛ Did you close the door? If you're using a 5 1/4-inch diskette, make sure you close the drive door by swinging that little tab downward.

☛ Is the diskette formatted? If this is a new diskette, you have to format it first in order to use it. Was the diskette formatted with the proper density? See Chapter 6 for help.

☛ Try taking the diskette out of the drive. Now, before you reinsert the diskette, give it a light tap on the side of your palm. This should reposition the diskette film inside, hopefully making it line up properly.

☛ Are you trying to save something onto the diskette? If so, make sure the diskette is not write-protected. See Chapter 6 for info. Also, are you sure you have enough room on the diskette to copy anything? See Chapter 12 for help on deleting files.

I Can't Get This Program to Start

If you've just installed a new program, sometimes getting it to start for the first time can be a pain. Look for these things:

☛ Did you install the program correctly? Did you follow the procedure in the manual, or did you simply copy the files from the diskette onto your PC? Most programs nowadays use an installation program to copy their files, create a working directory, and install a printer.

☛ Are you in the correct directory? Again, check the manual to find out what to type to start the program. You will probably have to type two commands: one to change to the correct directory, and the other to start the program. Remember to press Enter after each command.

☛ Is it a Windows program? If so, you need to start Windows first. Type:

   WIN

and press Enter. Look for the application's program group (a cute icon with the name of the application underneath), then double-click on it. It opens to reveal the application's icon. Double-click on it to start the program.

I Can't Get Anything to Print

Sometimes getting a new printer to work is hard, but here are some things you can try:

- ☞ Check the cable. Is it loose?

- ☞ Does the printer have power? Can you see lights?

- ☞ Does the printer have paper?

- ☞ Try pressing the Load/Eject/Form Feed button to try to feed your hungry printer with a sheet of paper.

- ☞ Is the printer on-line? Look for a button you can press.

- ☞ Turn the printer off and on to reset it. Sometimes, this is all it needs.

- ☞ Try printing a screen. Exit your program and then press the **Shift** and **Print Screen** keys at the same time.

- ☞ Can you print in any other program? If so, the current program may be installed with the wrong printer. If you have a program that can print, then check its setup and use the same printer model and computer port.

- ☞ If you're in Windows, check Print Manager. If necessary, select the print job from the list and click on Retry. If your PC's short on memory, sometimes Print Manager can't print. So exit other programs to free up more room.

- ☞ Try printing a file. Exit your program and type **PRINT C:\AUTOEXEC.BAT** and press **Enter**. If you see the message **Name of list device [PRN]**, just press **Enter**.

- ☞ Can you print at the DOS prompt, but not in the application? Your printer may not be installed properly for the application. Check the manual (yech) for instructions on how to install a printer.

How to Call For Help

When all else fails, it's time to call in the cavalry. Here's how to do that, without looking like a complete idiot:

☛ **As much as possible, know what's wrong.** Try to duplicate the problem before you call anyone over. Note exactly what happens. When does the problem occur? Are you doing something at the same time that the error occurs? Does it happen every time you do whatever? Do your other programs act funky, or is it just one in particular?

☛ **Make a list of what's new or different about your PC.** Chances are, whatever you just changed, added, or somehow made different is the culprit. If you've moved the PC, make a note of that, too.

☛ **Get your stuff together.** Gather your notes about the problem, then get other information together such as the type of PC you have, the amount of RAM, the type of CPU it uses, etc. If you have at least DOS 6, run Microsoft Diagnostics (see Chapter 28). if not, dig out your owner's manuals.

☛ **If you decide to call someone, call the right someone.** First, call a friend or co-worker who's good with PCs. They might help you narrow down the problem. Then, if you're having a problem with a program, call the program's tech-support line. If you're having trouble with the computer, the printer, or the modem, call the people you bought it from.

☛ **Call from a phone that sits next to your computer.** More than likely, the tech person you're talking to is going to want information you can only get while sitting at the PC, so move the phone over if you have to.

☛ **If you decide to take the PC in for repair,** make a backup of your hard disk if you can. Also, opt for a *diagnostic* first; they're cheaper, and they can tell you what's wrong. Next, replace whatever's bad instead of trying to get it fixed, and if possible, go ahead and replace it with the latest version. That way, you get a faster, happier PC out of the deal. A PC, fortunately, is really just a collection of parts that work together. (For example, you can easily replace the motherboard, without having to purchase a whole new computer. If your PC is slower than a 386, consider upgrading to a motherboard with a faster CPU while you're at it.)

Chapter 28
DOS 6 to the Rescue!

In This Chapter

- Looking under your PC's hood
- MSD, DOS 6's free diagnostic program
- Checking the hard disk's mental condition
- Removing nasty viruses
- Optimizing your hard disk so it runs like new, or something closely resembling it

You're having a bad day. Your boss handed you an already-overdue-but-dorko-can't-handle-it-so-will-you-fix-this project, and you sit down at your PC, determined to get through this day by *outliving* it, and *phhhht*. Nothing. So what do you do now?

Well, first, stop bothering me—it's not my problem. (Just kidding.) Now let's see what special things the DOS 6 somethings (DOS 6, 6.2, 6.21, or 6.22) can do to help.

Some of the things covered in this chapter are covered elsewhere in this book, so feel free to skip what you want. Just wanted to give you upgraders one place to find all the new DOS 6 stuff.

Some of the things covered in this chapter won't really fix a defunked PC, but they just might help you decipher enough about what's wrong to help the one that's trying to help you. Or they might prevent something bad from happening in the first place. If you don't have one of the DOS 6-point-something versions, I strongly urge an upgrade, because it contains lots of goodies (which you'll discover in this chapter) that make life with a PC almost bearable.

Enter Microsoft Diagonostics, Stage Right

One thing that's really annoying at times like this (besides the fact that there's something wrong with your computer *and you don't know what it is*) is a nerd who tries to help, but asks impossible questions such as "What kind of CPU does it have?" or "How much memory?" or "What's the BIOS date?" (If you knew that, you'd be repairing these puppies for a living, and not sitting there wondering what to do next.) But actually, in defense of all nerds everywhere, that kind of information *is* important for figuring out all sorts of problems. Trouble is, if the PC you're using was inherited from the last guy who had your job, chances are that no one knows much about what's inside.

That's why they make programs like MSD (Microsoft Diagnostics). If you have DOS 6-something, or Windows, you've got it. Just type: **MSD** and press **Enter**. You'll see a screen which looks (hopefully) like this:

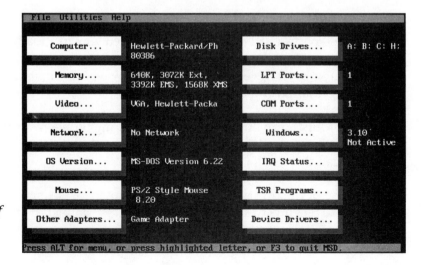

The inner workings of your PC. Scary, isn't it?

Poking Around

The main screen shows you the basics; for more info, you've got to do a little digging. For example, if you wanted the answer to that "What kind of CPU does it have?" question, you'd press **P** for Computer (or click on the box with your mouse-thingy), and you'd see more information related to the computer in general. Press **Escape** to return to the main section.

Be warned: most of this stuff has been declared dreadfully dull by the Surgeon General's office, and prolonged exposure should be avoided. When you're done poking, press **F3**.

Now, MSD is good for quite a few more things than telling you the obvious, like what kind of computer you have. MSD can also tell you what programs you have running in memory, where in memory they're located, and other geeky stuff like that. MSD can also *show* you what the contents of those programs are in memory, as well as the contents of anything else in memory.

> If your brain works anything like mine, you might want to print out this stuff so you don't have to memorize it. From the main screen, press **Alt+F** at the same time, then press **P**. Press **Enter** for a complete printout, or deselect the ones you don't want to print by pressing their highlighted letter, then press **Enter**.

Suppose you have a printer problem, for instance; your printer doesn't appear to be receiving any data at all (that, or it's on its twentieth coffee break of the day). Is it a printer problem—is the printer receiving the data, or is that data stuck inside the computer, waiting for a signal to move on? MSD can show you the contents of your *printer buffer* (the waiting room for data going to the printer). It can also show you what *port* your printer is connected to (LPT1: or LPT2:, for instance) and what *interrupt request line* (IRQ) is being used to address your printer.

Okay, okay, I'm getting too technical, if I'm starting to "IRQ" you, I'm sorry. It's just that, if you ever find yourself needing to know the answers to such puzzles, at least you could say I told you where to look.

Checking It Out with ScanDisk

ScanDisk is a DOS 6.2-something program which checks the status of your hard disk to verify that it's working more or less OK. You see, DOS has a rather bad habit of losing parts of files occasionally—usually parts that have been erased, but which (for some odd reason) are still there. Suffice it to say that ScanDisk can recognize a mess when it sees one, and for the most part, can fix it too.

To run ScanDisk, you must have DOS 6.2, 6.21, or 6.22. Type **SCANDISK** and press **Enter**. ScanDisk dutifully reports its progress as it pokes and prods your hard disk to see if anything is wrong.

Surface Scan, Anyone?

At the end of the session, ScanDisk will ask you if you want it to perform a surface scan. This is equivalent to having brain surgery to remove a headache. My advice is to just say No! by pressing **N**. (The exception here is if you've been experiencing weirdness deluxe, in which case, maybe brain surgery is necessary. Press **Y** for Yes. A surface scan sounds a bit like nails on a chalkboard—but any sounds you hear are normal—and takes awhile to perform, so sit back while the doctor does his work.)

There's Trouble Up Ahead!

ScanDisk may stop occasionally to consult with you. For the most part, pressing **Enter** resolves any questions about what option you should choose. Generally, the **Fix It** option is best, so select it, insert a blank disk (the "Undo" disk) when told, then let ScanDisk do its job fixing the problem.

If ScanDisk finds a lost chunk of a file, it will ask you what you want it to do. Since these long-lost file parts mostly come from dead files, **Delete** is usually the best option. If ScanDisk finds a lot of these "lost files" you may want to opt for saving them so you can take a look at these file bits and see if there's anything worth saving. For example, if you had lost an address file a few years ago, perhaps retrieving just a piece of it would help you put the pieces of your life back together (and get Aunt Jane off your back for not writing). For more info on this option, see Chapter 5.

Once ScanDisk is done, press **Enter** to view a log of what went on during the scan (ho hum). Press **Page Down** to view the entire log. Press **Enter** and you'll be whisked back Kansas and the main screen, where you can press X and click your heels three times to Exit.

Viruses Really Bug Me!

So what is a virus? Well, there are lots of cute names for the different types of computer viruses your PC might contract, but suffice it to say that you don't want your system to get one. They are sometimes real nasty critters who eat files for dessert and leave towels on the bathroom floor.

ScanDisk only checks one disk at a time, so if your PC has more than one disk, change to that drive by typing something like **D:** (insert the appropriate drive letter here), and pressing **Enter**. Then start ScanDisk all over by typing **SCANDISK** and pressing **Enter** again.

So now you're in a panic. Well, first, the good news: the chances of your PC getting a computer virus is about the same as somebody handing you tickets to the Super Bowl for free. Next, the bad news: if you swap a lot of disks with friends, or use software (especially games) that come from who knows where, or that someone gave you "for free" ("pirated" software—which you shouldn't be using anyway), you run a much higher risk of getting an "infection".

What to Do About Viruses

The best solution is to exercise a little bit of caution, which the DOS 6-somethings thankfully make very easy to do. If your PC is acting funny, chances are it is not a virus causing it, but a $2.00 part which will cost you $600 to replace. So relax!

If you want to know all about big bad viruses, check out Chapter 18.

If you want to be sure, run Microsoft Anti-Virus (if you have at least DOS 6) and check out your hard disk. Just type **MSAV** and press **Enter**. Click on the **Detect & Clean** doohickey, or press C to have MSAV clean your system. If it finds anything, follow the on-screen instructions, then call your Mom and tell her you just removed a virus (and you were out of chicken soup!). Press **F3** and **Enter** to exit MSAV when it's done.

Microsoft Anti-Virus checks out only one drive at a time, so if you have another disk drive, change to that drive by typing: **D:** and pressing Enter (use the correct drive letter here). Then type **MSAV** and press **Enter** to scan the new drive.

Getting Things Back in Order With Defrag

DOS is not a very tidy fellow. When a file is copied to the hard disk, it's placed into whatever spots seem handy at the time (such as behind the shower curtain or under the bed). Most files are split into sections and scattered hither and yon over the disk, making it harder for DOS to gather them all back up when the file is needed later. Why does DOS organize its files this way? Maybe DOS lives alone and just doesn't care.

This scattering of files over a disk is called *fragmentation*. Fragmentation slows down a poor little hard disk, making it huff and buff as its read/write heads scurry to put the file back together again. In addition, severe defragmentation can cause problems with some programs, such as Windows. So it pays to keep your hard disk in order.

Defrag works on one drive at a time, so if you have more than one hard disk, type DEFRAG followed by the new drive letter, and a colon, as in **DEFRAG D:**.

If you've got DOS 6-something, you can *defragment* your hard disk with Defrag. Although it can't find a mate for a lonely black sock, Defrag can reorganize the scattered pieces of each file so they are once again in adjoining sections on the hard disk. Just type **DEFRAG C:** and press **Enter**. This takes a while, so do it at the end of the day, or when you leave for lunch. If your hard disk is doublespaced, see Chapters 5 and 19 for more warnings.

The Least You Need to Know

☞ Microsoft Diagnostics tells you neat stuff about your computer such as what kind of CPU it has, etc.

☞ To run Microsoft Diagnostics, you need at least DOS 6. Type **MSD** and press **Enter**. Press **F3** to exit.

☞ ScanDisk comes with DOS 6.2-somethings, and it can perform a thorough check of your hard disk's condition. Type **SCANDISK** and press **Enter**. Press **X** to Exit.

☞ To scan for viruses if you have at least DOS 6, type **MSAV** and press **Enter**. Press **F3** and **Enter** to exit.

☞ To optimize your hard disk with at least DOS 6, type **DEFRAG C:** and press **Enter**. To defragment other drives, retype the command, substituting the C: for another drive letter.

A page is a terrible thing to waste.

Chapter 29

A DOS Command Reference That Even My Mother Would Love

Most DOS command references are complex, difficult to interpret, and almost impossible to understand unless you've had lots of experience using the command before. This command reference is different; it includes many examples, so you can get the command right the first time.

At the beginning of this part of this chapter, you'll find a guide to the commands you use every day. Other commands that you might be interested in are listed at the end.

Some Things You Should Know

Here's a quick review of some important concepts you need to know when working with DOS commands:

Remember to press Enter to execute a command. Until you press Enter, nothing happens.

DOS commands are tricky. Follow the examples carefully; don't add extra spaces.

The most common error message you get when using DOS commands is Bad command or file name. If you get this error message, you might need to set up a DOS path so that DOS can find the command. For now, type this:

PATH=C:\DOS

See Chapter 4 for more details. This kind of path is different from the one discussed in the next section, because it allows DOS to search only for program files (in this case, the external DOS command files). The DOS path command *does not* allow DOS to search for files or directories *you want it to do something to*; it only allows DOS to search for the files it can run.

Including a Path in a Command

A *path* is what DOS follows to find a file. You include a path in a DOS command, to tell DOS how to find the file or the directory you want it to use. It's like telling a friend how to find your house. A *path to a file* consists of three parts:

- The drive the file is located on followed by a colon, as in C:.
- A backslash (\), followed by the complete path to the file. Start with the parent directory. Then add another backslash, and a subdirectory name, if applicable. Finish up with a final backslash, as in **\PROJECTS\RESTOFUS**.
- End the path name with a file name or file specification, as in **CHAPTR29.DOC**.

The completed path looks like this:

C:\PROJECTS\CIGDOS\CHAPTR29.DOC

To create a path to a directory, follow this example, but leave off the extra \ and the name of a file.

C:\PROJECTS\CIGDOS

Include the path in a DOS command, instead of changing to the directory where the file is located. For example:

COPY C:\PROJECTS\CIGDOS\CHAPTR29.DOC A:

This command tells DOS to copy the CHAPTR29.DOC file from its directory to drive A.

Including DOS Wildcards

You can use DOS wildcards to specify more than one file to use in a single command:

- ☛ **The asterisk (*)** represents several characters within a file name. For example, *.DOC means "use files that have any first name, but a last name of DOC."

- ☛ **The question mark (?)** represents a single character within a file name. For example, JO?N.WK1 means "use files that begin with the letters JO, followed by any character, followed by an N, and the extension .WK1."

Use wildcards in place of actual filenames in a command, as in:

DIR *.WK1

This command tells DOS to list all the files in the current directory which end in .WK1.

DOS Commands You'll Really Use

You'll use the DOS commands in this section every day as you go about your business, which you'll get back to even sooner with these easy-to-follow examples.

CD (CHDIR)

Changes to a different directory.

Examples: CD\WORD   (changes to the directory \WORD)

CD\WORD\DOCS   (changes to the directory \WORD\DOCS)

What you should know: If you type just CD, DOS displays the name of the directory you are currently in. To change to a different directory, type **CD** (that's **CD** *backslash*) followed by the name of the directory to change to.

Where to go for more help: Chapters 7 and 13

CHKDSK

Displays available disk and memory space, and corrects disk errors for DOS versions 6.0 or less.

Example: CHKDSK C: /F

What you should know: That's **CHKDSK** *space* C *colon space forward slash* F. CHKDSK is an external command, so you're gonna need a DOS path to use it. See the earlier section. If you have DOS 6.2 or above, use SCANDISK. Otherwise, use CHKDSK periodically to check your hard disk for lost clusters and chains. (Lost clusters and chains are caused when DOS does not properly update its file tracking system.) DOS is sometimes a very bad housekeeper, so lost clusters and chains are normal; they are nothing to be afraid of. If CHKDSK converts lost clusters or chains to files, then use this command:

> **DEL C:\FILE????.CHK**

Where to go for more help: Chapter 5

CLS

Use anytime you want to clear your screen.

Example: CLS

COPY

Makes a copy (duplicate) of a file or files.

Example: COPY AUTOEXEC.BAT AUTOEXEC.SAV
(copies the file AUTOEXEC.BAT and saves the copy as AUTOEXEC.SAV)

Places a copy of a file in a different directory or disk.

Examples: COPY C:\MKTG\SALES93.WKS D:\SALES
      (copies the file SALES93.WKS to the D:\SALES directory)

      COPY C:\AUTOEXEC.BAT A:
      (copies the file AUTOEXEC.BAT to the A drive)

      COPY A:*.* C:\PROJECTS
      (copies all the files from drive A to the C:\PROJECTS directory)

      COPY C:\WORD\OLDFILE.DOC C:\PROJECTS\NEWFILE.DOC
      (copies the file OLDFILE.DOC to the C:\PROJECTS directory,
          and renames it NEWFILE.DOC.)

What you should know: The first part of the COPY command tells DOS the name (and directory path) of the file(s) to copy. The second part of the COPY command tells DOS the name of the drive or directory to copy the file to (along with a new name for the file, if you want). You can leave off part of the command if you happen to be in the directory that you are copying *from* or *to*, but that is generally confusing, so you're better off typing entire directory paths. Make sure you include a space after the word *COPY* and after the "copy from" section. Also, you can use DOS wildcards to specify more than one file to copy.

Where to go for more help: Chapter 11

DEL

Deletes a file or files.

Examples: DEL OLDFILE.DOC   (deletes the file OLDFILE.DOC)

      DEL *.* /P   (prompts before deleting all the files in
                            the current directory)

What you should know: If you have at least DOS 4, you can add /P to the end of the DEL command to be prompted before a file is deleted. You can also use wildcards with the DEL command to delete more than one file at a time.

Where to go for more help: Chapter 12

DELTREE (To use this, you need at least DOS 6.)

Deletes a directory and its subdirectories without having to remove the files first.

Examples: DELTREE C:\SALES93
(deletes the directory C:\SALES93)

DELTREE C:\PROJECTS\CIGDOS
(deletes the directory C:\PROJECTS\CIGDOS)

What you should know: You cannot undelete files if you also delete the directory in which they were located.

Where to go for more help: Chapter 13

DIR

Lists files in the specified directory or drive.

Examples: DIR /P   (one screen at a time)

DIR A: (list files on drive A)

DIR /W   (list files across the screen)

Lists files in a specific order (you need at least DOS 5 for these commands).

Examples: DIR /O:E (sorted by extension or type)

DIR /O:D (sorted by date)

DIR /O:S   (sorted by size)

Finds specific files (you need at least DOS 5).

Examples: DIR C:\LOST.DOC /S (finds all the files called LOST.DOC)

DIR C:*.BAK /S   (finds all the files with .BAK extension)

What you should know: You can use DOS wildcards to list specific files. Also, you can sort files in reverse order by typing a minus in front of the sort letter, as in –D.

Where to go for more help: Chapter 10

DISKCOPY

Makes a copy of a diskette.

Examples: DISKCOPY A: A:

DISKCOPY A: B:

What you should know: The first drive letter tells the location of the original, or source diskette. The second drive letter tells the location of the target diskette. Both drives must be the same size and density. If you have to use a single drive (like drive A), you'll be prompted when to switch disks back and forth. Start with the source disk in the drive.

Where to go for more help: Chapter 6

DOSSHELL (To use this, you need at least DOS 4.)

Starts the DOS Shell.

Example: DOSSHELL

What you should know: The DOS Shell is a graphical interface that allows you to perform common DOS tasks by selecting icons (pictures) instead of typing commands. The DOS Shell is easy to use, and great for beginners. The DOS 6.2-somethings do not include the DOS Shell, but you can order it from Microsoft.

Where to go for more help: Chapter 8

EDIT (To use, you need at least DOS 5.)

Creates or edits a text or a batch file.

Examples: EDIT C:\AUTOEXEC.BAT   (edits the file AUTOEXEC.BAT)

EDIT NEWFILE.TXT   (starts a new file NEWFILE.TXT)

What you should know: EDIT is a simple editor you can use to edit your CONFIG.SYS or AUTOEXEC.BAT files, or create simple batch files of your own.

Where to go for more help: Chapters 16 and 17

EDLIN

Creates or edits a text or batch file.

Examples: EDLIN C:\AUTOEXEC.BAT   (edits the file AUTOEXEC.BAT)

EDLIN NEWFILE.TXT   (starts a new file NEWFILE.TXT)

What you should know: EDLIN is a simple editor you can use to edit your CONFIG.SYS or AUTOEXEC.BAT files, or create simple batch files of your own. Use EDIT instead of EDLIN if you have at least DOS 5.

Where to go for more help: Chapters 16 and 17

EXIT

Returns to your application after using its temporary command prompt (DOS shell) to access DOS.

Example: EXIT

What you should know: A temporary command prompt allows you access to the DOS prompt without having to exit an application. For example, you can type a letter, use the DOS shell to format a diskette, then return to the application and save the file.

Where to go for more help: Chapter 24

FORMAT

Prepares a diskette for use.

Example: FORMAT A: /V

Creates an emergency diskette.

Example: FORMAT A: /S /V

Formats a double-density diskette in a high-density drive, using at least DOS 4.

Examples: FORMAT A: /F:360   (5 1/4-inch)

FORMAT A: /F:720   (3 1/2-inch)

Formats a double-density diskette in a high-density drive, using a DOS version prior to 4.

Examples: FORMAT A: /4   (5 1/4-inch)

FORMAT A: /N:9 /T:80 (3 1/2-inch)

Reformats a diskette that had been formatted previously, using at least DOS 5.

Example: FORMAT B: /Q

Formats a diskette unconditionally, using at least DOS 5.

Example: FORMAT B: /U

What you should know: You must format a diskette in order to use it the first time. Be sure to type the drive letter to format, and use only drives A and B. If you have at least DOS 5, you can unformat a diskette by using the UNFORMAT command.

Where to go for more help: Chapter 6

HELP (To use this, you need at least DOS 5.)

Accesses the DOS help system.

Example: HELP FORMAT (provides help on the FORMAT command)

What you should know: You can also type /? after a command to get help with syntax, as in **FORMAT /?**.

Where to go for more help: Chapter 9

MD (MKDIR)

Creates a directory.

Examples: MD C:\WORD\DOCS   (creates the directory
                                                        \WORD\DOCS on the C drive)

              MD TEMP   (creates the directory TEMP under
                                                        the current directory)

What you should know: MD creates a subdirectory *under* the current directory unless you specify a directory path.

Where to go for more help: Chapter 13

MOVE (To use this, you need at least DOS 6.)

Moves a file to a different location.

Examples: MOVE C:\TAXES\93BUDGET.WKS D:\NEW

              MOVE C:\WORD*.DOC C:\LETTERS

Renames a directory.

Example: MOVE C:\OLDDIR C:\NEWDIR

What you should know: You can move more than one file at a time by using DOS wildcards.

Where to go for more help: Chapters 11 and 13

RD (RMDIR)

Removes a directory, as long as it's empty of subdirectories and files.

Example: RD \PROGRAMS\JUNK   (removes the directory
\PROGRAMS\JUNK)

What you should know: Use the DEL command to remove its files, then use RD to remove a directory. If you have at least DOS 6, you can remove directories in one step by using the DELTREE command.

Where to go for help: Chapter 13

REN

Renames a file.

Examples: REN OLDFILE.DOC NEWFILE.DOC
(renames the file OLDFILE.DOC to NEWFILE.DOC)

REN 93*.WKS 94*.WKS
(renames files which begin with 93 and have an .WKS extension to files beginning with 94)

What you should know: You can't rename a file to the same name that another file is using; no two files in the same directory can have the same name. You can rename more than one file at a time by using DOS wildcards. If you want to rename a directory and you have DOS 6, see the MOVE command.

Where to go for help: Chapter 11

TYPE

Displays the contents of a text or a batch file.

Example: TYPE C:\AUTOEXEC.BAT | MORE

What you should know: That's the *pipe* character in front of the word MORE. It's usually found lurking above the backslash on the same key. It sometimes looks like a solid line, but most often like two vertical dashes.

Always include the | **MORE** filter with the TYPE command, or the contents of the file may scroll off the screen. Don't use the TYPE command on a program file (such as a file with an .EXE or a .COM extension) because all you'll get is a bunch of beeps and some weird characters.

Where to go for more help: Chapter 17

UNDELETE (To use this, you need at least DOS 5.)

Restores an accidentally-deleted file.

Example: UNDELETE C:\WORD\IMPTFILE.DOC

What you should know: Always try to undelete a file as soon as possible. Do not copy or create new files until you've recovered your lost file. Your chances of recovering a lost file are better if you establish a delete tracking system.

Where to go for more help: Chapter 12

UNFORMAT (To use this, you need at least DOS 5.)

Unformats an accidentally-formatted disk.

Example: UNFORMAT A:

What you should know: If a disk was formatted with the /U switch, it cannot be unformatted.

Where to go for more help: Chapter 6

VER

Displays the current DOS version.

Example: VER

What you should know: Many DOS commands are only available on recent versions of DOS. Use this command to determine the DOS version your PC uses.

Where to go for more help: Chapter 2 and 9

DOS Commands You'll Use Occasionally

Here are some less common commands that you may need now and then. Don't worry about learning them until you actually need them.

Command	What to use it for	Where to get more help
BACKUP	Saves duplicates of files as insurance against damage	Chapter 14
DATE	Enters or changes the system date	Chapter 3
DBLSPACE	Compresses disks (DOS 6 and 6.2)	Chapter 19
DEFRAG	Reorganizes a disk	Chapter 5
DOSKEY	Recalls previous commands	Chapter 4
DRVSPACE	Compresses disks (DOS 6.21 and 6.22)	Chapter 19
INTERLNK	Links two computers together for sharing files	Chapter 25
MEM	Checks memory usage	Chapter 20
MEMMAKER	Configures memory usage	Chapter 20
MIRROR	Enables delete protection	Chapter 12
MSAV	Protects against computer viruses	Chapter 18
MSD	Displays information about your PC	Chapter 28
MSBACKUP	Saves duplicates of files as insurance against damage	Chapter 14
PRINT	Prints text files (unformatted files)	Chapter 27

continues

continues

Command	What to use it for	Where to get more help
PROMPT	Changes the system prompt	Chapter 7
POWER	Helps to conserve power on a laptop	Chapter 25
RESTORE	Restores duplicates of files if originals become damaged	Chapter 15
TIME	Enters or changes system time	Chapter 3
TREE	Displays a listing of directories	Chapter 13
VOL	Displays the volume label of a drive	Chapter 6
VSAFE	Protects against computer viruses	Chapter 18

Speak Like a Geek: The Complete Archive

The computer world is like an exclusive club, complete with its own language. If you want to be accepted, you need to learn the lingo (the secret handshake comes later). The following mini-glossary will help you get started.

application   (1) The placement of shampoo on the head. (2) Also known as *program*, a set of instructions that enable a computer to perform a specific task, such as word processing or data management.

ASCII file   A file containing characters that can be used by any program on any computer. Sometimes called a *text file* or an *ASCII text file*. (ASCII is pronounced "ASK-key.")

AUTOEXEC.BAT   A special file that contains commands that are executed automatically when your computer is booted.

backing up   (1) The movement of my car when parked on a hill without the emergency brake. (2) A process that copies your files onto diskettes in a special compressed format. If something bad happens to the originals, you can restore your backed-up files (a process that uncompresses the files and copies them back).

backslash   The backslash (\) key represents the root directory in any DOS command. It's also used to separate the name of a parent directory from its subdirectory, as in C:\WORD\BOOK.

batch file A batch file ends in .BAT and contains a number of commands batched together in one file. You create batch files to perform several commands in sequence for you.

BIOS (basic input-output system) The BIOS (pronounced "BYE-oh-ss") controls input/ouput between the various elements that make up the computer, including disk drives, the printer, the ports, and the monitor.

bits (1) What I find at the bottom of the potato chip bag when I'm trying to pack lunch. (2) Short for **Binary digits**. Each bit is like a light switch: it's either ON (1) or OFF (0). Place eight bits in a row, and you form a *byte*, or a pattern that represents a single character, such as the letter J.

boot (1) What you really feel like doing to a computer that refuses to understand. (2) The process of starting a computer. The word *booting* comes from the phrase, "pulling yourself up by the bootstraps," a metaphor for what happens when a computer starts: first it gets power, then it checks itself out, then it loads DOS and awaits your command.

burn-in (1) What happens to my skin no matter how much suntan lotion I use. (2) Burn-in happens when the same image is displayed too long on a PC monitor. When other images are shown, the burned-in image is still there, like a ghost on the screen.

byte (1) What a baby will do nine times out of ten, if you stick a finger in its mouth. (2) A byte is the amount of space it takes to store a character, such as 1, Q, or $. A byte is made up of eight *bits*; for example, the byte 01000001 represents the letter A.

cache (1) A process which no one will perform on a two-party, out-of-state-check on a holiday. (2) See *RAM cache*.

CD-ROM (compact-disc read-only memory) A popular add-on for computers is a CD-ROM drive. With a CD-ROM drive, your computer can play ordinary CDs (music) and special computer CDs that store large complex programs or massive amounts of data. A single disc can store over 600MB of information. Pronounced "see-dee-RAHM."

click   To move the mouse pointer over an object or an icon, and press and release the mouse button once without moving the mouse.

client   (1) You, our beloved consumer. (2) On two computers linked though a cable, the client PC is the one which uses the services of the other PC. With two PCs linked through INTERLNK, the client is typically the laptop computer. See *server*.

CMOS (Complementary Metal-Oxide Semiconductor)   (1) That slimy stuff you find on rocks at the beach. (2) Pronounced "SEA-moss," CMOS is an electronic device (usually battery operated) that stores information about your computer. Information stored in CMOS includes the current date and time, and the number and types of disk drives your computer has.

cold boot   Same thing as booting; the process of starting a computer by turning the power on.

compressed drive   A drive whose storage capacity has increased because of a special program that uses a more effective method (than just DOS alone) of managing disk space.

compression ratio   The proportion of space a file uses on a newly *compressed drive*, as compared to the amount of space it used before the drive was compressed. A compression ratio of 2:1 is optimal.

CONFIG.SYS   A file that customizes your PC for the specific programs that you use by changing the system default values for certain parameters. The commands in the CONFIG.SYS file are executed automatically at system startup.

conventional memory   (1) Memory with no sense of "panache."
(2) The working area of the computer, or its "desktop." This is the part of RAM below 640K. Conventional memory is the most important memory because it's the only area of memory in which a program can run. It is the area of memory that DOS uses to manipulate data, run programs, and perform its tasks.

CPU (Central Processing Unit)   See *microprocessor*.

crash   (1) A sound you don't want to hear when you're moving your computer. (2) Failure of a system or program. Usually, you realize your system has crashed when the display or keyboard locks up. The term *crash* also refers to a disk crash or head crash, which occurs when the read/write head in the disk drive falls on the disk. This would be like dropping a phonograph needle on a record. A disk crash can destroy any data stored where the read/write head fell on the disk.

cursor   A horizontal line that appears below characters. A cursor acts like the tip of your pencil; anything you type appears at the cursor.

defragmentation   (1) What happens when you pull a sweater at one end. (2) When a file is copied onto a drive, parts of the file may be split over different sections of the drive in order to make the most effective use of available space. On an uncompressed drive, fragmentation can cause a drop in speed when accessing files. Defragmenting a drive causes the parts of files that were split up to be placed together.

default   (1) When it's not your fault. (2) The standards preset into your PC. With the CONFIG.SYS file, you can change these defaults.

density   A measure of the amount of data that can be stored per square inch of storage area on a disk. To understand density, think of a disk covered with magnetic dust. Each particle of dust stores one piece of data. No matter how large or small the particle, it still stores only one piece of data. With double-density disks, the particles are large, so the disk can hold fewer particles (less data). With high-density disks, the particles are small, so more particles can be packed in less space, and the disk can store more data.

Desktop   (1) That flat, rectangular surface which you can see when you push all those papers, cups, and candy wrappers onto the floor. (2) The "floor" in Windows upon which everything sits. When Windows is started, the Desktop occupies your entire screen; program windows (such as the one in which Program Manager runs) are arranged on the Desktop to suit the user.

desktop publishing (DTP)   A program that allows you to combine text and graphics on the same page and manipulate the text and graphics on-screen. Desktop publishing programs are commonly used to create news-letters, brochures, flyers, resumes, and business cards.

device drivers   (1) The guys who drive New York undercover cop cars. (2) Special programs which interpret commands for optional devices such as a mouse, network card, tape-backup, or a CD-ROM drive. Device drivers can also be used to configure memory (RAM) for special purposes.

dialog box   (1) The thing you speak into while ordering a hamburger at a local fast food place. (2) A dialog box is a special window or box that appears when the program requires additional information before executing a command.

differential backup   A type of backup that copies the files that have been changed since the last full backup.

directory   Because large hard disks can store thousands of files, you often need to store related files in separate directories on the disk. Think of your disk as a filing cabinet, and each directory as one of its drawers. By keeping files in separate directories, it is easier to locate and work with related files.

disk   (1) Something in your back which you don't want to slip. (2) A magnetic computer storage medium. See *floppy disks* and *hard disk*.

disk compression   Programs which store more information on a hard disk because they use a kind of "computer shorthand" that allows them to store data in less space than with DOS alone. If you use a disk-compression program, your hard disk can store nearly twice the data. DOS 6 and 6.2 come with a disk-compression program called DoubleSpace. DOS 6.22 comes with a disk-compression program called DriveSpace.

disk drive   (1) The main street in Silicon Valley. (2) A device that writes data to a magnetic disk and reads data from the disk. Think of a disk drive as a cassette recorder/player. Just as the cassette player can record sounds on a magnetic cassette tape and play back those sounds, a disk drive can record data on a magnetic disk and play back that data.

diskette   Another name for *floppy disk*.

document   Any work you create using an application program, and save in a file on disk. Although the term *document* traditionally refers to work created in a word processing program (such as a letter or a chapter of a book), *document* is now loosely used to refer to any work, including spread-sheets and databases.

DOS (disk operating system)   DOS, which rhymes with "boss," is an essential program that provides the necessary instructions for the computer's parts to function as a unit (keyboard, disk drive, central processing unit, display screen, printer, and so on). DOS interprets the commands you give your computer. Like a traffic cop, DOS controls the flow of information to each computer component.

DOS prompt   An on-screen prompt that indicates DOS is ready to accept a command. It looks something like **C>** or **C:**.

DOS Shell   The DOS Shell is a *graphical user interface* that keeps you safe and warm, miles away from the nasty world of the DOS prompt. Inside the DOS Shell, you can perform the same commands that you could outside the DOS Shell, but with greater ease (and understanding). See also *shell*.

double-click   To move the mouse pointer over an object or icon, and press and release the mouse button twice in quick succession.

drag   (1) Losing a winning lottery ticket. (2) Moving the mouse with the button held down. To drag the mouse, first move the mouse to the starting position. Now click and hold the mouse button. Move the mouse to the ending position, and then release the mouse button.

drivers   Special programs that tell your computer how to communicate with certain devices, such as a mouse. See *device drivers*.

EMS (expanded memory specification)   See *expanded memory*.

environment   (1) Something worth saving. (2) An *environment* is a setting in which you perform tasks on your computer. The DOS Shell, for example, uses a graphical environment that lets you enter commands by selecting pictures rather than by typing commands. This makes it much easier to use your computer (assuming you know what the pictures stand for).

executable file   A program file that can run (execute) the program. Executable files end in .BAT, .COM, or .EXE.

expanded memory   (1) Memory that needs to go on a diet. (2) A special kind of computer memory that is located on an expanded memory board or converted from extended memory. This type of memory cannot be used to run a program, but it can be used by programs for the temporary storage of their data. See also *extended memory*.

extended memory   Extended memory is the part of RAM above 1MB. Extended memory cannot be used to run programs, but can be used by programs to store their data temporarily. If needed, you can customize a portion of extended memory to act like expanded memory for use with programs that can use only expanded memory. See also *expanded memory*.

extension   (1) What the butler is always listening in on. (2) In DOS, each file you create has a unique name. The name consists of two parts: a filename and an extension. The filename can be up to eight characters. The extension (which is optional) can be up to three characters. The extension normally denotes the file type.

file   (1) What every prisoner wants to find in a birthday cake. (2) DOS stores information in files. Anything can be placed in a file: a memo, a budget report, or even a graphics image (like a picture of a boat or a computer). Files you create are called *data files*. Applications (like a word processing program, with which you can type letters and reports) are composed of several files called *program files*.

file allocation table (FAT)   A map on every disk that tells the operating system where the files on the disk are stored. It's sort of like a classroom seating chart.

File Manager   A program in Windows which enables you to perform basic file maintenance (copying, moving, deleting of files and directories) without actually succumbing to the DOS prompt.

fixed disk drive   (1) What your hard disk better be after it comes home from the repair shop. (2) A disk drive that has a nonremovable disk, as opposed to floppy disk drives, in which you can insert and remove disks. See also *disk drive*.

floppy disk drive   A disk drive that uses floppy disks. See also *disk drive*.

floppy disks   (1) Diskettes that have been left in the sun too long. (2) Small, portable, plastic storage squares that magnetically store *data* (the facts and figures you enter and save). Floppy disks are inserted into your computer's *floppy disk drive* (located on the front of the computer). (*Diskette* is a less confusing term.)

formatting   A process that prepares a diskette for use. Formatting creates invisible *tracks* (concentric circles) and *sectors* (pie-shaped wedges) on the surface of the diskette, creating a "map" that DOS can use for keeping track of where files are stored. The number of tracks and sectors that a diskette is divided into determines how much information it can store.

full backup   A type of backup that copies every file on your hard disk.

function keys   Some programs (including DOS) assign a special purpose to these keys (called the F keys because they all begin with F). There are 10 or 12 F-keys on the left side of the keyboard, or 12 F-keys at the top of the keyboard. F-keys are numbered F1, F2, F3, and so on. These keys are used to enter various commands in a program.

gigabyte   Roughly one billion bytes, or exactly 1,073,741,824 bytes.

graphical user interface (GUI, pronounced "goo-ey")   (1) Tar on a hot day. (2) A type of program interface that uses graphical elements, such as icons, to represent commands, files, and (in some cases) other programs. The most *popular* GUI is Microsoft Windows.

graphics mode   A display mode that uses pictures in its display, rather than just text and simple lines. Graphics mode makes the display attractive, but not all monitors and video cards support it.

hard disk   A nonremovable disk drive that stores many megabytes of data. Because it is fixed inside the computer (see *fixed disk drive*), it performs quicker and more efficiently than a floppy disk.

hardware   The physical parts of a computer (such as the *monitor*, the *disk* *drives*, the *CPU*, and so on). The programs you run are electronic, rather than physical; they're known as *software*.

icon   (1) What that little train was always saying: "I think icon, I think icon." (2) A graphic image that represents a command, such as saving or printing. An icon can also represent an object, such as a file or a diskette.

incremental backup   A type of backup that copies only the files that have been changed since the last full or incremental backup. Available only with MSBACKUP command.

initialize   (1) What Hollywood stars do when they get too big to sign a complete autograph. (2) To reset a computer or program to some starting values. When used to describe floppy or hard disks, the term means the same as *format*.

Insert mode   The default typing mode for most word processors and text editors. Insert mode means that when you position your cursor and start to type, what you type is inserted at that point.

jump term   (1) A word that emits a small electrical charge when you use it. (2) A highlighted term in the DOS 6 help system that, when selected, "jumps" to a related section of the help system.

kilobyte   A unit for measuring the amount of data. A kilobyte (K) is equivalent to 1,024 bytes.

laptop   A portable computer about the size of your lap. Other portable computers include notebooks, palmtops, and PDA (personal digital assistants). Laptops cost a lot more than regular desktop computers, presumably because they have to get people with really tiny hands to assemble them.

logical drive   (1) A type of drive that only Spock could love. (2) A section of a hard disk or memory that is treated as a separate disk and is assigned its own letter. For example, you may *partition* your hard drive into logical drives C, D, E, and F. It's still one disk, but it is partitioned into logical drives.

lost clusters and lost chains   (1) These are probably with my other sock.

(2) Lost clusters and chains are pieces of files that have been "lost" by DOS. When you delete a file, it is not actually erased; instead, the reference to the file's location is erased. If a file's location is erased from the file listing, but its address is still marked "used," you get a lost cluster. You can also get a lost cluster if you reboot while a file is being written to disk. If several of these clusters occur together on the disk, you get a lost chain.

megabyte   A standard unit used to measure the storage capacity of a disk and the amount of computer memory. A megabyte is 1,048,576 bytes (1000 kilobytes). This is roughly equivalent to 500 pages of double-spaced text. Megabyte is commonly abbreviated as MB, M, or (not as often) Mbyte.

megahertz   (1) The type of car they use at funeral parlors down in Texas. (2) The speed with which a CPU processes information, abbreviated Mhz. For example, a 486 30 Mhz CPU runs about half as fast as a 486 66 Mhz CPU.

memory   (1) Something that, as I get older, I keep losing more and more. (2) Electronic storage area inside the computer, used to temporarily store data or program instructions when the computer is using them. The computer's memory is erased when the power to the computer is turned off.

memory-resident program   See *TSR*.

menu   (1) A listing of high-priced food items which, when served, bear little resemblance to their descriptions. (2) A list of commands or instructions displayed on the screen. Menus organize commands and make a program easier to use.

microprocessor   (1) A food processor with only one setting. (2) Sometimes called the central processing unit (CPU) or processor, this chip is the computer's brain; it does all the calculations for the computer.

modem   An acronym for MOdulator/DEModulator. A modem lets a computer send and receive data through an ordinary telephone line.

monitor   A television-like screen that the computer uses to display information.

mouse   (1) The last name of a little guy named Mickey. (2) A mouse is a device that moves an arrow (a pointer) on the screen. When you move the mouse, the pointer on the screen moves in the same direction. Used instead of the keyboard to select and move items (such as text or graphics), execute commands, and perform other tasks. A mouse gets its name because it connects to your computer through a long "tail" or cord.

MS-DOS (Microsoft Disk Operating System)   See *DOS*.

multitasking   (1) What you should not do while driving a car. (2) The capability to run two programs at the same time. Some programs, such as the DOS Shell, allow you to switch between two or more programs, but do not allow a program to perform operations in the background. This is called *task-switching*, not multitasking.

network   (1) How to find out what's *really* going on in the office. (2) Connecting several PCs together for the purpose of sharing information and printers. In a local area network (LAN), the connected PCs are located in the same building. In a wide area network (WAN), the connected PCs can be located thousands of miles apart.

Overtype mode   The opposite of *Insert mode*, as used in word processors and text editors. Overtype mode means that when you position your cursor and start to type, what you type replaces existing characters at that point.

parameter   A part of a DOS command that tells it which files, directories, or drives to work with.

partition   A hard disk drive can be divided (or *partitioned*) into one or more drives, which DOS refers to as drive C, drive D, drive E, and so on. (Don't be fooled; it's still one disk drive.) The actual hard disk drive is called the *physical* drive; each partition is called a *logical* drive.

path   The route that DOS travels from the root directory to any subdirectories when locating a file. Think of telling a friend how to find your house. A complete path looks like this: **C:\WORD\DOCS\CHAP01.DOC**.

PC-DOS   IBM's name for its version of MS-DOS. PC-DOS is designed to run exclusively on IBM PCs.

peripheral   The system unit is the central part of the computer. Any devices that are attached to the system unit are considered *peripheral* (as in "peripheral vision"). Peripheral devices include the monitor, printer, keyboard, mouse, modem, and joystick. Some manufacturers consider the keyboard and monitor as essential parts of the computer rather than as peripherals.

pipe character   The character (I) that controls the flow of information between two DOS commands, as in **TYPE AUTOEXEC.BAT I MORE**.

ports   The receptacles at the back of the computer. They get their name from the ports where ships pick up and deliver cargo. In this case, the ports allow information to enter and leave the system unit.

POST (Power-On Self Test)   (1) The part that holds up a fence. (2) A series of internal checks the computer performs on itself whenever it is booted. If the test reveals that any component is not working properly, the computer displays an error message on-screen giving a general indication of which component is causing problems.

program   (1) What you can't tell the players without. (2) A set of instructions written in a special "machine language" that the computer understands. Typical programs are word processors, spreadsheets, databases, and games.

program file   See *file*.

Program Manager   The main program in Windows. Program Manager organizes your programs and keeps track of the ones which are running. In Windows, you start and stop your programs through commands you issue to Program Manager.

prompt (1) Something the pizza delivery man is usually not. (2) A message from DOS letting you know that it is waiting for a command. When you type a command, it appears next to the prompt on the screen. Typical DOS prompts include **C>** or **C:\DOS>**.

pull-down menu Contains the selections for a main menu command. This type of menu, when activated, is pulled down from the main menu bar, in much the same way a window shade can be pulled down from the top of a window frame.

random-access memory (RAM) A state of *very* temporary electronic storage, where your computer keeps data it is working with. Any information that the computer needs to use (data, programs, even DOS commands) must be placed in RAM so the computer can access them. When you turn the computer off, it forgets everything in its memory—so you need a permanent means of storing data you want to keep: either on a *hard disk* or on a *diskette*.

RAM cache An area of RAM (memory) which stores copies of the most-often-requested files. Files in RAM are quicker to access than files on the hard disk. By keeping often-requested files in RAM, your PC's hard disk can retrieve those files a whole lot faster. A RAM cache can also be used to collect files that need to be written (saved) on the hard disk, so this procedure can be done in one step (instead of lots of short trips to the hard disk to save one file, then another).

rebooting The process of restarting a computer that is already on. Press **Ctrl+Alt+Delete** to reboot. Also known as *warm booting*.

redirection symbol Used in a command to send the output of that command to another device, a file, or another command, instead of displaying the output on the monitor. The DOS redirection symbol is the greater-than sign (>), and it is by the name of the device, the file, or the command you want to direct the output to, like this: **DIR > PRN**.

restoring files Backing up your files is a process that copies files onto diskettes in a special compressed format. If those files get damaged somehow, you can restore them through a reverse process (restoring) that decompresses the backed-up files and copies them back to the hard disk.

ROM BIOS See *BIOS*.

root directory   The main, or central, directory. All other directories branch off from the root.

server   (1) With two PCs linked with INTERLNK, the server is typically the desktop PC. The server PC provides the resources (files, disks, or printer) that the client PC uses. (2) A network server provides centralized resources for everyone attached to the network: files, programs, disks, and printer.

scroll   To move text up/down or right/left on a computer screen.

shell   (1) What Sue sells by the seashore. (2) A program that lets you choose operating-system commands from a menu. DOS shell programs make the operating system easier to use. (3) A temporary DOS prompt, provided through a command within an application. A temporary DOS prompt allows the user to access DOS without having to exit the application itself. Type **EXIT** to return to an application after using the temporary DOS prompt.

software   (1) Ware that's been washed in Downy. (2) Any instructions that tell your computer (the *hardware*) what to do. There are two types of software: operating system software and application software. Operating system software (such as *DOS*) gets your computer up and running. *Application* software allows you to do something useful, such as type a letter or save the whales.

subdirectories   Means the same thing as directories. The prefix *sub* is used to emphasize the fact that all directories are subordinate to the root directory. Sometimes the word *subdirectory* describes a directory under another directory.

surge protector/power strip   A special kind of power strip that protects your PC against sudden power surges.

switch   (1) A pretty good movie starring Ellen Barkin. (2) The part of a DOS command that modifies the way in which the command is carried out. Switches are always preceded with a forward slash (/). For example, the DIR command has a switch (/W) that lists files going across the screen instead of down.

temporary DOS prompt   A special part of a regular application that allows the user to perform needed file-maintenance functions without actually exiting an application.

text file   A type of file that contains no special formatting (such as bold), but simply letters, numbers, and such.

text mode   A display mode that uses text and simple lines or boxes, rather than pictures. Text mode can be used with almost any monitor and video card and is especially useful for those that do not support graphics.

TSR (terminate and stay resident)   Special programs that start and then "go to sleep" until they are reactivated by a special key combination.

uninterruptible power supply (UPS)   A battery-powered device that protects against power spikes and power outages. If the power goes out, the UPS continues supplying power to the computer so you can continue working, or safely turn off your computer without losing any data.

upper memory   (1) Memory that's tough to reach without a ladder. (2) The area of RAM between 640K and 1MB. This area is reserved for DOS.

video card   A circuit board in your computer that works with your *monitor* to project images on your screen.

virus   A computer virus is a program that vandalizes your system. The worst viruses destroy data and render your computer helpless. Others display strange messages, but do no damage. A virus can enter your system through an infected diskette or an infected file that has been downloaded (received through a modem) from another computer. An anti-virus program monitors changes to your files and alerts you to the presence of a virus.

volume label   A brief description or name for a disk, recorded electronically on the disk itself during the format process. A volume label displays when DIR is used to list the files on the disk.

warm boot   See *rebooting*.

wildcard   A wildcard is used to represent characters within a filename.

Wildcards create a general filename pattern so that several files can be used with a single DOS command. There are two DOS wildcards: the asterisk (*), which represents several characters within a filename, and the question mark (?), which represents a single character. Think of a wildcard character as a "wild card" in a game of poker. If the Joker is wild, you can use it in place of any card in the entire deck of cards.

windows   (1) Something I don't do. (2) A box that is used to display information in part of the screen. With a capital W, a nickname for Microsoft Windows, a *graphical user interface* program (see *GUI*).

write-protect   To prevent a computer from adding or modifying data stored on a disk.

WYSIWYG   (1) Phyllis Diller's hair. (2) Pronounced wizzy-wig. Short for What You See Is What You Get, an acronym which describes a program's capability to display your document on-screen, in a manner which resembles what it will look like when printed.

Index

W

Who cares what you think? WE DO!

We take our customers' opinions very personally. After all, you're the reason we publish these books. If you're not happy, we're doing something wrong.

We'd appreciate it if you would take the time to drop us a note or fax us a fax. A real person—not a computer—reads every letter we get, and makes sure that your comments get relayed to the appropriate people.

Not sure what to say? Here are some details we'd like to know:

- ☛ Who you are (age, occupation, hobbies, etc.)
- ☛ Where you bought the book
- ☛ Why you picked this book instead of a different one
- ☛ What you liked best about the book
- ☛ What could have been done better
- ☛ Your overall opinion of the book
- ☛ What other topics you would purchase a book on

Mail, e-mail, or fax it to:

Faithe Wempen
Product Development Manager
Alpha Books
201 West 103rd Street
Indianapolis, IN 46290

FAX: (317) 581-4669
CIS: 75430,174

Special Offer!

Alpha Books needs people like you to give opinions about new and existing books. Product testers receive free books in exchange for providing their opinions about them. If you would like to be a product tester, please mention it in your letter, and make sure you include your full name, address, and daytime phone.

The Complete Idiot's Guides to Computer Topics

More Fun Learning from Alpha Books!

If you liked this *Complete Idiot's Guide*, check out these other completely helpful books!

The Complete Idiot's Guide to PCs, New Edition
ISBN: 1-56761-459-0
$16.95 USA

The Complete Idiot's Guide to Windows, Second Edition
ISBN: 1-56761-546-5
$16.95 USA

The Complete Idiot's Guide to DOS, Second Edition
ISBN: 1-56761-496-5
$16.95 USA

The Complete Idiot's Guide to the Internet, Second Edition
ISBN: 1-56761-535-X
$19.95 USA

Look for these books at your favorite computer book retailer, or call 1-800-428-5331 for more information!

Also Available!

**The Complete Idiot's Guide
to 1-2-3, New Edition**
ISBN: 1-56761-404-3
Softbound, $14.95 USA

**The Complete Idiot's Guide to
1-2-3 for Windows**
ISBN: 1-56761-400-0
Softbound, $14.95 USA

**The Complete Idiot's Guide
to Ami Pro**
ISBN: 1-56761-453-1
Softbound, $14.95 USA

**The Complete Idiot's Guide to
Buying & Upgrading PCs**
ISBN: 1-56761-274-1
Softbound, $14.95 USA

**The Complete Idiot's Guide to
Computer Terms**
ISBN: 1-56761-266-0
Softbound, $9.95 USA

**The Complete Idiot's Guide
to Excel**
ISBN: 1-56761-318-7
Softbound, $14.95 USA

**The Complete Idiot's Guide
to Internet**
ISBN: 1-56761-414-0
Softbound, $19.95 USA

**The Complete Idiot's Guide
to The Mac**
ISBN: 1-56761-395-0
Softbound, $14.95 USA

**The Complete Idiot's Guide
to VCRs**
ISBN: 1-56761-294-6
Softbound, $9.95 USA

**The Complete Idiot's Guide
to WordPerfect**
ISBN: 1-56761-187-7
Softbound, $14.95 USA

**The Complete Idiot's Guide to
WordPerfect for Windows**
ISBN: 1-56761-282-2
Softbound, $14.95 USA

**The Complete Idiot's Guide
to Word for Windows**
ISBN: 1-56761-355-1
Softbound, $14.95 USA

**The Complete Idiot's Guide
to Works for Windows**
ISBN: 1-56761-451-5
Softbound, $14.95 USA